D0877559

Greece & Rome

NEW SURVEYS IN THE CLASSICS No. 39

ROMAN LANDSCAPE: CULTURE AND IDENTITY

BY
DIANA SPENCER

Published for the Classical Association
CAMBRIDGE UNIVERSITY PRESS
2010

CAMBRIDGE UNIVERSITY PRESS
The Edinburgh Building, Cambridge CB2 8RU, United Kingdom
32 Avenue of the Americas, New York, NY 10013-2473, USA
477 Williamstown Road, Port Melbourne, VIC 3207, Australia
Ruiz de Alarcón 13, 28014 Madrid, Spain
Dock house, The Waterfront, Cape Town 8001, South Africa

www.cambridge.org
Information on this title: www.cambridge.org/9781107400245

First published 2010 (Greece & Rome 56)

Printed in the United Kingdom by Bell and Bain, Glasgow, UK

A catalogue record for this publication is available from the British Library

ISBN 9781107400245 (paperback)

For Wilf – waiting farther down the line

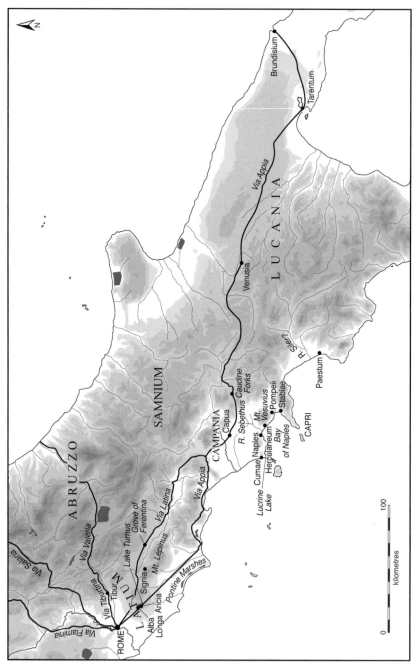

Figure 1 Italy: Rome and the south.

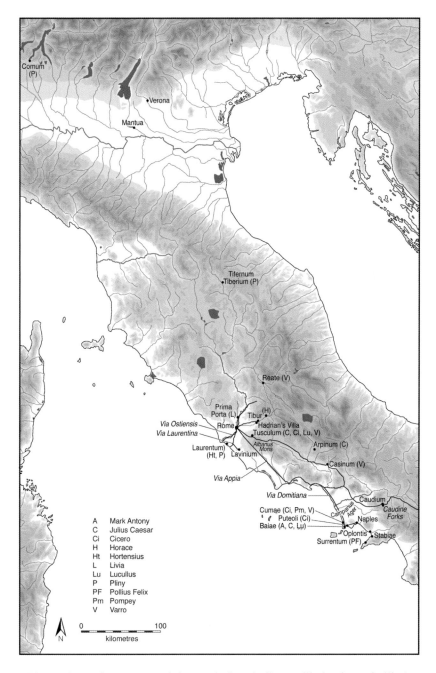

Figure 2   Italy: Rome and the north (key indicates likely sites of villas).

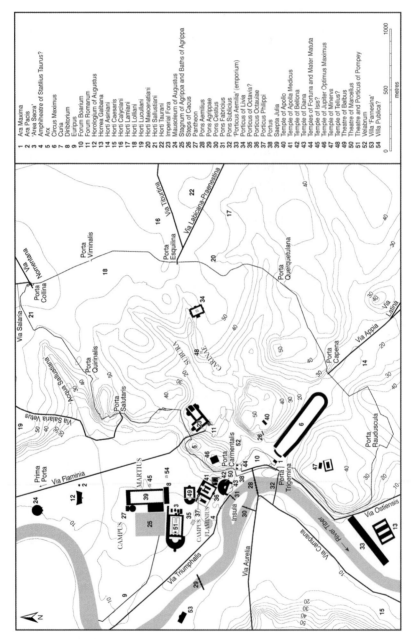

1	Ara Maxima
2	Ara Pacis
3	'Area Sacra'
4	Amphitheatre of Statilius Taurus?
5	Arx
6	Circus Maximus
7	Curia
8	Diribitorium
9	Euripus
10	Forum Boarium
11	Forum Romanum
12	Horologium of Augustus
13	Horrea Galbana
14	Horti Asiniani
15	Horti Caesaris
16	Horti Calyciani
17	Horti Lamiani
18	Horti Lolliani
19	Horti Luculliani
20	Horti Maecenatiani
21	Horti Sallustiani
22	Horti Taurani
23	Imperial Fora
24	Mausoleum of Augustus
25	Stagnum of Agrippa and Baths of Agrippa
26	Steps of Cacus
27	Pantheon
28	Pons Aemilius
29	Pons Agrippae
30	Pons Cestius
31	Pons Fabricius
32	Pons Sublicius
33	Porticus Aemilia '(emporium)'
34	Porticus of Livia
35	Porticus of Octavia?
36	Porticus Octaviae
37	Porticus Philippi
38	Portus
39	Saepta Julia
40	Temple of Apollo
41	Temple of Apollo Medicus
42	Temple of Bellona
43	Temple of Diana
44	Temples of Fortuna and Mater Matuta
45	Temple of Isis?
46	Temple of Jupiter Optimus Maximus
47	Temple of Minerva
48	Temple of Tellus?
49	Theatre of Marcellus
50	Theatre of Balbus
51	Theatre and Porticus of Pompey
52	Velabrum
53	Villa 'Farnesina'
54	Villa Publica?

Figure 3 Augustan Rome (here and in Figure 5 the contour lines draw on Haselberger, Romano, and Dumser 2002).

CONTENTS

ACKNOWLEDGEMENTS

Many people have helped to bring this book to life, but particular thanks go to John Taylor (the *New Surveys* series editor) who believed in it from the start, to Classics and Ancient History students in the Institute of Archaeology and Antiquity (University of Birmingham), who have had a lot of the explanations tried out on them, to Michael Sharp, Sue Tuck and Liz Hanlon (Cambridge University Press), to CUP's two anonymous readers (not all of whose thoughtful and provocative suggestions could be fitted in), and to Hester Higton for thoughtful and highly efficient copy-editing. Throughout the process of writing this *Survey*, Gideon Nisbet has read successive drafts repeatedly and (most importantly) with ongoing enthusiasm: everyone should have such an excellent support system.

Writing a book that criss-crosses disciplines is always challenging. The Society of Architectural Historians awarded me a Samuel H. Kress Foundation Fellowship, which, with a little extra help from the University of Birmingham (whose support also allowed me to visit many of the exhibitions alluded to in the notes), enabled me to participate in Mantha Zarmakoupi's panel 'The Roman Luxury Villa: An Ongoing Affair of Architecture and Landscape' at the Society's 2009 Annual Meeting, in Pasadena, California. There I had a chance to test some of the ideas in Chapter VI on an ideal audience, and thanks are also due to staff at the Huntington Library and Gardens in San Marino, who provided me with a reader's ticket and full access to the research facilities during my stay. Getting to grips with time and relativity proved in every sense much easier thanks to recommended reading suggested by Brian Cox.

Making site visits has been one of the joys of working on this topic: another exceptionally useful research trip was facilitated by Valeria Brunori, Fine Arts Curator at the US Embassy in Rome, who made it possible for me to visit the landscape frescoes still *in situ* beneath the Embassy and was extremely generous with her time on more than one occasion. Agnese Pompei arranged to have the Aula Adriana (Horti Sallustiani, Rome) opened up for me – an ideal opportunity to get a sense of the scale of the ancient site, and of the subsequent topographic changes. Colm Molloy's wonderful flat in Rome provided an idyllic base for a month-long stay, which made all the difference. A sequence of Italian visits (in particular) to Frascati, the Veneto, and the Villa Medici in Rome also helped to make real many of the issues graciously summed up for me by Professor Laurie Olin, based on his work on the hermeneutics of ancient landscape design in Renaissance and later Italian villa culture.

The Classical Association has made the illustrations possible through a very generous grant, and my Birmingham colleague Henry Buglass has (yet again) undertaken exceptional work on maps and plans.

Various people have made significant contributions to the practicalities of obtaining the images and permissions. Thanks are due to Carmel Byrne and Elaine Harte (Powerscourt House and Gardens, Co. Wicklow, Ireland), to Elena Obuhovich (The State Hermitage Museum, St Petersburg), to Jessica Robinson (The J. Paul Getty Trust, California), to René Seindal, to the Soprintendenze for Rome and for Naples and Pompeii, to Kristen Wenger (the British Museum, London), and to Katherine Wodehouse (the Ashmolean Museum, Oxford).

LIST OF ILLUSTRATIONS

ABBREVIATIONS

ANRW   Temporini, H. and Haase, W. (eds.) 1972–. *Aufstieg und Niedergang der römischen Welt.* Berlin, Walter de Gruyter.

LTUR   Steinby, E. M. (ed.) 1993–2000. *Lexicon Topographicum Urbis Romae* I–VI. Rome, Laterza.

OLD   Glare, P. G. W. (ed.) 1982. *Oxford Latin Dictionary.* Oxford, Clarendon Press.

Journal abbreviations follow the scheme in *l'Année Philologique*

PREFACE: KEY TERMS

This is a set of terms that recur in the main text (shown in bold at first use) and it makes a useful toolkit when studying landscape – it should be read through before proceeding to Chapter I. The chapter of first use in the main text is indicated after each entry. Bold terms in the text cross-reference head-word entries.

aesthetic(s) – relating to sensuous perception; an approach to studying the nature of beauty (*Chapter I*).

anthropomorphic – like a human in shape, behaviour, motivation, or other characteristics (*Chapter II*).

autarky – self-sufficiency; the ability to rely on one's own resources; by implication, self-control (*Chapter II*).

autochthonic – indigenous; aboriginal; native to a land or region (*Chapter I*).

axial line – direct or unimpeded line between two points in three-dimensional space, and the associated visual field; important for studying **space syntax** (*Chapter IV*).

chronotope – a literary critical term designating the complementary and culture-specific relationship between time and space that gives meaning to narrative and plot; made famous by Mikhail Bakhtin in the 1930s (*Chapter IV*).

code-switching – using more than one communication code (e.g. language, grammar) within a conversation or other form of **discourse**; important in socio-linguistics and translation studies (*Chapter V*).

cognitive linguistics – a branch of study that developed in the 1970s, and that examines the organizational principles of language with special emphasis on the relationship between linguistic structure (e.g. syntax, morphology), meaning, and use (*Chapter I*).

deictic – specification of a shared cognitive field relative to space, time, and context; implies taking into account the points of view of both the speaker (or author) and the audience (*Chapter IV*).

dialectic – using logical discussion to examine the nature of truth, or a practice, or an opinion (*Chapter V*).

discourse – employed by post-structuralism to mean language (written, spoken, or visual) or a system of ideas in use within a particular set of contexts (historical, social, and ideological) (*Chapter I*).

ekphrasis – the literary description of a work of art (*Chapter III*).

entropy – a measure of randomness in a system; the tendency of systems to move from the less probable (order) towards the more probable (disorder) (*Chapter II*).

episteme – an idea-set of beliefs, categories, and assumptions comprising or dominating knowledge or understanding (of a subject) at a given time (*Chapter I*).

epistemology – a philosophical approach to defining what knowledge is; analysis of the nature of knowledge and how it is defined; hence **episteme** (*Chapter II*).

ethnography – the (comparative) description of particular human societies (typically, communities or nations); hence 'ethnographic' (*Chapter III*).

ethnology – the (comparative) study of particular human societies (typically, communities or nations); hence 'ethnological' (*Chapter I*).

ethnoscape – a space given shared meaning as a territory by a community; a space that a group, defining itself ethnically, sees as providing a shared frame of reference and point of origin (*Chapter I*).

fat (convex) space – **semiotically** dense, taking significant conceptual effort to move through because of, for example, unfamiliarity (taking an unknown route from *a* to *b* appears to take longer than a return trip from *b* to *a* that traces the same route); complex **isovists** (perhaps including signage requiring interpretation, visually rich buildings, or monuments); or the appearance of interim destinations or blocked routes (**axial lines**) requiring decision-making; key term in **space syntax** (*Chapter I*).

focalization – in narrative theory, this is typically the presentation of a scene through the perception of one character or persona, or from a particular point of view; hence 'focalize' (*Chapter I*).

the Gaze – from psychoanalytic theory (developed by Jacques Lacan), and also important in post-colonial criticism, this defines what happens when we recognize an ideal self in an external object (e.g. in a mirror, in a movie), and become aware that what we see appears to look back at us (or configure how we look at it). Hence we realize that, even when we think that we define and control the external material world in our own terms, it inevitably exercises control over us and our responses. See also *voyant-visible* (*Chapter I*).

hegemony – leadership or dominance imposed by one group within a community or federation; hence 'hegemonic' (*Chapter V*).

hermeneutic(s) – (drawing meaning from) the study of (the process of) interpretation (*Chapter I*).

hyperreal(ity) – as used in postmodernism, signifies an object or site that creates a vivid illusion of authentic reality; the illusion is flawed only because the effect is too good to be true; for example, it totally fulfils one particular audience's expectations of what 'reality' ought to be, to the exclusion of other perspectives; typically discussed in terms of the **simulacrum**; see Eco 1986 (*Chapter V*).

iconography – a set of recognizable images or symbols associated with a particular subject or person; hence 'iconographic' (*Chapter I*).

ideology – a complex of ideas or a conceptual scheme reflecting and/or serving the needs of an individual or group; an acculturated belief-system by which an individual/group makes sense of the world; hence 'ideologically' (*Chapter III*).

interdisciplinary – looking at the connections linking different fields of study and applying critical methods and approaches from a range of disciplines (*Chapter I*).

intratextuality – approaching a **text** as a segmented unit composed of parts, prioritizing the interest and autonomy of those parts, and exploring how the parts do or do not relate to each other (and the whole); hence, 'intratextual(ly)' (*Chapter II*).

isovist – entire visual field accessible from a specified point in space (significant for studying **space syntax**) (*Chapter IV*).

labor – Latin term – physical toil (*Chapter I*).

lieux de mémoire – **ethnographically** qualified zones saturated with shared (typically historical) meanings that define a group, culture, or people; made famous by Pierre Nora; variously translated as 'sites' or 'realms' of memory (*Chapter I*).

locus amoenus – Latin term – a **trope** signifying a charming, pleasant, and delightful place; a highly wrought **scenographic** franchise (*Chapter I*).

meme – a persistent idea or cultural practice transmitted across a civilization or population (e.g. urban legends, catchphrases, trends) (*Chapter II*).

methodology – a group of critical approaches used in a particular field; implies consideration of the suitability and implications of the choice of particular methods of study or analysis (*Chapter I*).

mnemotechnic(s) – (the process of) structuring memory using patterns of ideas or associations in order to aid recall (*Chapter V*).

narratology – the theory and analysis of how stories are told (structure, narration, stylistic features, etc.) and how this affects the way in which they are perceived and understood (*Chapter IV*).

natura – Latin term – (the power that determines) the way things inherently are; (what directs natural processes in) the physical world (*Chapter I*).

negotium – Latin term – etymologically, a combination of the negative *nec* and *otium*, therefore an activity that, by contrast, is 'not leisure'; it typically refers to business undertakings (*Chapter I*).

nexus – a network, or a point of convergence (*Chapter I*).

ontological – relating to ontology, which is the study of the nature of existence or reality (*Chapter IV*).

otium – Latin term – **semiotically** complex, denoting both productive and wasteful leisure (*Chapter I*).

palimpsest – a reused writing surface from which earlier writing has been incompletely erased and so remains visible; in critical theory, a place, object, or entity with more than one available layer of meaning, or where earlier patterns or arrangements continue to show through the most recent layer (*Chapter V*).

phenomenology – theoretical approach prioritizing the analysis of subjective (or first-person) experience, typically of an 'object' or phenomenon; hence 'phenomenological' (*Chapter I*).

praxis – practice developed from a theory or informed by a particular cultural context; sometimes denotes speech as action *(Chapter III)*.

prosopopoeia – (literally) putting on a mask and speaking as if someone else; orators loved this dramatic effect, which put all the great men of history at their disposal (*Chapter V*).

scenography – the construction, representation, and description of (often performative) space; typically implies a theorized or critically alert approach to the qualities of perspective and point of view; compare *skenographia* – ancient theatrical set-design or scenery (*Chapter I*).

scopophilia – deriving (sexual) pleasure from looking at something or someone; voyeurism; frequently, the (male) **Gaze** as a means of objectification; hence 'scopophiliac' (*Chapter V*).

self-fashioning – designing a persona (or image) for oneself that fits in with a set of social norms (see Greenblatt 1980) (*Chapter I*).

semiotic(s) – the interpretation of signs and symbols (see Barthes 1967) (*Chapter I*).

simulacrum – in philosophy, something which gives the appearance of reproducing a real entity but is in fact not related to or dependent upon any original external model; associated with postmodernism's **hyperreal**; see Webography: Oberly (*Chapter III*).

somatic – relating to the body as an entity defined by a dialogue between biological factors, environment, and perception (*Chapter II*).

space syntax – a theoretical approach for defining and analysing space systematically by seeing how and where a space's **axial lines** intersect, and how the resulting zones reflect and establish patterns of human use and interaction (*Chapter I*).

subaltern – a socio-culturally subordinate group of people, discourse, or point of view (*Chapter III*).

syncretism – the harmonization, reconciliation, or fusing of diverse ideas and practices (*Chapter II*).

taxonomy – the practice and science of classification into ordered and often relational groups or categories (*Chapter II*).

teleology – in philosophy, an interpretive system that explains events in terms of purpose and causation; often used to explore the idea of progress in the study of history, where it denotes purposeful linear momentum towards a set goal (*Chapter IV*).

text – an item of cultural production (often, but not necessarily, written) which is susceptible to critical analysis (*Chapter I*).

trope – a motif or recurrent theme, often involving figurative language; traditionally, a turn of phrase using words non-literally (e.g. metaphor) (*Chapter I*).

voyant-visible – simultaneously seeing and being the object of sight (coined by Merleau-Ponty, and connected to **the Gaze**; see also Heisenberg's Uncertainty Principle – the observer affects the observed) (*Chapter II*).

way-finding – the process whereby an individual or group recognizes and imposes meaningful patterns on their surroundings in order to navigate their environment (see Lynch 1960) (*Chapter IV*).

I INTRODUCTION: SURVEYING THE SCENE

Landscape...contains a multitude of meanings, all of which revolve around human experience, perception and modification of the world.[1]

What is landscape? Was there a concept of landscape in ancient Rome? Analysing the cityscape is now an established trend in the study of Rome and, since the 1990s, scholarship has explored the idea that thinking about the topography of the city of Rome encourages a more wide-ranging exploration of what being Roman was all about.[2] Taking a broader approach, this *Survey* tackles the **semiotics**[3] of a set of described, depicted, and three-dimensional landscapes where the emphasis is on a collaboration between nature and humankind. The timeframe is the late Roman Republic and early Principate, an era of change and reconstitution, when defining what being Roman meant was high on many agendas. This is also an era that offers the best possible scope for exploring a fascinating and diverse range of emblematic natural and manmade environments, taking in some of the most famous (but also some more unexpected) scenes in Roman literature, art, and architecture, closing with Hadrian's out-of-town landscaped villa near Tibur.

'Landscape' means something different from 'environment' or 'space': it foregrounds cultural context and emphasizes the relationship between humankind, nature, and the inhabited world. It also prioritizes **aesthetics** and the relationship between observer and observed (**the Gaze**).[4] To investigate 'landscape' in ancient Rome means recognizing the diverse palette of ideas, traditions, and cultural assumptions that 'landscape' trails now.[5] For this reason, this *Survey*'s Preface presents

---

[1] Alcock 2002: 30. See also La Rocca 2008: 7–13.

[2] See e.g. C. Edwards 1996, developed recently by Royo and Gruet 2008: 377.

[3] Chandler 2007 is a good introduction. Eco 1984 is readable, and still influential.

[4] Wylie 2007 (check 'Index' *s.v.* 'gaze') briefly introduces a range of applications relevant to landscape study.

[5] Sampling key trends in landscape study from the last thirty years: Meinig 1979b; Daniels and Cosgrove 1988; Hunt 1991; Bender 1993; Ingerson 1994; Mitchell 1994b; Tilley 1994; Hirsch and O'Hanlon 1995; A. Miller 1995 (survey article); Schama 1995; Olwig 1996; Cosgrove 1998; Spirn 1998; Birksted 2000; Fritter 2002. Wylie 2007 efficiently sums up, whilst Elkins and DeLue 2008 collect up most of the key current thinking on 'landscape' in a broad

a tool-kit of key terms that will crop up as we analyse the building blocks of what makes a Roman space into 'landscape'. As we proceed, you will also encounter samples of a range of **methodologies**, selected to show different ways of exploring how landscape and identity came together in the late Republic to form a key **discourse** in Roman culture and society.[6] Over the course of six chapters, this *Survey* suggests that studying what 'landscape' means now and might have meant then sheds light on some of the most urgent issues confronting wealthy, educated, ambitious, and politically minded citizens during this era – for example, historical destiny, citizen identity in a time of rapid cultural change, and the relationship between *labor, otium*, luxury, and the search for the best of all possible worlds. Testing these approaches on a wider range of sites and **texts**, and following up on the different and often **interdisciplinary** methodologies in more depth, will be up to you.

Broadly speaking, Western usage makes 'landscape' a term for defining interest in a space, and this convention gained popularity in England via a vogue for sixteenth-century Flemish and Dutch art.[7] The sixteenth and seventeenth centuries also saw northern European artists travel to Rome to study new masterpieces funded by wealthy patrons, often visually referencing the scenery of classical myth and the increasingly available physical traces of ancient Roman civilization. 'Landscape' painting in this era was radical in bringing to centre stage what had previously featured only as background noise for medieval art's religious main events: hills, trees, streams, meadows, buildings (see cover picture), scenes from daily life. Studying and working amid classical ruins (and the archaeological finds that were emerging) and new buildings whose structure and form drew heavily on classical models, artists reinvented antiquity as a panoramic pattern book for reflecting on and delighting in human progress. Renaissance humanism had helped to fix classical antiquity more generally in the Western consciousness, and Grand Tourists of the eighteenth and nineteenth centuries made direct connections between intellectual development, sightseeing, ancient ruins, and an aesthetics or ethos of place (see

sense. The journals *Landscape Research* (from 1968) and *Studies in the History of Gardens and Designed Landscapes* provide snapshots of changing approaches.

[6] Huskinson 2000a presents the back story concisely. Hodos 2010 sums up strategies for understanding ancient identity.

[7] Big names include Paul Bril (1553/4–1626), Pieter Bruegel the Elder (*c.*1525–69), and Joachim Patinir (*c.*1485–1524). Andrews 1999 is the best introduction to how landscape features in Western art. Cf. Cosgrove 1998: 1, 16 (on the terminology).

Figures 6 and 7).[8] The Romantic movement's fascination with the unknowability and awesome power of nature (the Sublime) took this a stage further.[9] Romanticism's enthusiasm for landscapes stripped of human figures, but occasionally populated with ruinous symbols of antiquity's decline, helped to display nature's triumph as the ultimate landscape artist. This back story inevitably colours our attempts to relate modern and ancient understandings of 'landscape'.[10]

The material remains of what we might term 'real' ancient Roman landscapes often present only a fragmentary and even unintelligible story, and interpretation involves us in the processing of data – inevitably a subjective activity.[11] Archaeological techniques including geophysical surveying and aerial photography can help map plantings and hard- and soft-landscaping, but to interpret the resulting stratigraphy, post holes, pollen, and organic remains meaningfully, and to work out how and why particular landscapes mattered, we need to turn to surviving designed 'texts' – literary, material, and visual – which communicate Roman understanding of what makes a space interesting enough to be tagged as 'landscape'.[12]

This chapter's opening quote cues up some core approaches, including Lefebvre's influential definition of space as the product of what we perceive (our understanding), what is represented (what we are shown), and how we experience our environment.[13] Chapters II, III, and IV tackle Roman ideas of landscape thematically as a product of aesthetics, of hard work, and of time. Chapters V and VI propose chronologically organized literary and material cultural case studies as starting points for relating symbolic and real-life landscapes. Fortunately, Classical texts are well served with online resources. For texts (and translations), the Webography points you to *Lacus Curtius*

---

[8] Chard 1999 is the major study.

[9] Andrews 1999: 129–49 sums up on landscape and the artistic Sublime.

[10] We return to landscape art in Chapter VI. Consult Warnock and Brown 1998, or Azara 2008 for different (more totalizing) takes on 'landscape'.

[11] Renfrew 2005 sets out the problems of identification of original meaning for sites and objects.

[12] Bahn 1996 introduces what archaeology does; for impressive coverage, see Renfrew and Bahn 2008. Anschuetz, Wilshusen, and Scheick 2001 introduce key approaches for landscape archaeology. The approaches to studying classical archaeology outlined in Alcock and Osborne 2007 are particularly useful – see J. L. Davis 2007 and Hurst 2007 for the practicalities. More generally, Barker and Lloyd 1991 collect up case studies. Von Stackelberg 2009 demonstrates just how hard it is to draw all the elements together. Useful online fora are provided by *Archaeolog* and *Archaeology News* (see Webography). Harvey 2009 introduces important issues for studying material culture.

[13] Lefebvre 1991: 1–67.

and the *Perseus Digital Library*, and, for Latinists, *The Latin Library*. Chapter VI flags up additional resources for tackling material and visual cultural sites.

Approaches: ethnology, aesthetics, and the language of space and place

We can start by investigating some of the ways in which Romans understood the relationship between human authority, provident, eternal ***natura***, and wilderness. By the end of this chapter we will have a sense of how and why 'landscape' works as what Soja terms a 'realandimagined' space within which to dig deeply into Roman identity.[14] Barthes, for example, suggests that conservative mythologization of 'Nature' has often made an ideal alibi for explaining and justifying the status quo – a position we will see prefigured in elite Roman interest in the land and its use.[15] Schama, too, sees myth-making at work, although we might question his certainty that 'Landscapes are culture *before* they are nature; constructs of the imagination projected onto wood and water and rock.'[16]

Schama makes landscape an end-product of culture, but exploring ancient models of landscape shows that it is rarely this straightforward. Whether or not their identity is an imaginary construct, Romans conceptualize it at least partly as a response to topographic referents (the Seven Hills, Troy, the Tiber, Italy) identified as significant or meaningful for some reason.[17] Putting these ideas together, we have a model whereby claiming a space as 'landscape' immediately changes both the space and those who attach symbolic meaning to it. One task of this *Survey* is therefore to tackle the **hermeneutics** of landscape. Looking at hermeneutics pushes us to investigate how landscape produces and is also a product of culture, and to identify how and why defining space as 'landscape' poses perennially and cross-culturally interesting questions.

Harris's definition of landscape is useful here: 'a wide range of outdoor forms and spaces including, but not limited to, parks, urban

---

[14] Soja 1996: 11.
[15] Barthes 1993: 53, 142.
[16] Schama 1995: 61, emphasis added. For a more gardenist perspective (and an introduction to one of garden history's big names, Geoffrey Jellicoe), see Jellicoe, Waymark, and Jellicoe 1995.
[17] Snyder 1990 exemplifies how a contemporary spin on this might work.

open space, cemeteries, monument sites, estates, and gardens of all sizes and types'.[18] What these spaces have in common is that they are all composed of places, typically identified by toponyms, demarcated by walls or boundaries, and semiotically framed. They affect those who visit or inhabit them in ways more or less determined by culture and design. There is 'art' in their construction, and further artfulness comes into play in describing and representing them. What none of these landscapes suggest is raw, unmediated, or unconsidered space, and Andrews takes the artfulness a stage further when he observes that 'a "landscape", cultivated or wild, is already artifice *before it has become the subject of a work of art*'.[19] This is important for our purposes: works of art rather than direct experience are our primary way into the subject of ancient landscape.

If we view landscape as a set of places, we need to decide what 'place' means. Augé's **ethnological** approach adds value at this point. He proposes that a 'place' is somewhere occupied by a group of people who

defend it, mark its strong points and keep its frontiers under surveillance, but who also detect in it the traces of chthonian or celestial powers, ancestors or spirits which populate and animate its private geography...

The ethnologist...sets out to decipher, from the way the place is organized (the frontier always postulated and marked out between wild nature and cultivated nature, the permanent or temporary allotment of cultivable land or fishing grounds, the layout of villages...in short, the group's social, political and religious geography), an order which is all the more restrictive – in any case, the more obvious – because its transcription in space gives it the appearance of a second nature... Foundation narratives are...narratives that bring the spirits of the place together with the first inhabitants in the common adventure... The social demarcation of the soil is the more necessary for not always being original...

The indigenous fantasy is that of a closed world founded once and for all long ago... Everything there is to know about it is already known: land, forest, springs, notable features, religious places, medicinal plants, not forgetting the temporal dimension of these places whose legitimacy is postulated, and whose stability is supposed to be assured, by narratives about origin and by the ritual calendar. All the inhabitants have to do is *recognize* themselves in it when the occasion arises.[20]

In effect, Augé is describing an **ethnoscape**: a space where memory and imagination join forces in visualizing a shared, communal

---

[18] Harris 1999: 434; this useful survey offers concise access to issues treated in more detail by big names such as Conan, Hunt, Mitchell, and Soja.

[19] Andrews 1999: 1, emphasis added.

[20] Augé 1995: 42–4, emphasis original. Ingold 2000 (parts 1 and 2) takes a similar approach for a spin.

interpretation of the world.[21] Augé's reading sharpens our understanding of a recognizably Roman mindset, as sketched for example by Varro in the later first century BCE. The dedicatory opening to book 3 of his 'handbook' *De re rustica* (*On Country Matters*) observes that, by tradition, two modes of life are available: rural or urban. There is, moreover, 'no doubt but that these are separate not just in terms of *space* [*locus*], but also as a function of the different *chronological* [*tempus*] origins of each'.[22] Country life – a pre-urban landscape – is, he says, the most ancient; there never was a time when fields (*agri*) ripe for cultivation (*colo*) were not immanent within the landscape (*terra*). Varro's vision of an archaic countryside suggests that Roman agribusiness in its purest form is in effect tracing a natural blueprint. From time immemorial, he hints, a Roman's *raison d'être* was to perform a set of practices bound up in a **nexus** including habitation, cultivation, and worship.[23] Neither Varro nor Augé appears to be talking about aesthetic approaches to the environment, nor describing and responding to its 'natural' beauty. This is not landscape as art, or in the Romantic tradition, but an ethical, practical, and political relationship between humankind and the spaces that we inhabit – our ethnoscapes.[24]

As recent philosophical inquiry into the aesthetics of nature has made increasingly clear, however, addressing aesthetics can improve our methodological focus:

the mistaken search for a model of the correct or appropriate aesthetic appreciation of nature reflects a lack of recognition of the freedom that is integral to the aesthetic appreciation of nature, a freedom which means that much more is up to the aesthetic observer of nature than of art, a freedom which is one aspect of nature's distinctive aesthetic appeal.[25]

Berger's influential study of *Ways of Seeing* explained how all observation is conditioned in some sense, but Budd's focus on nature suggests that

---

[21] A. D. Smith 1999: 150–2. This also ties in with Lefebvre 1991, where space is defined and analysed as a social construct. B. Anderson 2006 provides a lucid and comprehensive overview of key issues.

[22] Varro, *Rust.* 3.1.1.

[23] Ibid., 3.1.3, 4. The verb '*colo*' draws together these meanings and more. See the lengthy *OLD* entry, which also includes 'embellish', 'practise', and 'inhabit as a god'. Roman thought on nature filters through Beagon 1992. Peterson 2001: 51–61 sums up trends in defining how 'the human story' relates to 'the earth community' (60).

[24] See also Casey 1993: 188.

[25] Budd 2002: 147–8, see also 19–23 (the extent of our knowledge of nature affects our experience and judgement) and 110–48 (a lively survey of contemporary approaches).

Figure 4 Tivoli, Grand Cascade. As we know from the Younger Pliny (*Ep.* 8.17), the River Anio (Aniene) was accustomed to wreak periodic havoc upon the estates of Tibur. Pope Gregory XVI's rerouting of the river (in 1835, after particularly disastrous floods in 1826, which washed away part of the town), forming this new 'grand' cascade, dramatically changed the aural and visual qualities of the relationship between the citadel and its most characteristic feature: water. It provided viewers with a dramatic new 'natural' water feature, whose flow and impact was in fact configured by hydraulic engineering (via a tunnel); this view presents the waterfall as a natural phenomenon. Cf. Figures 6 and 7, which appear more 'staged', and make a feature of human intervention in the landscape.

one way in which we enjoy 'natural' scenery is because we *imagine* it to offer raw material for expressing our individuality, free from the constraints of an author's, painter's, or designer's vision (compare Figures 4, 6, and 7).[26] In terms of cultural geography, changing the focus from 'seen' to 'seeing' (passive to active) turns 'nature' from art to raw material, downplaying the idea that 'nature' means the same

[26] Berger 1972.

thing to everyone. By prioritizing interpretation, this approach creates what Wylie terms 'the landscape way of seeing'.[27] Looking at 'nature' makes artists of everyone. Even a primarily utilitarian landscape still offers scope for this kind of aesthetics because we enrich these spaces, too, with our own prior experience, our visual or **iconographic** memories, needs, and desires. In this way, Budd (2002) and Cooper (2006) develop a **phenomenological** approach also exemplified in Meinig (1979a), recognizing that the eye of the beholder is what unlocks the meaning of three-dimensional landscapes. This process of interpretation rooted in a shared semiotic system is what gives real and symbolic substance to how we perceive the natural world.

Semiotics are also important for Spirn, who argues that 'the meanings landscapes hold are not just metaphorical and metaphysical, but real... Landscape has all the features of language. It contains the equivalent of words and parts of speech'.[28] The complex semantic background to Spirn's position is described by Fauconnier, a major figure in **cognitive linguistics**:

Understanding the linguistic organization involved [in metaphor, metonymy, and other rhetorical devices] leads to the study of domains that we set up as we talk or listen, and that we structure with elements, roles, strategies, and relations. These domains – or interconnected *mental spaces*, as I shall call them – are not part of the language itself, or of its grammars; they are not hidden levels of linguistic representation, but language does not come without them.[29]

Fauconnier's 'mental spaces' are hugely useful for tackling textual landscapes and, as we shall see, three-dimensional space has its own grammars and vocabularies. Cognitive linguistic terminology intersects here with another recently burgeoning theoretical approach: analysis of **space syntax**. Hillier is a key player in this field, and his interest in deconstructing (or parsing) the rhetoric(s) of space offers significant strategies for understanding what landscape means for Rome. Hillier and Hanson's **'fat space'** model encourages us to think harder about the assumptions and connections that we make when we read about or move through culturally and intellectually resonant spaces, rich

---

[27] Wylie 2007: 92, 93 (55–93 provides a detailed overview).
[28] Spirn 1998: 11, 15. See Wylie 2007: 80–1 (summary discussion).
[29] Fauconnier 1994: 1, emphasis original. Dennett 1991 and Varela, Thompson, and Rosch 1991 address cognition more generally. V. Evans and Green 2006 provide an excellent introduction to cognitive linguistics. See also Harnad 1987; Gärdenfors 2000. Looking at Rome, see Leach 1988: 74–8.

with semiotic meaning.[30] A final way into this field is through the terminology of cultural memory.[31]

Like all discourse, memory relies upon and is generated by the manipulation of symbols: we perceive a 'thing', compare it relationally to other 'things' in our mental library, and define or 'tag' it accordingly.[32] Individual or personal memory weaves together our personal tags and our individual experiences. Communal memory might be expressed as operating at the intersections *between* personal memories; this kind of memory is consensual, and assumes groups of people with shared or agreed responses to (or memories of) particular events, images, ideas, or entities (**epistemes**). Cultural memory, for the purposes of this book, is concentrated specifically in the collaborative production of memory and identity within a society or group: shared ideas and practices are explained and memorialized when recast as stories, and, in repeatedly telling the stories, their formulaic (and often highly conservative) qualities tend to dominate.[33] For ancient Rome, this is especially useful when thinking about shared values such as ancestral custom (*mos maiorum*) and its connection of citizen identity with the landscapes of Rome and Italy.[34] Through shared values and associations, we see how spaces become places and how monuments of all kinds take on semiotic weight, in a manner explored (for France) in Nora's ***lieux de mémoire***.[35] Using this approach encourages us to place emphasis on the hermeneutic and **epistemological** relationship between the topographic entity (tree, tomb, road, temple) and its *agreed* meaning, value, and significance. Again, Lorrain's sketch of Aeneas and the Sibyl (cover illustration) offers an excellent example. We must always remember, however, that ascribing meaning and staking a claim to

---

[30] Set out in Hillier and Hanson 1984. Hillier and Penn 2004 address problems with the model. For its application to antiquity, see Grahame 2000. On the implications for archaeology, see Lock 2009. Drawing these strands together, see the introductions to Barnes and Duncan 1992, and Duncan and Ley 1993.

[31] Developed by the Egyptologist Jan Assmann (usefully summarized in Assmann 1995; explored in more detail in Assmann 2006), this approach draws on the formulation 'collective memory', for which see Halbwachs 1992. A connected idea, 'social memory', is introduced by J. Fentress and Wickham 1992.

[32] Small 1997 provides an authoritative overview focusing on ancient memory, drawing on Yates 1966. See also (e.g.) Bergmann 1994; Farrell 1997; and Walter 2004: 155–79. Flower 1996, 2006 discusses specific instances of how memory and culture intersect.

[33] See Wachtel 1990 (on the Holocaust); Zerubavel 2003 (on the patterns that structure the creation of 'history').

[34] See Treggiari 2003, on Cicero.

[35] See Nora 2001 and (for a practical example) Roncayolo 2006.

landscape and imbuing sites with cultural significance is never value-neutral.[36]

The politics of charm

Gardens and landscapes (parks, rustic imagery, and *trompe-l'oeil* vistas, often with a mythological or fantastic theme) become central to elite cultural production and consumption at Rome during a time of great change (the late Republic and early Principate).[37] Varro represents a turning point in a tradition whereby Rome's natural environment overwhelmingly signifies productivity, ethnicity, political and social identity, and power. These themes often have aesthetic implications, but there is yet another kind of landscape, one where (the right sort of) sensory gratification and relaxed pleasure is the priority. The key term for this kind of landscape is **locus amoenus**. An example from Cicero clarifies its meaning, showing how cultural context and hermeneutics coloured Roman perception:

> *quibus quaeris, idque etiam me ipsum nescire arbitraris, utrum magis tumulis prospectuque an ambulatione ἀλιτενεῖ <u>delecter</u>. Est mehercule, ut dicis, utriusque loci tanta amoenitas ut dubitem utra anteponenda sit.*   Cic. *Att.* 14.13.1 (Puteoli, April 44 BCE)

[in your letter] you ask (thinking I won't know the answer) whether there's more <u>pleasure</u> in the hills and the view, or in the *maritime* promenade. It's just as you say: there is so much damn charm in both places that I am in doubt as to which should rate higher.

Writing from delightful seaside Puteoli (see Figure 1), Cicero seems at first to engage straightforwardly with his friend Atticus' evaluation of the relative attractions and merits of particular places. Caesar's assassination, however, overshadows the letter – Tatum (2006) sums up the political background effectively. Cicero is in a tricky political position: struggling to reach an accommodation with Mark Antony (then consul), when his inclination is towards Brutus' faction. Reading context in makes Cicero's aesthetic deliberation, with its Greek loan-word hinting at a wider Mediterranean perspective, seem less

---

[36] S. Jones 1997 is an excellent introduction to the politics of ownership of the material past.

[37] For a working proposition of the relationship between the garden and the broader idea of landscape, see Hunt 1999 (or 2000: 2–29). On out-of-town villa landscapes, see Littlewood 1987 and Purcell 1987b. Jashemski 1981 summarizes key features of peristyle gardens.

straightforwardly descriptive and appreciative. As he goes on to say, in the world after Caesar, choosing one's position has become a matter of urgency.[38] *Amoenitas* evokes a particular kind of phenomenological charm linked to physical and sensory comfort (so Cicero is also conjuring up a sensory environment and embodied practice), while also calling to mind a highly literary, Hellenistic panorama focused on the scenes of pastoral verse.[39] Literary pastoral, newly fashionable at Rome, deploys a **scenography** where playing with ideas of rusticity equals sophistication; paradigmatic landscape **tropes**, drawn most famously from Theocritus, offer Romans a new way of thinking about their relationship with the land, mapping it onto a specifically Greek topographic imagination, and giving a Hellenic flavour to the Gaze between Rome and Italy.[40] A *locus amoenus* is not, then, awe-inspiring or terror-inducing in the way that a 'sublime' place is, but it does conjure up a range of cultural anxieties that add ethical chiaroscuro to the light and shade of pastoral's typical landscapes.[41]

Suburban landscape parks form a backdrop to this trope, and became particularly significant in the characteristic late Republican culture of display.[42] In Rome's Campus Martius (see Figure 3), new monumental and decorative spaces included Pompey's carefully planned entertainment complex. Later designed landscapes that were open to the public included Agrippa's leisure centre (baths, gardens, exercise spaces) and the landscaped environs of Augustus' Mausoleum. Rather than adding self-promoting elements piecemeal to the cluttered Campus, Pompey (and then more comprehensively Augustus) completely remodelled a vast chunk of it as a kind of theme park, telling a story (as we will see in Chapter VI) about personal power and

---

[38] Cic. *Att.* 14.13.2.

[39] On landscape as a function of human existence, see Ingold 2000: 55.

[40] See Chapter II. Theocritus, from Syracuse, was writing in the early third century BCE. Hellenistic literature was hugely significant in the development of Roman culture; Gutzwiller 2007 introduces the key figures and Gruen 1992 sets out how Roman culture responded. On what's often termed the 'imperial gaze', Wylie 2007: 126–36 sets out key issues.

[41] *On the Sublime*, attributed to Longinus (dating to perhaps as early as the first century CE), makes sublimity primarily a rhetorical quality. McEvilley 2001: 60–77 summarizes the Sublime from Romanticism onwards; Stafford 2001 offers a quirky modern example. Giesecke 2007: 49–51 outlines the danger, mystery, and human helplessness lurking in classical Greek representations of nature. Cf. the first-century-BCE Roman poet-philosopher Lucretius' pragmatic division of the world into three, out of which the 'wilderness' is useless to humankind (5.200–17); see Schiesaro 2007, and Porter 2007.

[42] See Chapter VI. Grimal 1984:110–36 usefully surveys likely locations for the main late Republican *horti* (estates). What is 'culture'? Wallace-Hadrill 2008: 3–37 sums up.

magnificence.[43] In concrete terms, the cosmocratic and imperializing motifs that saturated Pompey's theatre and garden complex would also make clear that stepping in was to enter a different version of Roman space.[44] Purpose-designed public landscapes were paralleled by an alternative gesture: throwing open one's private gardens (as Caesar did, in his will). Horace's use of Caesar's Gardens as a topographic signpost ("'I want to look up someone you don't know / he's ill, flat out, way across the Tiber, near Caesar's Gardens'") suggests that they quickly became a landmark fixture in the city, but, like Pompey's, they remained a place distinct, offering something different from what had traditionally characterized everyday urban experience.[45] Horace uses them conceptually to distance the speaker's destination (within the poem) from the city centre.

Far from offering a natural or idyllic contrast to the city, designed landscape in this sense tells an explicitly civic and political story, closely tied up in the political and social changes of the late Republic and early Principate. Urban development of the Campus Martius in particular seems to have presented a fresh way of constructing Roman identity as a function of a developing dialogue between landscape, architecture, and monuments. This newly developing identity prioritized a union of nature and artifice in the service of the changing political landscape, one which was not exclusively focused on the nostalgia-tinted patriotism that coloured Rome's ancient political heart (the Capitoline Hill and the Forum).[46] Elite villas and landscape parks also aggressively colonized the suburbs, transforming potential farmland into a zone for the cultivation of meaning. Famous estates (*horti*) nestling barely outside the city of Rome in the mid-first century BCE included those of Maecenas, Lucullus, and Sallust (see Figure 3).[47] Traces of the kinds of debate that their luxury may have provoked filter through the criticism and mockery that the

---

[43] On theme-park landscapes, see Young and Riley 2002. Favro 1996: 24–41, 252–80 imaginatively describes two strolls through ancient Rome.

[44] See Kuttner 1999a; we examine Pompey's Porticus garden in Chapter VI.5.

[45] Hor. *Sat.* 1.9.17–18. On Caesar's gardens, see Coarelli 1996; Papi 1996; D'Arms 1998; Haselberger, Romano, and Dumser 2002: 142–3. On Horace's satire, see Welch 2001.

[46] Zanker 1988: 73–6, 141–4; Favro 1996: 40, 144–216. Spirn 1998: 240–65 discusses the polemic qualities of landscape, ranging widely through the nineteenth and twentieth centuries. One aspect of the Augustan Campus that has cast a long shadow is the sundial (*horologium*). On its original form, see e.g. Heslin 2007; see also online resources, e.g. Webography: *Museo dell'Ara Pacis*; Neilson (contemporary comparison); *Solarium/Horologium Augusti* (University of Oregon).

[47] The Horti Sallustiani feature in Chapter VI.5. On the *horti* of Lucullus, see Broise and Jolivet 1987, 1996, 1999; on the *horti* of Maecenas, see Häuber 1996, 1998. For both, consult Haselberger, Romano, and Dumser 2002: 144–5.

ostentatiously private, secluded luxury parks and villas of Campania could sometimes inspire. Moving forwards a century or so, we can see how these kinds of criticism feed into and colour the senatorial vitriol and disgust that greeted Nero's decision not to rebuild his home in the form of a traditional townhouse (*domus*) after the great fire of 64 CE but instead to redevelop a whole city-centre zone as a new urban form, part imperial residence, part villa – his Domus Aurea (Golden House).[48]

The anxieties associated with luxury estates and their impact on traditional morals feed into and upon a stereotype: Roman **self-fashioning** as a community of farmer-citizens whose identity was rooted in working the land.[49] Sallust eloquently sums up in nostalgic reactionary terms how this relates to cultural fracture in the first century BCE: imperial expansion from the mid-Republic onwards had led to Romans losing touch with the countryside. A weakened relationship with the land, however imaginary, threatened the **autochthonic** qualities of Rome's historical imagination and impaired access to a collective historical memory.[50]

Picking up on Nora's terminology again, we can read landscape as a 'site of memory' giving access to *priscae uirtutes*, ancient and fundamental qualities of the ideal Roman.[51] Roman origin myths traditionally fixate on teasing out the relationship between citizenship and the pastoral quality of the pre-urban city-site. Wachtel comments on this kind of topographic yearning to map identity to place: 'it is… possible to search for the original world by looking there where it authentically was, by returning to those places where the ancestors

---

[48] See Favro 1996: 39, 176–80. For detail, see Grimal 1984: 109–66; and for analysis, see Wallace-Hadrill 1998b. Examples of ancient criticism of luxury estates can be found in Cic. *Leg.* 2.2, *Q Fr.* 3.1.5; Hor. *Carm.* 2.15, 18 (cf. Sen. *Ep.* 89.21); Mart. 12.50, 57, 66; Ov. *Fast.* 6.639–48; Sall. *Cat.* 12.3; Sen. *Controv.* 2.1.13; Suet. *Calig.* 37, *Ner.* 31; Tac. *Ann.* 3.55, 15.42; Varro, *Rust.* 3.3.6–4.3. A Second Sophistic perspective is found in Plut. *Vit. Luc.* 39.2–3. On Nero, see Elsner 1994. Nevertheless, Roman authors blow hot and cold on this topic, praising luxury estates when it suits (C. Edwards 1993: 137–72), e.g. Vitr. *De arch.* 6.5.1–2. For images of excavated rooms from Nero's Domus Aurea today, see Webography: Curran; recent discoveries (September 2009) online via the Ministero per i Beni e le Attività Culturali.

[49] E.g. Varro, *Rust.* 2, *Praef.* 1–2; cf. Cato, *Agr.*, *Praef.*

[50] Sall. *Cat.* 2–3, 10–13. Discussing Varro, *Rust.*, Green 1997: 432–3 suggests that elite anxiety configured such shifts as relocating political power from Rome to the culturally supercharged estates, making urban life hard to justify (see also Howe 2004). Dench 2005: 37–92 provides a detailed summary discussion.

[51] Nora's *lieux de mémoire* interrogate the relationship between place, ethnicity, and politics; his project undertook 'to achieve a close link between a *general* problematic of memory with the particular thematic of "places"' (2001a: xx, emphasis original). See also Farrell 1997, and Gowing 2005 passim.

lived'.[52] Viewed retrospectively in terms of mythic history, inhabiting and contemplating this site by the Tiber where Rome would be built is always a process of colonizing a landscape of ancestral exile. Telling stories about the authentic ancestral city-site brings into sharp focus the loss of the new settlers' *ur*-city (Troy): only as a result of Troy's destruction and Aeneas' exile, in mythic terms, can Roman landscapes come into being. This is set out most clearly in Virgil's *Aeneid* (as we investigate in Chapter IV): Rome – Troy refounded – is what Aeneas and the Trojans have in their sights even as they gaze across the countryside of Latium and Campania.

This tension informs the sometimes paradoxical connections between cultivated landscapes and historical process in late Republican authors as seemingly disparate as Catullus and Varro. An idealizing traditionalist such as Cato might, writing in the early second century BCE, still imagine an ideal Rome whose primary function was to be the tactical headquarters of an agrarian people, providing infrastructure and coherence for its primarily agricultural citizenry, but he seems to have been swimming against the tide even then. Rome's success as a city and imperial centre inevitably made it impossible for *every* citizen to count a farm in Latium or even Campania (core 'Roman' agricultural territory) as their own 'home'. Moreover, an increasing body of 'Romans' in the new provinces might never experience Italian landscapes (or the myth-saturated topography of Rome) at all.

Perceptions of this shift are very much in evidence in Virgil's *Eclogues*, where nostalgia-soaked rural aesthetics gain political bite and a public edge, setting city and countryside on a collision course.[53] These poems **focalize** urbane, Roman, and political poetics through an Arcadian perspective, using shepherds with artfully Greek names and Hellenic landscape backdrops to discuss some of the most urgent issues facing Rome in the wake of decades of civil war. They work, intermittently, within an environment that fuses real-life changes in land use with a highly intellectual sensibility. Their speakers communicate stripped-down Roman problems using self-consciously literary language, and re-imagine pastoral concerns and activities through a Hellenistic filter. In this way, landscape in the *Eclogues* showcases how 'Greek culture leaves its mark on Rome at every moment we can document'.[54]

---

[52] Wachtel 1990: 124.
[53] See Leach 1974. Skoie 2006 explores Virgil's city/country clash in depth.
[54] Wallace-Hadrill 2008: 25.

When Spirn comments that 'to call some landscapes natural and others artificial or cultural misses the truth that landscapes are never wholly one or the other', the *Eclogues*' tightly scripted blend of reality and artifice has got there first.[55] Their oppositional foci (*labor* plus **negotium** versus *otium*) are ideally united in the concept of landscape – a space that combines aesthetic and sensory pleasure in the essential beneficence of 'nature', with strategies for investigating human mastery of nature's unknowability. As Gowers observes (of gardening): 'there is always a tension between control and runaway fertility'.[56] As we shall see, controlling nature – whether physically, or conceptually as an object of study or a visual field, or artistically – is central to what landscape means in ancient Rome, and underpins its significance as an area for study. Hence the search for a Roman sense of landscape illuminates and enriches understanding of their world and its differences from and similarities to (y)ours. We may not feel fully comfortable with Fairclough's early twentieth-century observation that 'the ancient Greeks and Romans did not differ essentially from modern people in their appreciation of the world of nature', but we will see how contemporary experience of landscape and the environment continues to echo tropes and archetypes that were already in play two thousand years ago.[57]

---

[55] Spirn 1998: 24.
[56] Gowers 2000: 141.
[57] Fairclough 1930: 251.

II LANDSCAPE AND AESTHETICS

Ac principio terra uniuersa cernatur...uestita floribus herbis arboribus frugibus, quorum omnium incredibilis multitudo insatiabili uarietate distinguitur. Adde huc fontium gelidas perennitates, liquores perlucidos amnium, riparum uestitus uiridissimos, speluncarum concauas altitudines, saxorum asperitates, inpendentium montium altitudines inmensitatesque camporum...   Cic. *Nat. D.* 2.98

In the first place, the whole world is subject to our gaze...clothed with flowers, grass, trees, grain, all of which are incredibly numerous and relentlessly varied and diverse. Add to these unceasing cool springs, the pellucid streams of rivers – their banks clothed in vivid greenery – the deep vaults of caves, the cragginess of rocks, the peaks of sheer mountains and the immeasurability of plains...

Defining a space as landscape suggests that it is visually distinctive and interesting, that it attracts the eye, and engages the senses and faculties. Agriculture (or productivity) can be one important feature of what makes space into land and divides it up into -scapes and territories, but it is not always the main issue.[1] Typically, classical texts featuring something akin to our 'landscape' showcase the natural environment supporting, threatening, or ornamenting human existence.[2] So at the beginning of the Graeco-Roman tradition we see that the landscapes of Homeric epic, or pastoral verse (for example, the Hellenistic poets Bion and Theocritus), gain order and meaning from the inclusion of human figures, but they also contribute atmosphere and a distinctive sense of place that enriches the stories that play out against them.[3] Chapter I introduced one particularly delightful and hugely popular topographic trope: an idyllic space where sensory and aesthetic

---

[1] Venturi 1989; M. Carroll 1992.

[2] An excellent example is Cic. *Nat. D.* 2.87: the structure of the world could not have been bettered in respect either to utility or beauty (another good example is Ov. *Fast.* 4.125–9). Compare how Thoreau – a philosophically inclined naturalist and author – characterizes the American wilderness as 'necessary...for a resource and a background, the raw material of all our civilization'. Thoreau is useful as an example of someone describing landscape in terms that Cicero might recognize (e.g. 2004: 39–40). For an introduction to Thoreau's pastoral, see Yu 1996; on reading Thoreau against contemporary critical theory, see Bennett 2002. On 'Greek' poetic landscapes, A. Parry 1957 gets things started.

[3] Gill 1995: 67–89 sums up on nature's ethics and norms. See also Giesecke 2007: 35–41; Osborne 1992. For background, see Hes. *Op.* 'Natural environment' is rarely a neat translation for *natura* (Pellicer 1966). To compare the pragmatics, see Alcock, Cherry, and Davis 1994.

qualities encourage harmony between humans and nature. The *locus classicus* or touchstone for this *locus amoenus* is Plato's dialogue *Phaedrus*. Famously, this dialogue riffs on a very specific landscape scene, one which was to have an intense and far-reaching effect on subsequent landscape discourse, and which provides an ideal point of departure.[4]

A day out with Socrates

Strolling with a philosophically inclined friend, Phaedrus, along the lovely banks of the river Ilissos outside Athens, Socrates is moved by the beauty spot to extol its spreading plane tree, the shade and fragrance provided by the blossoms, the delightful chill of the stream, the cooling breeze, the summery chirruping of the cicadas, and the gently sloping bank. These are the 'natural' features. This is not, however, by any stretch of the imagination, an untouched and unrefined 'wilderness'.

For a start, the sensory and intellectual (or **somatic**) impressions described by Socrates are dependent upon human experience and agency (the water is cold, we learn, because Socrates dips his foot in it); **epistemology** (the particular placement of statues and offerings allows Socrates to infer that the place is sacred to nymphs and Achelöos); **taxonomy** (this is a summer scene – sounds are being made by cicadas, a cooling breeze is welcome); and desire for physical gratification (the sloping grassy bank presents a perfect headrest). Secondly, **anthropomorphic** gods and goddesses (Hera, Dionysus, riverine deities) are key presences in the scene. By recalling and alluding to them, Socrates pulls extremes of free and controlled sexuality into the picture, and implicitly hints at a tension between civic and rustic order (Hera; Dionysus) and wild nature (Dionysus; the nymphs).[5] Socrates benefits intellectually from the controlled distance from Athens offered by this charming spot (like Rome's portico gardens, it offers a getaway where one can stroll, converse, and think), but the site itself also gains significance precisely as a day trip recalled in a literary dialogue.[6] Philosophically cultured and textualized memory transforms Socrates'

---

[4] Pl. *Phdr.* 230b2–c5 (set in the late fifth century BCE, but probably composed in the first half of the fourth century). Rosenmeyer 1969: 179–203 is still the best introductory discussion; Ferrari 1987 discusses the whole dialogue in depth; Hass 1998 summarizes what *locus amoenus* denotes and evokes. M. Edwards 1987: 267 draws out Christian use of the topos.

[5] Dorter 1971 provides a clear reading of the imagery involved.

[6] Hindin 2008 shows how memory is key to the perception of beauty in this dialogue.

delightful day out from an instance of serendipity into a privileged site visit. In the process, it prefigures the role of cultivated nature in the great Athenian philosophical schools such as the Academy and Lyceum.[7]

We also see echoes of this in Epicurean philosophy. The site of the Hellenistic philosopher Epicurus' Athenian philosophy garden remains uncertain. Writing in the mid-first century CE, Pliny the Elder makes Epicurus' Garden – in effect, a landscaped, outdoor setting for philosophical study – the inspiration for the luxury estates beloved of Rome's wealthy families.[8] In the wake of Epicurus, the close association of philosophy with withdrawal to a quasi-natural, out-of-town site of intellectual cultivation, combined with the productive agricultural associations of growing-your-own, gained momentum. We have few contemporary descriptions of how Greek philosophers used landscape and garden settings, but the association is strongly reflected in the settings for 'doing' Greek philosophy as described in (much) later authors – Lucretius, Cicero, Plutarch, Diogenes Laertius, among others. Romans enthusiastically redrafted and gave new context to Greek philosophy by locating it in the colonnaded gardens of suburban and rustic villas (see the frescoed garden in Figure 9), blending the traditional agricultural focus of the villa with Greek civic architectural form (the stoa). Cicero's work suggests that how humankind related to nature was also a hot topic conceptually in the late Republic. His *De natura deorum* (probably set in the late 70s BCE) has Balbus, a Stoic, say that human intervention transforms nature's landscape into an *altera natura* (an 'other' or alternative nature), recalling Augé's 'second nature' quoted in Chapter I.[9] In his dialogue *Academica* (set in the late 60s BCE), Cicero himself comments that 'there is a kind of natural fodder for the spirit and intellect in the study and contemplation of nature'.[10] Missing from this reading, however, is the 'wilderness' aesthetic.[11]

---

[7] Osborne 1987: 168–9 discusses the schools' natural settings and provides an excellent contextualizing overview of classical Greek rural landscapes. Giesecke 2007: 88–91 connects 'garden' philosophy to Athens and its aftermath at Rome. See also Alcock 2007.

[8] Plin. *HN* 19.50–1, discussed briefly by von Stackelberg 2009: 10–11. On Epicurus' Garden, see now D. Clay 2009. Cic. *Fin.* makes it a landmark. On Epicureanism, see Sharples 2006: 226–32. Cima and La Rocca 1998 is a go-to collection on what 'garden' means at Rome.

[9] Cic. *Nat. D.* 2.152.

[10] Cic. *Acad.* 2.127.

[11] Cf. Garrison 1992, a contrasting reading of 'bad' nature in Augustan literature – published just when global warming, natural disasters, and international eco-politics were gaining headline status; Stibbe 2009 develops this angle.

Wild at heart

Untamed 'nature' was often associated with the god Dionysus (Bacchus). It is particularly significant for our investigation of landscape that a key quality in Dionysiac worship was going out of the *polis* and into the unknown, 'up the mountain'.[12] These trips are emblematic of the alien, ecstatic, or frenzied qualities that gave Dionysus added bite as a god: his cult drew together forces of **entropy** and order and encouraged cult worshippers to act in a manner appealing to the increasingly urbanized fourth century BCE and onwards – though there is no clear evidence that cult followers made actual rather than symbolic excursions to wild mountains and caves.[13] Just the idea of going to the wild lands induced enough of a *frisson* of mystery and danger. Some of the most potent **memes** circulating in the Hellenistic world drew together Dionysus and the king who tried to outdo him, Alexander the Great, to show how, even in the here and now, exceptional, semi-divine mortals could still hope to experience the world of myth.[14] After Alexander's death, these memes spread and developed in the super-states carved up by his successors, and enthusiasm for exuberant Dionysiac imagery made his cult a pan-Mediterranean winner.[15]

The cult's popularity inevitably filtered into Roman experience, in particular in the years after the First Punic War.[16] It made for a potent mix: a god-king-commander encouraging his own worship and imprinting his ethos onto strange new worlds, exotic civilizations, and wild territories. This imagery increasingly fitted Rome's status as the new imperial power and, by the first century BCE, Dionysiac motifs had become high fashion in the decor of luxury villas.[17] Cultural **syncretism**

---

[12] Eur. *Bacch.* 977–86, 1043–52.

[13] See Bérard and Bron 1986. See also Paus. 3.24.3–4 (Dionysian landscape), 5.19.6 (Dionysus on the chest of Kypselos; cf. Paus. 10.23.1–7 on the god Pan). Alcock 1993: 200–10 discusses rural cults and the sacred landscape. On performance and the Hellenistic Dionysiac cult, see e.g. Kuttner 1999b: 102–5.

[14] Burkert 1985: 291 argues that a lack of fixed cult centres made Dionysus particularly interesting when worldviews were expanding and societies fragmenting and reconfiguring. For Alexander's epic Dionysiac quest, see e.g. Arr. *Anab.* 5.1; also Gallini 1970: 97–155.

[15] Jaccottet 2003 analyses wide-ranging inscriptional evidence; Burkert 1985: 290–6 considers Dionysiac cult as a pre-Hellenistic mystery religion. On Dionysus in the Hellenistic world, see concisely Mikalson 2006: 209, 211–12, 214–15, 221; on ancient Greek religion more generally, see Bremmer 2004 (excellent introduction) and Mikalson 2005.

[16] See e.g. Bruhl 1953; Gallini 1970: 11–52; Foucher 1981.

[17] Wyler 2008 sums up (in French) on Dionysus in Roman villas, but is less attentive to the spatial dynamics of villa use (on which see e.g. J. T. Smith 1997). In English, Beard, North,

and growing interest in explaining Rome's rise to power probably enhanced the lure of Dionysus towards wide-ranging significance. His diverse sexual and political associations bundled paradoxical notions of personal **autarky** (putting individuals in control of their own destiny and salvation), ecstatic freedom, and uncompromising autocracy. Despite Rome's suppression of cult practices by senate decree in 186 BCE,[18] Bacchic nature continued to feature in Roman cultural production. It offered something of the mystery and danger associated with the natural environment in Homer, and hinted at aspects of the sublime (as later described by Pseudo-Longinus).[19] It also keyed into Epicurean philosophy's paring away of the fears and tensions associated with civilization in order to plug all entities directly into the elemental cosmos. Finally, it offered scope for Stoic philosophers to speculate on the beneficence of nature in particular contexts, its relationship with divine reason, and how best to live in harmony with the universe.[20]

The complex flourishing of Bacchic nature in Roman culture is complemented by the success of one influential strand in Hellenistic 'nature' discourse: pastoral verse. Theocritus' *Idyll* 7 is the most perfectly realized Greek example, reinventing a landscape immediately recognisable from *Phaedrus*, and showcasing just how amenable the franchise was. Pastoral verse came to Rome complete with tightly controlled numinous qualities and delightful rustic landscapes replete with amenity value, but still offering thrilling hints of wilderness just offstage.[21] This aspect is exemplified in the frightening, off-kilter

and Price 1998: 161–6 take Pompeii's Villa of the Mysteries as a case study; Wyler 2006: 224–8 examines Dionysus at Rome's Villa 'Farnesina'.

[18] *S. C. de Bacchanalibus*; writing in the late first century BCE, Livy (39.8–19) makes this a sensible response to a contagious, Greek underground cult. The reasons for the Senate's action probably related to political instability at Rome. Takács 2000 summarizes lucidly. See also Gruen 1990; Pailler 1988; Beard, North, and Price 1998: 92–6. Pagán 2005: 50–67 explores the literary angle (cf. Bacchus' walk-on at Lucr. 5.743; Liber/Bacchus in Ov. *Fast.* 3).

[19] Porter 2007 is the ideal introduction. [Longinus] *Subl.* 9.8 refers to Homer directly (the purity and majesty with which Homer's description of the sea endows Poseidon). Innes 2002 discusses [Longinus] *Subl.* 15.6: Bacchic frenzy on a Euripidean mountain is preferable to an Aeschylean palace. Compare the more familiar model: Verg. *Aen* 8.349–50; Schrijvers 2006 shows how this plays out in Silius Italicus (late first century CE).

[20] See Segal 1963. On Plato, Aristotle, and Epicurus in these terms, see e.g. Gill 1995 (on the norms of nature). For Stoicism, the whole cosmos was a living and coherent entity. M. J. White 2003: 124 summarizes Stoicism's rejection of value-neutrality when investigating nature. Rosenmeyer 1969: 181–203 examines the unity of nature (humans, cosmos) in pastoral.

[21] See also e.g. Bion's poetry; evocative scenes in Ap. Rhod. *Argon*. On Horace's melding of Bacchic and pastoral nature, see Leach 1993; Spencer 2006. Cf. Lucretius' primal landscape (Lucr. 5.925–1010). Petsalis-Diomidis 2007 explores the relationship between landscape and (divine) epiphany.

locus amoenus imagined in Apollonius' third-century-BCE epic poem *Argonautica* (2.727–51), where the scenography embodies nature's implacability and destructive potential. Apollonius achieves this effect through subversion of the same pastoral tropes we first met in Plato – shade, the spreading plane, woodland, rocks, slopes, and a river. Just like the Theocritean landscapes, this conjures up intense sensory responses: emotive triggers draw the audience into the frame. Here, however, the familiar sites induce a frisson of tension between macrocosmic order (the sun always rises; waves break against the shore; summer follows spring) and the microcosmic vagaries of individual human interventions and attempts to control nature.[22]

Evidence for the attractiveness of pastoral's combination of wild and tamed nature crops up not just in literature but also, as recent studies have emphasized, in visual culture, in particular as subject material for domestic landscape frescoes.[23] In fact as reinvented at Rome, the signs of pastoral become memes in a multimedia discourse that shapes, reflects, and interrogates culture. This sits well with a comparison of memes to genes: (landscape) memes generate (Roman) culture by replicating and evolving just as genes create organisms.[24] Pastoral's internal logic, as influentially recast for Rome by Virgil, turns away from both physical and intellectual labour and conjures up a nostalgic, melancholy Golden Age scene of freedom, pleasure, and ease.[25]

Perhaps a decade or so after Virgil's *Eclogues*, Horace *Odes* 2.19 presents an excellent example. The poet gazes beyond the confines of fields, groves, and woodland, fixing his eyes instead on remote crags. Here Bacchus is in control, hinting at a challenging, entropic, and dangerously wild landscape of the imagination. Horace's attempts to

---

[22] E.g. the cave is Hades', the river turns out to be the Acheron. The landscape is personalized and ethicized by the introduction of animating descriptors, and by the ways in which nature threatens and saves groups of passers-through. M. F. Williams 1991 looks generally at landscape in Apollonius. Cf. Livy's description of the landscape of the Caudine Forks (9.2.6–9, 9.3.1–3), useful when we look at Columella in Chapter V.3.

[23] Recognizably 'landscape' scenes become iconographically significant in the early first century BCE (the so-called 'Second Style' frescoes). Ling 1977 is a usefully concise, if dry, starting point (Peters 1963 is also still important); Mazzoleni and Pappalardo 2004 offer lavish illustrations; Chapter VI investigates further (see Figures 13–16). On the interplay between literary and visual pastoral, see e.g. Leach 1974: 70–112; 1988: 27–72, 197–306; 2004: 123–52; and (looking at Greece and Rome) La Rocca 2008. See also Conan 1986; Mitchell: 1986: 47–50; Bergmann 1991, 1992, 1995a. More generally, see Daniels and Cosgrove 1988.

[24] Adapting Taylor 2002: 229.

[25] Scully 1988 assesses the tension between cities and Golden Age discourse. A. T. Smith 2003: 105, 109–11 offers useful methodological caveats against swallowing whole the textual, elite, oligarchic presentation of this nexus. Papaioannou 2003 discusses Virgil's Evander (*Aeneid*) and the Golden Age. Contrast Evander in Ov. *Fast.* (Fantham 1992).

conjure up Bacchic nature are heavily indebted to the kind of consensual and shared 'memory' of what the untamed and dehumanized nature that we have been exploring ought to look like.[26] It becomes landscape rather than a non-place by dint of shared understanding of topoi that can signify 'wilderness' – Bacchus and rocky crags. This is 'wilderness' as one might see it painted on a Roman villa wall, and description in Latin codifies it as Roman space.[27] Slipping between Bacchus and Liber as names for the god enhances the sense of cultural duality (Greek/Roman), and the landscape's malleability is emphasized when we hear how Bacchus/Liber (in the spirit of Roman engineering) can reroute rivers and tame the sea. This is also a landscape of plenty (springs flow with wine, and streams with milk; honey pours from cavities in the trees) but it is a plenty that serves the god's purpose, not humankind's.[28] In this, if anything, its unknowability or at least strangeness is most obviously located. Here, the *locus amoenus* trope disconnects Horace's villa and country landscapes from their tenuous connection with the reality of life on the farm. The intellectual and aesthetic complexity of these landscapes obeys no rational pattern of spatial organization to suit a productive and profitable villa.[29] In this, as in other Latin literary pastoral texts, artfully wild but intrinsically productive and fertile nature frames and nourishes the figures that populate it, enabling them to compose music and song while participating in a world that straddles myth, history, and reality.[30]

Meaning, morality, and beauty

The *locus amoenus* is at least notionally a scene within which poets and philosophers find that verse and thought come naturally and with divine support. Pastoral verse imagines a rustic landscape populated by poet-shepherds whose favoured mode of expression is song; and Roman bucolic poets such as Virgil and (a century or so later)

---

[26] Alcock 1993: 24–32, 53–4, 80–92, 201–2 traces perceptions of rural Greece under Rome. Pentheus is name-checked at Hor. *Carm.* 2.19.15.

[27] Hor. *Carm.* 2.19.1, 7, 17–18. Cf. the late first-century-BCE landscape with Perseus and Andromeda from the Villa at Boscotrecase, Campania (Metropolitan Museum of Art, New York, cat. 20.192.16).

[28] Hor. *Carm.* 2.19.10–12, 18.

[29] Frischer, Crawford, and de Simone 2006 present an excellent overview of what the reality of an estate such as Horace's might have been like.

[30] Segal 1981: 226 comments on the mystic qualities of this poem.

Calpurnius Siculus continue this trend. The pleasurable qualities of pastoral's *locus amoenus* are often associated with the trials of love, sex, and literary composition, which in turn draw in Venus, fertility, and the process of authorship – a *locus* (place) gains *amoenitas* (delightfulness) by being rendered in words, conceptualized, or depicted, and through engendering or inspiring composition.[31] Latin literary pastoral explicitly and often self-consciously negotiates the boundaries and shared spaces of rural and urban ways of life and attitudes to the world.

Virgil's *Eclogues* present landscapes 'charged with human feeling', and these ten short poems' contribution to understanding how humans respond to and inhabit a fragile environment under threat from political and social change has generated voluminous scholarship.[32] Like the *Eclogues*, rustic landscapes in Ovid's *Metamorphoses* mark another key phase in the development of pastoral, showcasing the complex symbolism of a countryside that is both archetypal and constantly in a state of flux, always subject to the demands of narrative and context.[33] Latin literary pastoral also gains a visual vocabulary in dialogue with the kinds of pattern-book rusticity on display in fashionable wall-painting from the first centuries BCE and CE. Pastoral in itself, however, is not our main focus here. Instead, in this and the next section I suggest three less obvious authors who sample elements of pastoral in ways that show its wider impact, specifically, how landscape marries aesthetics and morality more generally in Roman discourse: Catullus (mid-first century BCE), Horace (late first century BCE), and Statius (late first century CE).

...landscape acquires significant organization as a result of certain extrinsic and intrinsic factors... The frame literally defines the landscape, both in the sense of determining its outer limits and in the sense that landscape is constituted by its frame...the landscape

---

[31] On authorship in pastoral, see Breed 2006. Definitions of pastoral were key to twentieth-century scholarship (e.g. Empson 1935; Rosenmeyer 1969; R. Williams 1973; Poggiolo 1975; Halperin 1983; Loughrey 1984; A. Patterson 1987; Gutzwiller 1991; Alpers 1996; Hubbard 1998; Gifford 1999; Marx 2000 [1964]; see now Fantuzzi and Paphangelis 2006). On reception, see e.g. A. Patterson 1987; Skoie and Velázquez 2006; Paschalis 2007.

[32] Alpers 1979: 231. Hardie 1998: 5–27 introduces concisely; Martindale 1997b sets the *Eclogues*' politics of pastoral into the European tradition. Segal 1981 influentially draws Virgil and Theocritus together. On contextualizing landscape in the *Eclogues*, see Leach 1974; Geymonat 2000. Putnam sums up the tensions: Virgil will make pastoral's woods 'worthy of a consul, performing the impossible through song' (1970: 137).

[33] Ovid's *Metamorphoses*, too, have a lengthy bibliography. For Ovid's landscapes see Grimal 1938 (examining links with landscape art); H. Parry 1964; Segal 1969; Hinds 2002 (setting Ovid within a tradition of landscape reception); and Newlands 2004 (connecting Ovid's landscapes with those of Statius). Useful and accessible on Calpurnius Siculus are Leach 1973, 1975; P. J. Davis 1987; Newlands 1987; Mackie 1989; Hubbard 1996; R. G. Mayer 2006: 453–63.

may also be internally focused and organized by its relation to what is non-landscape – a human figure in heroic action, for instance… Remove the frame…and the landscape spills into a shapeless gathering of natural features. It has nothing to contain or shape its constituents, nothing to environ, nothing for which to be a setting, nothing to supplement.[34]

Catullus 61 locates us in the ultimate 'framed' poetic landscape – Greece's Mount Helicon, sacred to the Muses and complete with springs and grottoes. This mythic landscape is not just an idyll (literally, a 'little picture'); it also stimulates its audience to think about the more contained scenography of the garden (invoked by the presence of Venus, the protector of *horti*).[35] Recent study of what gardens mean and represent in Rome helps decode Catullus' poem.[36] At its heart is a bride-to-be, like a blooming hyacinth in a rich man's charming garden.[37] Marriage is entwined here with visual pleasure, sexuality, and fertility, zoning the garden as a place where the family is collectively sustained and nurtured. The poem is saturated with fruitful, Golden Age symbolism and vivid colour. Gardens, like families and marriages, are also strictly contained sites. As literary constructs and physical spaces they associate the cultivation of food with the pursuit of wisdom, and Catullus' heavily symbolic set-up signals that his carefully framed scene is designed to make us think about the constituent elements in society, and how best to foster a positive relationship between individual and collective, human and nature.

Roman interest in the biographical qualities of the relationship between nature and cultivator (we grow like our gardens and vice versa) suggests that Catullus' link between gardens, marriage, and childbearing is particularly meaningful for understanding how families thrive and endure.[38] This poem's optimistic vision is,

---

[34] Andrews 1999: 5.

[35] Varro marks Venus as a natural fertility goddess (e.g. *Rust.* 1.1.6; cf. *Ling.* 6.20); the other, and obvious, late Republican comparator is Lucretius' Epicurean poem on what makes the world go round, i.e. categorizing 'Venus' appropriately (see Gale 1994: 67, 71, 153, 211–31). Lucr. 5.907–15 sends up a ludicrously exaggerated Golden Age, and then (5.945–52) reinvests it with 'rational' pastoral sensibility (cf. the Platonic Lucr. 2.29–33). On Lucretian landscapes, see e.g. Gillis 1967; De Lacy 1964; and concisely, Giesecke 2007: 128–34. Virgil's didactic landscapes (Verg. *G.*) are very much in tune with this.

[36] Chapter VI returns to gardens. In brief: Beard 1998 has proved influential on how and why gardens matter; Zanker 1988: 285–91 concisely sums up on cultural production; Pagán 2006 strolls through some famous textual gardens; von Stackelberg 2009 prioritizes spatial analysis. Jashemski 1979 is encyclopaedic on the gardens of Pompeii and nearby towns; Grimal 1984 catalogues Roman garden texts and sites; Andreae 1996 is less detailed, but well illustrated.

[37] Catull. 61.87–9.

[38] Pagán 2006: 13–14 provides a taste of the debate.

however, immediately reworked at 62.38–44.[39] Here, the natural and unmediated beneficence of the breezes, the sun, and showers is no adequate substitute for the lord of the manor's lack of attention to his plot. This is a garden in which the natural order of things is out of sync with human behaviour. As in poem 61, a flower stands apart, but here it has no proper context for display, thus cancelling its aesthetic value. It is an object of desire, but in this '*hortus saeptus*' (*enclosed* garden) there is little hint of sustaining productivity, or civic or social duty.[40] Pushing the imagery hard, we might see Catullus alluding pointedly to a differently framed 'enclosure'. We do not know when construction commenced on Caesar's Saepta Julia in Rome (see Figure 3), eventually completed by Augustus' aide Agrippa in 26 BCE, but Cicero's allusion in 54 BCE puts it in Catullus' mix.[41] More straightforwardly available as an associative allusion is the Republican Saepta (or Ouile, 'sheepfold') that it replaced. This was where the *comitia centuriata* met, and 'chutes' funnelled citizens (like sheep) into the appropriate spaces for casting their votes.[42] No such communal 'productivity' characterizes Catullus' enclosure, and beauty alone is not enough to make such landscapes viable.

In *Epistle* 1.14, Horace presents himself as an enforced exile – trapped in the city by his friend Lamia's grief after a bereavement and longing for a return to the autarky that the countryside seems to offer.[43] This is in contrast to his addressee, his estate manager (*uilicus*), who suffers this exile in reverse (sequestered at Horace's country property). Horace describes this rejuvenating estate as woodland (*siluae*) and a smallholding (*agellus*), and comments that only hateful business affairs (*negotium*) can drag him from there to Rome.[44] In his mind's eye, this delightful and ethically idyllic space is characterized specifically as the opposite of wilderness:

> …*Nam quae deserta et inhospita tesqua*
> *credis, amoena uocat mecum qui sentit, et odit*
> *quae tu pulchra putas.*   Hor. *Epist.* 1.14.19–21.

---

[39] Cf. a similar image at 11.21–4.

[40] On gardens and fences, see Pagán 2006: 10–12; von Stackelberg 2009: 21–4, 66–72.

[41] Cic. *Att.* 4.16.8.

[42] The *comitia centuriata* (Centuriate Assembly) was a political assembly, for the purposes of which the citizen body was divided into six property classes that generated 193 block 'votes' (the 'centuries'). Its first-past-the-post system favoured wealthier citizens' interests.

[43] Hor. *Epist.* 1 was probably published *c.*20/19 BCE.

[44] Ibid., 1.14.17.

...For that which is a desert and inhospitable wilderness
in your eyes, becomes a delightful spot when he who thinks like me
   describes it, and hates
the very thing you think beautiful.

The rural landscape is, here, one without urban amenities – no cantinas or taverns, no sex for sale, no entertainers (set out in the complaints of the estate manager, *Epist.* 1.14.21–6). Horace quickly moves to overwrite these 'criticisms' by sketching in the idyllic rustic archetypes that might by contrast characterize the country life of his implied (that is, elite, intellectual) audience: a modest meal, a refreshing doze on the grassy riverbank, and perhaps the prospect of some light work shifting turfs and stones later (cf. Figures 13 and 15). This imagined task draws Amphion into the poem and, by allusion, Horace also evokes Orpheus, the quintessential musical celebrity fatality.[45] In myth, Zeus's son Amphion used his lyrical talent to help build the walls of Thebes, moving rocks through music alone. Horace's poem conjures up the scene, but his versified earth- and rock-moving has neither the grandeur of epic nor any impressive outcome. Making Amphion and Orpheus points of reference for a gentleman-farmer's rustic idyll emphasizes how much of a literary cliché the topos of country retreat as private kingdom had become by the late first century BCE. It also hints at the impossibility of turning back the clock to recover a notional lost world of authentic *labor* and frugality. Civilization is the defining context for this kind of landscape. Here in Horace, the country landscape is most productive when helping him to write (we see this motif later with Pliny in Chapter V), and he writes because – as he tells it – his career at Rome (rewarded by the grant of a country estate, from his patron Maecenas) depends on his literary skills. The lines quoted above emphasize the subjective and imaginary nature of these literary landscapes.

Layers of meaning

Jumping forward to the 90s CE, Statius' *Woodland* (*Siluae*) collection of poems shows the symbolic potential of case studies of individual

---

[45] Ibid., 1.14.35, 39. A significant intratextual link is to Hor. *Ars P.* 395 (cf. *Carm.* 3.11.2, and see also Ov. *Ars am.* 3.321–5 and Prop. 3.2.5–6). Stat. *Silv.* 2.2.62 offers a similar combination of '*saxa*' and '*moueo*' (Statius' referent is Pollio *qua* Amphion). Linking Amphion and Orpheus, see e.g. Cic. *Arch.* 19; Paus. 6.20.18. Frazer 1992 teases out 'pastoral' as a villa quality.

plants in a visually rich landscape. *Siluae* 2.3 imagines an aetiology for a plane tree on the Roman estate of one of Statius' wealthy dedicatees, Atedius Melior.[46] The poem ranges through the prehistory of urban Rome's landscape, exploring the local sites before they were enclosed by Melior's boundaries.[47] This landscape showcases an alternative version of the intense relationship between person and place that we saw in Catullus' marriage poem (61), and hints at similarly embedded ethical qualities. Melior and his landscape are inextricably linked, as set out in the opening lines' juxtaposition of terms and elision of syntax, and intertwining of man and tree:

> *Stat* quae *perspicuas* *nitidi* Melioris *opacet*
> *arbor* aquas *complexa* lacus;   Stat. *Silv.* 2.3.1–2

> *There stands* one which to the *pellucid* waters of *gleaming* Melior *gives shade*:
> *a tree embracing* a pool;

The first words of these two lines strike the eye. The tree marks a fixed point: it stands, controlling the landscape vignette (emphasized when the eye spots the embracing '*complexa*'). Where the first word plants the tree, the last word of that line gives us the 'pastoral' clue: this is a tree designed to give shade; unsurprisingly it turns out to be one of pastoral's favourites, a (water-loving) plane, implicitly flagged up by the last word of the sense unit ('*lacus*'). *Perspicua* and *nitidus*, juxtaposed, mark a contrast to the shade that syntactically closes the embrace on Melior: the two terms imply something very similar, connecting gleaming Melior with the luminous clarity of the pool, which turns out eventually to be both refuge and prison for a nymph fleeing the god Pan. This is a refined landscape of hills, streams, and groves – a god-haunted, mythic landscape, familiar from pastoral (as Pan's presence emphasizes). But it is not just a titillating and artful pastoral scene. The explicit setting amid Rome's seven hills makes a difference (see Figures 3 and 5). For Hardie,

the poem operates with a twofold set of metaphorical equivalences...constituting the aetiological deposit, as it were, of the mythic narrative...the closing description of... Melior reflects aspects of the ensemble of tree and pool, and of the narrative thereby

---

[46] On Melior, see Nauta 2002: 226–7. See also Myers 2000, 2005.

[47] Hardie 2006 is a key recent discussion. Echoes of late-first-century BCE literary landscapes abound in Statius; Vessey 1981: 46 comments on similarities with Ov. *Met.* 5. 572–642; see also Newlands 2004. Keep an eye out for echoes of Tib. 2.5.23–56, Prop. 4 (*aetia*, 'origin stories'), and Verg. *Aen* 8 – see Chapter IV. Rea 2007 sets up the big issues for the Palatine.

memorialised, with the further result that the two framing descriptions, of physical landscape feature and abstract qualities of the soul, also reflect each other.[48]

The shifting points of view in this poem encourage us to read **intratextually**. We are offered an array of different perspectives on the plane tree and its site, each one actualizing a different experience of the landscape.[49] We first see the tree primarily as a function of Melior himself: tree and man share a characteristic sparkling liquidity which is set off by their shady setting. The tree's shape and alignment then render a naturalistic scenography, voiced by the narrator:

> ...quae robore ab imo
> <in>curuata uadis redit inde cacumine recto
> ardua, ceu mediis iterum nascatur ab undis
> atque habitet <u>uitreum</u> tacitis radicibus amnem.   Stat. *Silv.* 2.3.2–5.

> ...from the base of its trunk
> it is bent into the waters, then it turns back, with crown erect
> towards the heights, just as if from the midst of the waves it was born afresh
> and living with hidden roots in the *glassy* stream.

Vitreus echoes *perspicua* (line 1), but otherwise this could stand as a straightforward nature description. Reading on, Pan becomes the aggressive agent of change. Now we see the fleeing nymph Pholoë running from her pursuer, through woods and streams, catching glimpses now of his shaggy legs, then of his horns. As the focalizing subject, her headlong flight takes her into explicitly proto-Roman and therefore implicitly civilized urban space. She passes (and is visible from) the 'warlike grove of Janus', the dark country seat (*rus*) of Cacus, the agricultural landscape of the Quirinal, before ending up in the Caelian wilderness (that is, where Melior's estate 'now' sits), exhausted.[50] Statius' toponyms suggest temporal flux with historical

---

[48] Hardie 2006: 208. See also Vessey 1981: 51.

[49] E.g. Stat. *Silv.* 2.3.1–5 (omniscient narrator), 6–8 (poet), 10–17 (Pholoë), 20–6 (Diana), 39–42 (Pan-as-gardener), 43–52 (Pan-as-lover), 53–61 (personified tree). Hardie 2006: 213 suggests a more monological reading, emphasizing the primacy of Statius' poetic voice. Merleau-Ponty's formulation of the **voyant-visible** is useful here (1964 or, more challengingly, 2002; cf. Varela, Thompson, and Rosch 1991).

[50] Stat. *Silv.* 2.3.10–14. Janus' grove is a puzzle – no other references exist. Janus is very much in the air in the *Siluae*: he was an important feature of Domitian's new Forum Transitorium (a reconfigured Temple of Janus Quirinus [Geminus] where the Argiletum entered the Forum Romanum), and *Siluae* 4.1 makes Janus the protagonist, with an encomium of Domitian taking up twenty-six of that poem's forty-seven lines. Janus' bellicosity crops up again in Statius' paean to the new Via Domitiana (4.3.9); see also 1.6.3; 4.2.60–1. As suggested e.g. by Virgil (*Aen* 8.82)

eras blending into one another: Janus' grove conjures up a wooded landscape (perhaps the Quirinal slopes) as backdrop, yet also suggests a discrete and managed copse (rather than uninterrupted forest) and evokes contemporary Rome's temple – three phases in the taming of this scene. The Quirinal itself features not as a woody hill but as a farmscape, hinting at Melior's estate in its future, but also representing a stark contrast for any readers familiar with the hill in the mid-first century CE; by then the hill was quite built up, including mixed-use urban units (*insulae*) and luxury housing.

Cacus, a popular monster in Roman mythic history, was memorialized in urban Rome by a flight of steps climbing the Palatine from the Circus Maximus valley. His seat in the country is hard to pin down, located variously in antiquity on the Palatine or the Aventine. Here I tend to favour the Palatine, both because of the 'steps' and because the Aventine is already in play (as tagged by Diana). Out hunting Aventine deer, Diana spurs Pholoë on with a well-aimed arrow (2.3.20–30) into the pool's dubious refuge. Cacus' gloomy domain marks a contrast to the light, translucent qualities of the pool/Melior nexus and, by inference, stands in opposition to Melior's own dwelling. Melior's plot straddles a range of semiotic systems. Sited on a former wilderness, which is now zoned urban (Caelian), it is characterized by pastoral scenography and located in a historically rural landscape; yet the estate is far from being a country villa.[51] Finally, it is described as a *tesca*: an inhumane desert or wilderness.[52] Into this scene runs semi-anthropomorphic Pan, too late:

> *primaeuam nisu platinum, cui longa propago*
> *innumeraeque manus et iturus in aethera uertex,*
> *deposuit iuxta uiuamque aggessit harenam*
> *optatisque aspergit aquis…* Stat. *Silv.* 2.3.39–42

with an effort, a sapling plane – with a long stem
and countless twigs, and a crown en route to the heavens –
he planted next [to the pool], and he packed in fertile sand
and sprinkled longed-for water…

---

and Ovid (*Fast.* 1.243–4; 3.71–2), the site of future Rome, and indeed Latium as a whole, was typically envisaged as forested. See e.g. Hardie 1992; Carandini 2007 (archaeological focus); Rea 2007 (literary analysis).

[51] See Plin. *HN* 36.48.

[52] Stat. *Silv.* 2.3.14. A disputed archaic term (*OLD s.v. tesquum*) – see also Hor. *Epist.* 1.14.19; Luc. 6.41; cf. Varro, *Ling.* 7.10–11.

These lines, echoing lines 2–5, ramp up the artifice of the location. Pan the garden-protector has landscaped the wilderness, articulating how much less autochthonous it is than its first, magisterial appearance suggested. This quasi-technical exegesis cuts to the heart of Roman interest in landscape. There is real hard graft involved: even for Pan it is an effort to get this sapling uprooted and replanted, to make expert choices of sand to dig in, and to moisten. His choice of specimens combines aesthetics and scientific husbandry: the young tree is clearly healthy and vigorous, but it will also be the best possible plane tree by being stereotypically tall and leafy, and therefore generative of that cliché: pastoral shade. Pan is engineering a Pan-friendly landscape.

The following lines mark a further change in perspective. Pan becomes the active looker (rounding out his role as **voyant-visible**): he apostrophizes the newly planted tree, using his role as its cultivator to instantiate his longing and as a kind of pledge of his protection for all time (2.3.43–52). This is where Statius locates the heart of the *aition* ('origin story'): Pan has told the tree to bend down and caress unkind Pholoë's shadowy couch, tipping the water with its leaves and protecting her from the fiery heat of the sun, as well as from cruel hail. Explaining its upward turn involves a further change of focalization: Pan's desire animates the tree, which in turn bends into the pool and then resurfaces, transformed into a wholly different tree.[53]

This plane presents a direct phenomenological link between first-century-CE reality, the landscapes of Athenian philosophy, complex Hellenistic literary sensibility, and the mythic qualities of Rome's origins in a pre-urban world. Pan's laborious cultivation of the plane tree reminds the reader of the essence of what a villa estate should be about (production, fertility) but, because Pan's crop is a plane, the only produce he can expect is related to *otium*: intellectual (like Socrates), or personal (shade in which to recline), or literary (Pan's role as subject and inspiration for composition). From Plato to Statius, this chapter has suggested some ways in which aesthetic qualities can highlight a tension between fruitfulness and sterility, *labor* and *otium*, and this is where we will start in Chapter III.

---

[53] Stat. *Silv.* 2.3.53–61. There are some oddities, but the overall meaning seems clear.

III THOSE HAPPY FIELDS? DIY LANDSCAPING

nos campis nos montibus fruimur, nostri sunt amnes nostri lacus, nos fruges serimus nos arbores, nos aquarum inductionibus terris fecunditatem damus, nos flumina arcemus derigimus auertimus, nostris denique manibus in rerum natura quasi alteram naturam efficere conamur.   Cic. *Nat. D.* 2.152

We enjoy the produce of the plains and the mountains, *ours* are the rivers, *ours* the lakes. *We* sow crops and trees, *we* give fertility to the land by controlling the waters. *We* contain, straighten, and divert the course of rivers, and so with *our own* hands *we* try to fashion a kind of other nature, within the nature of things as they stand.

Chapter II outlined how literary pastoral scenography makes for an often visually delightful but also heavily symbolic ethnoscape, ideally suited to the exploration of red-hot political, civic, and socio-cultural issues. The signs of pastoral provide props and a set for the rustic, artful, and occasionally (naïvely) politicized figures that populate and give Roman meaning to an imaginary and leisurely rural world, superficially very different from daily life. This chapter explores how pastoral imagery can also help us to think about a different aspect of what made for enjoyable Roman space: the sight of a productive agricultural landscape.

The practical realities of everyday life, shadowy presences for the most part in pastoral verse, strengthened family networks that linked city to countryside dynamically, connected family business to family smallholding, and plugged villa estates and farms into the rural economies and local politics.[1] The artificial quality of Latin literary pastoral's tropes encourages investigation of the semiotics of language and the values embedded in linguistic choices (Virgil's *Eclogues* present a Graeco-Roman scenography, scripted in Latin, whose protagonists answer to Greek names). Yet it also flags up the mechanics and implications of cultural change (why should Latin literature interest itself in forms rooted in the Greek world?), and what constitutes the daily grind of being Roman and working in the countryside in troubled times (from herding animals peripatetically, to knuckling down to plough, sow, and harvest, not necessarily inhabiting

---

[1] See Tacoli 1998; Scheidel 2004.

a 'family' or hereditary property, right through to dispossession and economic migrancy). In this way, literary pastoral's landscapes engage with Roman experience and even demographic mobility much more vividly and complicatedly than we might at first imagine. They also mediate between the contrived extremes of agricultural and urban life so popular in late Republican discourse, where the contrast typically invokes disquiet at a newly mobile society, one insufficiently signed up to traditional values and customs.[2]

The nostalgic and conservative qualities of pastoral's evocation of a vanished world of natural harmony can invoke a sense of loss, as set out influentially by Empson in 1935. This reconfigures the hard work and sense of place associated with agriculture, smallholdings, and family farm as signs of a vanished, easy relationship with the natural environment that humankind can no longer access.[3] Golden Age imagery at Rome in the late first century BCE had its origins in the Hesiodic notion that if humankind works hard and behaves righteously, a (less god-haunted and mystical) version of a Golden or 'Saturnian' Age can be recuperated.[4] Once we shift genre, however, we can find out how this works in more practical terms. Humankind's relationship with nature as set out in Cicero's *de Natura Deorum* (quoted above) reinvents the natural world as a kind of DIY store – raw materials primed for the right, skilled, and equipped labourer.[5] The people best qualified to get the most from these materials are most likely to be those who inherited the land once worked by Saturn's people, the site of his ideal political state: Italy.[6] This way of thinking suggests (as we saw hinted at by Varro, in Chapter I) that, rather than struggling against the momentum of history to recreate a lost world of Golden Age leisure, Romans simply need to dig in, to develop a close working

[2] Chambers 1994: 5–6 defines migrancy as 'a movement in which neither the points of departure nor those of arrival are immutable or certain...[a migrant is] simultaneously "inside" and "outside" the situation at hand'. Maggiulli 1995 painstakingly surveys the representation of vegetation and flora in Virgil; see also F. Jones (forthcoming).

[3] On loss in Verg. *Ecl.*, see e.g. Segal 1965. On their intertwining of politics and Arcadia, see e.g. Otis 1963: 135–6; Pöschl 1964; Putnam 1970: 20–81. Leach 1974: 113–42 reads *Eclogue* 1 lucidly in these terms. See also Wallace-Hadrill 1982.

[4] See Hes. *Op.* 116–19, 225–37; Pl. *Leg.* 4.713B–714A. Segal 1963 tackles the issues for Greece. Compare Verg. *Aen* 8.321–5 (and see R. F. Thomas 2004–5 on Saturn). R. Evans 2003 is the best introduction for utopian landscapes and Rome.

[5] Cic. *Nat. D.* 2.150–52 (cf. 2.87, 158 – on beauty and natural bounty). Nevertheless, 'natural' things are also better than things created by 'art' (2.87). *ANRW* ii.37 presents a wide range of approaches to Roman technology, science, land use, and more. Hughes 1994 introduces key themes for studying ancient ecology and human impact on the environment.

[6] Verg. *Ecl.* 4.6; *Aen* 8.329, 11.252. See e.g. R. F. Thomas 1982: 93–107; Zetzel 1997; Dench 2005: 63, 152–221.

relationship with their ethnoscape and make the most of what a unified Italy has to offer.[7]

Livy's history of Rome provides excellent examples of how Romans saw their city and its site as a kind of time machine. His identification of contemporary sights and monuments deeply embedded in Roman history gave a sense of synchronicity to what counted as Roman space, and how one defined and inhabited it. This phenomenological quality, giving memory a tangible place in the cityscape, helped Livy to give physical reality to the relationship between history and contemporary life.[8] Livy tells how, after Rome's sack by the Gauls (390/389 BCE), the patriotic hero M. Furius Camillus successfully spoke against a proposal to relocate the community to nearby Veii. Camillus generates a complex historicizing scenography in order to show Romans that their city and its physical site are their identity: one cannot successfully separate the two.[9] As Livy's Camillus observes, the hills, plains, woods, and river that define urban Rome's site are just as significant as the manmade structures; moreover, the earliest Romans were a ragbag mix of exiles (*conuenae*) and shepherds.[10] Migrancy and shepherding were the two *authentic* rustic lifestyles that made Rome's foundation possible, but it was only when the soon-to-be-urban space they came to share was rewritten as fatherland or native soil (*patria, solum*) and motherland (*terra, mater*) that 'communities of shared memory' transformed the disparate individuals into a citizen-family.[11]

The politics of agricultural landscape

Roman legends and Roman institutions show a disposition towards a pastoral longing for nature in their idealization or preservation of associations with nature in the past. The founders of Rome were inhabitants of a pastoral world.[12]

---

[7] The vision set out at Verg. *G.* 2.173.

[8] Jaeger 1997 takes this approach; Spencer 2007 examines one example, Livy on the Lacus Curtius. For the key issues more generally, see Gowing 2005 and Stein-Hölkeskamp and Hölkeskamp 2006.

[9] Livy 5.32–55; Camillus' key lines: 5.51.1–54.7. On this episode, see e.g. Kraus 1994; Feldherr 1997; Jaeger 1997: 89–93.

[10] Livy 5.54, 5.53.8–9.

[11] S. Jones 1997: 1, part of an important discussion of how digging up the past, in various senses, contributes to nationalism. Moatti 2006 teases out some related issues for Rome.

[12] Leach 1974: 57.

Pastoral symbolism continued to influence Roman responses to the natural environment, even when the focus was on the reality of a mixed agricultural community, a group of flesh and blood individuals who needed physical sustenance supported by hard graft in order to survive.[13] Varro, writing shortly before Virgil and Livy, and perhaps with tongue in cheek, is keen to scrutinize the 'strange hostility to civilization' that characterizes the nostalgic, ultra-traditional position whereby farmers are the only remnants of Saturn's race.[14] Rather than griping about how country values have been corrupted by urban sophistication, Varro foreshadows Livy by focusing on a different dichotomy: agriculture, the world of the farmer-colonist (*agricola*, *colonus*, and *arator* – farmer, cultivator, colonist, or ploughman), is set against, although still intertwined with, the world of pastoral (*opilio*, *pastor*, herdsman).[15]

Filtering through Varro's farming treatise we see an intense and close relationship between those cultivating the land (although his characters are what we might term 'gentleman farmers') and those working the urban, political, and commercial angles. Both constituencies are directly connected to the land and territory in ways that are quite different from the literary pastoral lifestyle – shepherds may have founded Rome, Varro observes, but it was only through combining animal husbandry with the organized and managed territorialism of agriculture (distinct from pastoral's 'range') that Rome became a city-state.[16] Varro's subjects – wealthy landowners (more or less involved in cultivating the fields) and city folk alike – behave inappropriately at times and need guidance if a balance between different kinds of landscape (subsistence agriculture, surplus economics and clearance for grazing, field systems, pasture, and woodland) is to be maintained. Nevertheless, he still makes an overlap between the two communities clear: socially and politically, territory defines them.

All texts, however apparently immersive or transparent, are **ideologically** framed in some way. This holds good for visual and representational depictions of landscape just as much as for literary ones, and as we investigate approaches rooted in Italy's landscapes we should briefly revisit how frames affect our understanding of space.

---

[13] Garnsey 2000 gives a sense of the Italian agricultural landscape. Linderski 2001 sums up how (market) gardening continued to figure in daily Roman life.

[14] Freud 1963: 24–5.

[15] Varro, *Rust.* 2 *Praef.* 4–5; 3.1.7.

[16] Varro, *Rust.* 2 *Praef.* 1–2, 4; 3.1.3–5; 1.2.12–28. Cf. Marx 2000: 22–3.

At its most basic level, a frame delineates that around which it draws a line. The lines drawn by literary pastoral prioritize distance, both temporal and physical (pastoral scenography and points of reference are Hellenic, its world accessible primarily as an echo of what might once have been). The lines drawn by texts interested in agronomy are rather different. The world of Roman *labor* evoked in the late Republic is still typically imbued with nostalgic historical qualities, but its primary frame of reference is the here and now, and the questions it poses about cultural identity relate directly to developing interest in **praxis** (practical ethics and hard graft) in an intensely Roman way.[17]

Cities rely on surplus food, and prosper when linked directly to an intensively farmed landscape for supplies, but they also function as markets for (and therefore as suppliers of) manufactured and imported goods. Italy's countryside was thoroughly and successfully farmed, and 'city' and countryside were interdependent in practice, despite the oppositional quality that characterizes literary discourse.[18] As Roman power expanded through the Italian peninsula, Roman practice officially recognized distinctions in the rural landscape by categorizing arable and grazing land differently – in legal and religious terms centuriation was a feature of agricultural land only, leaving the pastoral landscape unmodified.[19] This sits well with the differences imposed by genre on verse pastoral and prose didactic agricultural vistas.

Even though Virgil found interest in pastoral's mobile scenography and transcultural archetypes (the cool breeze on a hot day; leafy shade; singing rustics; caves, hills, and streams) as a stage for posing Roman questions, there is also a sense that grappling with the really difficult dilemmas facing Romans as a community required a landscape defined by Roman power, knowledge, know-how, and hard work. Landscape, we might argue, '*circulates* as a medium of exchange, a site of visual appropriation, a focus for the formation of identity'.[20]

---

[17] Hes. *Op.* sits squarely behind Roman agritexts; in practice, see e.g. Cic. *Nat. D.* 2.150, *Off.* 1.69–73, 2.3, 2.60.

[18] Spurr 1986 draws together archaeological survey and detailed analysis of the ancient agronomists; on oppositionality, S. H. Braund 1989 is a good starting point.

[19] Centuriation marked up and divided out the land prior to the foundation of a colony. It started to become a feature of the Italian landscape in the late fourth century BCE. See concisely Gargola 2004. Nicolet 1991: 149–55 discusses the politics; Dilke 1971 is still useful, but see now Campbell 2000. Varro, *Ling.* (e.g.) 5.32–7, *Rust.* 1.9.2, and Frontinus, *De arte mensoria* (*On the Art of Surveying*) root surveying in the pre-Roman world. Cuomo 2000 shows the benefits of revisiting Frontinus, who flourished in the later first century CE.

[20] Mitchell 1994b: 2, emphasis original.

Virgil went on to explore this in verse in his *Georgics*, but prose
farming handbooks in particular offer an intriguing literary equivalent
to centuriation's agenda. The ostensibly practical handbook, with its
overtly organizational and didactic agenda, sets up a frame of reference
for structuring and managing a farm, and offers the prospect of well-
informed control over plantings, field systems, and accommodation.
Centuriation's squared-off grids redefined space as cultivated Roman
territory, and *limites* or survey lines running east–west and north–south
generated ideologically framed scenes tagged to the relevant local
Roman urban foundation. If land could not be cultivated, then the
syntax of centuriation had no symbolic meaning or relevance as a way
of demonstrating control over space. Conversely, if a farming manual
could create an orderly frame for animal husbandry, then pastoral,
too, could take root and be confined. The implicit yet commonplace
frame for Roman agritexts is therefore that most characteristic Roman
imperializing practice: centuriation.

Drawing on Said's postcolonial approach, Cuomo reads centuriation
as an act of 'geographical violence'.[21] From the point of view of the
'colonized' or **subaltern** groups, this is surely the case: 'there is no
document of civilisation that is not at the same time a document of
barbarism', and the process of civilizing and rationalizing a landscape
is never without consequences.[22] That these consequences need not be
brutal nor destructive, however, is key to the conclusion summed up
by Bergmann: 'productive villas belonged to a spatial and economic
network, created by the Roman system of land-allotment (centuriation),
combining town, suburb, and agricultural land'.[23]

Reading Varro highlights the diversity of the connections that were
in play between place and ethnicity, and hints at another aspect of
the tension between regional and citizen identity in the late Republic.
Rome's foundation and success inevitably overwrote many local
ethnographic traditions but, in the best postcolonial manner, Italy
'wrote back' in the first century BCE, just when what it meant to
be Roman was being challenged by the increasing polyphony of an

---

[21] Cuomo 2000: 190, quoting and redeploying Said 1993: 271.

[22] Benjamin 1999: 248 (written in Paris, 1940). Compare this with the Highland Clearances
in nineteenth-century Scotland, or the processes for allocating land to Native American peoples;
for example, the General Allotment Act (1887) assumed that assimilation and civilization of
native peoples would proceed quickly if individual ownership of land parcels was made the
norm, and traditional activities such as of hunting, gathering, and fishing were discouraged.

[23] Bergmann 2007: 236. Terrenato 2007 emphasizes centuriation as a conceptual and
physical imposition of meaning.

empire that stretched beyond the peninsula.[24] From Varro (probably from Reate), through Catullus (Verona), and Cicero (Arpinum), to Virgil (Mantua), and Horace (Venusia), landscapes in the literature of the late Republic are always the product of a conversation (or even conflict) between different flavours of Roman identity. As Cicero expresses it, Roman citizens have two homelands: the city of Rome itself and their place of birth.[25] Virgil, too, has a go at interrogating and collapsing distinctions between core representatives of citizen ethnicity: Sabines, Etruscans, Romans, and Saturn's people.[26] These literary accounts seem to evoke a first-century-BCE Zeitgeist, exploring commonality between the Italian peoples as a whole, but also touting the idea of a broadly positive continuum, grafting a Romanized present onto the hardy 'native' stock of archaic, agricultural, ethnographically diverse Italy.[27]

Latin texts interested in farming juggle with pastoral and agricultural frames and thereby encapsulate a range of key issues, including the politics of allocation of Roman land and citizenship. The surplus farming model takes for granted a market economy, and so the city always lurks behind descriptions of pasturage, rows of vines, grids of olives, or fields of corn. In the most basic sense, then, such texts are documents of civilization because their end product (crops, meat, cheese) is what keeps the city or colony in business.[28] They are also documents of civilization in another sense: their alternative vision of what constitutes commercially savvy pastoralism (guidance on meadows, grazing, small-animal husbandry) implicitly points up the artifice of literary pastoral's shady afternoons and singing shepherds. In doing so, they remind readers that both didactic and pastoral are literary genres, and equally in the business of creating their

---

[24] Ashcroft, Griffiths, and Tiffin 2002: 8–11. Key studies for postcolonialism include Spivak 1987: 197–221; Bhabha 1990a; Brennan 1990; Renan 1990; Said 1993; Bhabha 1994 (chapters 7, 9, 11); B. Anderson 2006. The Italian tensions of the early first century BCE form an important backdrop here: see Brunt 1965b; Oakley 1993; Gabba 1994; and (in detail) Mouritsen 1998. Jehne and Pfeilschifter 2006 present an array of up-to-date approaches.

[25] Cic. Leg. 2.5. Morley 2003 discusses migration to Rome as imperial capital; Farney 2007: 5–26 is useful on the dilemma of 'two homelands' for most Romans.

[26] Verg. G. 2.532–40. His Aeneid, of course, widens the scope by exploring Trojan and Greek origins as well.

[27] Zerubavel 2003 uses the term 'time map' to define this kind of strategy. On the Roman and Italian background in Virgil, see Toll 1997; Ando 2002; Witek 2006 (immensely detailed). On Italian ethnic diversity and the ethnographic tradition, see R. F. Thomas 1982: 1–7, 100–2; Zetzel 1997: 188–94; in detail, Dench 2005: 227–79; Farney 2007.

[28] E.g. Verg. G. 2.513–15. Cf. R. F. Thomas 1982: 51–60, drawing Horace (e.g. Carm. 2.6) and Virgil together; and on Verg. G. 2.458–540, see Kronenberg 2000.

own agenda-driven universes. Just like literary pastoral, agronomic handbooks look to a literary form that flourished in the Hellenistic world.[29] Scripting farming as the ultra-Roman way of life is therefore also a way of writing into being a network of intellectual and cultural connections between Rome and the Mediterranean. In turn, the Italian communities fighting for full citizenship in the early first century BCE were themselves also struggling to maintain unique identities, including a significant Greek heritage, particularly in the south. This approach encourages us to keep in mind the close connections drawn between identity and ethnicity, and the concepts of landscape, land use, territory, and empire.[30]

The need to balance urban and rural modes of citizenship and cultivate lines of communication is reflected in day-to-day Roman experience. The urban religious calendar, full of rustic festivals, is one example. Archaeological studies now also emphasize how diverse and flexible the relationship between cities and countryside was, and Roman road-building practice was gradually shrinking the gap between capital, countryside, and other urban centres, making for what might be termed a new 'travelling culture'.[31] The result helped to transform the peninsula. The centuriated landscape, criss-crossed by local tracks and Roman road networks, opens up the subject matter of key Roman documents such as Cato's *De agricultura* (*On Agriculture*), Virgil's *Georgics*, and Varro's *De re rustica*. Virgil's *Georgics* in particular have become emblematic of a friction between nostalgic yearning for a simpler world of shared values (Rome's notional *mos maiorum*) and the intellectual fireworks generated by wealth, political change, and cultural exchange within a developing pan-Mediterranean empire.[32]

In Virgil's *Georgics* we see a spectacular demonstration of how stereotypically stolid Roman farming can also occupy the forefront

---

[29] For farm management texts, Xen. *Oec.* is always a key point of reference.

[30] On networks, settlement, and the environment in the Mediterranean, see Horden and Purcell 2000: 89–172. On archaeology's usefulness for understanding demography, see Gualtieri 2008; Pelgrom 2008 (especially on land division); Rathbone 2008; Witcher 2008; Yntema 2008.

[31] Clifford 1997: 17–46. On roads, see Laurence 1999. Dyson 2003 surveys trends in archaeological study of the city/countryside nexus. See also Purcell 1987b, 1990; Witcher 2005, 2009; Terrenato 2007. Two valuable case studies are della Portella 2004 (Via Appia) and Bjur and Santillo Frizell 2009 (Via Tiburtina).

[32] Hardie 1998: 28–52 introduces Verg. *G.* concisely. R. F. Thomas 1995 looks at city–country tensions. Batstone 1997 investigates how and why (teaching) farming moves to centre stage, and summarizes key bibliography. More generally, on nostalgia and religion with reference to literature of agriculture, see Feeney 1998: 133–66. On Rome's ancestors' everyday presence in Augustus' era, see Wallace-Hadrill 2008: 213–58.

of Mediterranean intertextual culture.[33] Recent study of Cato's much earlier *De agricultura* shows Virgil's approach slotting into a developing Roman discourse linking the teaching of farming lore to cultural self-fashioning.[34] Reading Cato in this way we find an ideal figure for testing a nostalgic model of what landholding meant in the mid-second century BCE. What we find is that, a century before Varro, Cicero, and Virgil, Cato's addressee (the would-be landowner) still has to be pestered into getting his hands dirty.[35] Cato's rustic agricultural landscape of clearly defined estates is relentlessly communal in its frame of external reference (*'uicinis bonus esto'*, 'be a good neighbour', 4); it is also curiously (and surprisingly) semi-detached, to the point of isolationism. Neighbours figure only as potential resources for the canny landowner, or as purchasers of his produce; the estate itself is populated only by slaves and functionaries.[36]

Cato's assumptions and advice conjure up a world perhaps just as imaginary as that of literary pastoral: one in which the familial and familiar qualities of the countryside are increasingly unavailable to many. In this landscape, transmission of land from father to son is not functioning smoothly, nor meshing with already nostalgic visions of how land and family inform on each other. The emerging agenda hints that the know-how of authentic rustic life has somehow come unstuck from a generation confronting a country scarred physically and culturally by war, even though the real paradigm shift in the balance between agriculture and warfare probably began in the fourth century BCE, when longer campaigns, farther from home, became more common.[37] We shouldn't read too much into it but, having emphasized the long-term investment in place required for successful cultivation of asparagus, Cato's closing apophthegm concerns curing meat: *Roman* salt (wit, or ingenuity?) interspersed with rigorous and

---

[33] Emphasized in e.g. R. F. Thomas 1988 and Farrell 1991.

[34] E.g. Reay 2005.

[35] Cato, *Agr.* 3, cf. 39. Reay 2005: 344–5 outlines the argument that the addressee in section 3 changes from owner to overseer, but rightly concludes that there is nothing in the logic or syntax of the text to promote this reading (2005: 346–9). The direct address to the overseer (Cato, *Agr.* 5) makes this particularly clear.

[36] Contrast Hes. *Op.* 343–60. Even Cato's lone designated female is a housekeeper (*Agr.* 143). The relentlessly masculine character of this imagined estate is surprising, too, in the context of one obvious model, Xen. *Oec.* (addressed to his wife – a topos picked up by Varro). Purcell 1995 offers a corrective vision of how things might have worked in practice.

[37] Rosenstein 2004: 35. Although Cato's agritext was probably completed not long before his death (149 BCE), his vision conjures up an ideally Roman world of earlier days. See e.g. *Agr.* 1.2, where the perfect paterfamilias is intimately acquainted with the minutiae of the villa estate, and is in a position to teach the overseer his job.

regular arrangement and rotation of the hams, concludes with a kind of bathhouse treatment (chill them, scrape them, sponge them, smoke and oil them). The now impervious hams leave the hopeful landowner with a double vision of himself and his produce merging on the ideal estate. Consuming fertile Italy's produce means communing, in this sense, with a traditional farming ethos: a way of eating oneself victoriously into authentic Roman identity. Cato's envoi, thus, offers the ultimate in self-sufficiency, and self-care.[38]

Thoreau commented that 'A sentence should read as if its author, had he held a plough instead of a pen, could have drawn a furrow deep and straight to the end.'[39] Setting aside nostalgia, this remark suggests other reasons why agricultural landscapes were so interesting. Textualizing farmland (that is, turning it into something to be read and interrogated, and which generates meaning) is about exerting epistemological control over the source of production. Surviving texts show agriculture as a subject that allows and encourages investigation of how knowledge, and in particular the one right way of doing things, is transmitted. This does not just have to be about the mechanics of centuriation, measured fields, serried ranks of vines, or furrowed earth (as in Cato's exhortation not to introduce a varied pattern when ploughing, or Frontinus' detailed study of surveying practice); a more symbolic form of squaring off is also in evidence.[40]

Virgil starts his *Georgics* with a pun: by making it the song of (what makes) happy/manured (*laetae/laetamen*) fields (*segetes*), he personifies fields as participants in the poem's unfolding project of cultivating a shared Roman identity.[41] He seems to be making the agricultural landscapes of Italy complicit in their own Romanization, and hints of this recur in the opening lines of *Georgics* 3 (3.1–41). This well-known passage connects rustic and public cult deities (Pales, Apollo), the Hellenic landscapes of epic and Arcadia (Mount Lycaeus), the craft of poetry, Octavian, and his influential friend Maecenas, and makes all of them subject to an imperializing (poetic) gaze. Virgil gathers up a diverse array of keynote images, sites and places, and cultural touchstones and reorganizes them into one metapoetic

---

[38] Cato, *Agr.* 162.
[39] Thoreau 2004: 107.
[40] Cato, *Agr.* 61.2.
[41] Lyne 1974: n. 9 explains. Johnson 2004: 79, discussing Perkell 1989, comments that *Georgics* 4's gardener 'needs to create beauty, to make beauty', but without friendship (i.e. a social network) the scene remains sterile. On Virgil's agriscapes, see Leach 1988: 144–93.

scheme given shape in the heavily symbolic marble temple that he writes into existence at Mantua (his home town) by the river Mincius. This notional temple's location is, we hear, a verdant plain (*campus*). Virgil has already characterized Mantua as unlucky in losing its plain to the programme of veteran settlement in the late 40s BCE (*G.* 2.198), and here we find a militaristic and triumphant temple replacing the food that the land might have produced. A back story of pre-existing patterns of land use or local cult is absent; instead, the plain is saturated in the civic Roman imagery of conquest and imperialism.[42] From a distant Roman point of view, of course, the kind of meaning generated by the imagined monument is far more immediately productive. It shows an extreme vision of the Roman operating system appropriating and silencing local Italian perspectives, and using a Hellenizing scenography to give weight to the new model of authority. Local boy Virgil has lavishly recoloured Mantua's productive territory as part of his literary career towards Rome.

Selling the idea of hard work

We tackle the other big names – Varro and Columella – in Chapter V, so let's see here how labour and agriculture feature in landscapes from two less obvious authors: Catullus and Lucretius. In Catullus 64 (as is also evident in Virgil's *Georgics*), even hard work is not always enough to guarantee nature's benevolence or even benign indifference to the human condition.[43] On display instead is a tension between Golden Age enjoyment of the land's natural bounty (by natural right, Rome enjoys the fruits of empire) and a post-Golden Age need for relentless *labor* simply to maintain it as a viable human environment. As in Lewis Carroll's 'Red Queen' hypothesis, one has to run as fast as one can just to stand still: simple survival takes up every joule of energy that humankind possesses.[44] Here, then, we see a highly mannered, literary response to what is overwhelmingly a Roman imperial perspective on how country and city relate to one another.

---

[42] Harrison 2005 succinctly introduces Virgil's 'temple' as an allusion to Augustus' Mausoleum. See now Meban 2008.

[43] See e.g. Verg. *G.* 3.478–566.

[44] L. Carroll 2007: 24–5. Cf. Van Valen 1973. Cicero's vision is different: *Nat. D.* 2.98–100, 131 makes the world of *labor*, a world conceptualized via Roman praxis, the ideal and, indeed, strikingly lovely state of affairs.

Ultimately, attempting to recreate a Golden Age experience of the land results in a **simulacrum**, a fantasy version of an ideal countryside, not a return to a lost mythic world. The persistence of such fantasy landscapes in elite culture (see cover image, and Figures 6 and 10), combined with the reality of change in Roman politics and the city's demography, suggests at least two models for viewing the countryside: first, as a place where relentless hard work was the norm if any produce was to reward the landholder, but where 'bad' landholders (not 'people like us') were unwilling to accept the moral responsibility of the practicalities of estate management; second, as a place where *labor* was once not necessary (in a lost Golden Age), but which no longer sustained humans spontaneously or worked with them collaboratively owing to a decline in human morals (the wrong sorts of people gaining land and misusing the power it offered). Neither is wholly satisfactory, and these extreme positions hint at cultural stereotyping: the politics of land use as a weapon in a battle for authority. Hence, as Catullus 64's crisis point – Peleus and Thetis' wedding day – approaches, we find cultivation of the land abandoned, and for all the wrong reasons. The tone suggests that this is not a legitimate day off from the farming calendar but a complete change in lifestyle, with significant consequences.

> *Deseritur Cieros, linquunt Pthiotica Tempe*
> *Crannonisque domos ac moenia Larisaea.*
> *Pharsalum coeunt, Pharsalia tecta frequentant.*
> *rura colit nemo, mollescunt colla iuuencis;*
> *non humilis curuis purgatur uinea rastris;*
> *non glebam prono conuellit uomere taurus;*
> *non falx attenuat frondatorum arboris umbram;*
> *squalida desertis rubigo infertur aratris.*   Catull. 64.35–42

Cieros lies abandoned, they leave Phthiotian Tempe
and the houses of Crannon and the walls of Larisa.
Gathering at Pharsalus, they crowd out the Pharsalian roofs.
Nobody tends the countryside, and the necks of the young bulls grow soft;
the low-lying vines are not cleared with curved hoe;
the bull does not shear the clod with angled blade;
the sickle does not thin the shade of leafy trees;
degrading rust attacks the abandoned ploughs.

This desolation is intensified on reaching the royal palace: opulent, gleaming with precious metals (including gold) and the regalia of monarchy.

ipsius at sedes, quacumque opulenta recessit
regia, fulgenti splendent auro atque argento.
candet ebur soliis, collucent pocula mensae,
tota domus gaudet regali splendida gaza. Catull. 64.43–6

but in his residence, in whatever direction the opulent palace
stretches out, it glistens with dazzling gold and silver.
Ivory shines from the seats, cups add glitter to the table,
the whole house rejoices in the resplendent treasury of royalty.

Immediately after this description, Catullus segues into the famous **ekphrasis** that details the myth of Ariadne's catastrophic elopement and destructive passion.[45] These lines play to a reading of Catullus 64 as a closural narrative, where humankind finds out what happens when the productive struggle of cultivation is abandoned. Rather than ease and tranquillity, the end of *labor* signals civic and communal dislocation, destructive passion, families ripped apart and identities shattered. The conclusion of the ekphrasis ends the human celebrations, ushering in Catullus' gods (64.278–302) and with them a very different landscape: the palace becomes a pleasure garden. Chiron's 'woodland gifts' ('*siluestria dona*', 64.279) turn the produce of hills, river valleys, and fields into confused and disorderly garlands ('*indistinctis...corollis*', 64.283): must-have party accessories rather than practical equipment. The river god Peneus brings the signs of pastoral: an uprooted beech, a vigorous laurel, nodding plane, poplar, and high-flying cypress. All these he weaves lavishly around the house, enclosing it with constricting foliate swags.[46] Catullus' vision suggests that these gifts of the gods overwrite human achievement even as they set a scene of relaxation and plenty.[47] The luxurious landscape that the gods' control generates requires no *labor*, but it also leads to no optimistic outcome or fruitful future. In the poem's closing lines we hear that Tellus (the Earth) is 'steeped in impious wickedness'.[48]

Lucretius' philosophical poem *De rerum natura* (*On the Nature of Things*) is intensely interested in how humankind relates to nature, and presents a very different Golden Age prospect from what we saw in Catullus 64. Huge, tough figures rove the landscape like

[45] Krieger 1992 homes in on topographic ekphrasis. Elsner 2007 shows how Catullus' ekphrasis works in dialogue with contemporary Roman wall-painting.

[46] Catull. 64.278–93.

[47] Cf. the very different but contemporary take on a resolutely post-Golden Age world (where seafaring is highlighted as a key activity) at Cic. *Nat. D.* 2.151–2, 161–2.

[48] Catull. 64.397. Cf. Catull. 68b.51–72. Tellus' Roman temple is the setting for Varro, *Rust.* 1.

wild beasts; the plough and agriculture are unknown, and instead humans nose out berries and snack on acorns washed down with draughts of river water.[49] The relationship between mortals and the natural environment in Catullus 64 straddled the worlds of *labor* and Golden Age bounty, encouraging us to recognize when we are well off. In Lucretius' scenography, the notion of Golden Age concord and freedom is taken to its unpleasant extreme: his archaic, anarchic, and instinctual humans cannot enjoy the harmony of their existence because they are barely conscious in human terms. This pre-laborious landscape is meaningless, a world without memory.[50] Inhabiting the woods, forests, and mountain caves, humans have no concept of time and are more likely to be eaten or die of injuries than of old age.[51] Even so, a kind of naturally inspired progress eventually makes humankind capable of ascribing names and agreeing on meanings.[52] Consciousness and memory together – and thereby humanity and, ultimately, Roman identity – are only possible in a laborious world where work depends on experience and therefore on knowledge and continuity of practice.[53]

To conclude with a return to the practicalities, by the time of Cato's youth, urban Rome was the symbolic and patriotic centre-stage of a state on the verge of radical imperial change. The iconographic and architectural forms that came to characterize 'Rome' and that rolled out across the landscape in the guise of Romanization were distinctly hybrid and semiotically Hellenistic in many respects.[54] Important studies emphasize how a symbolic tension between reality, myth, and culture underpins both everyday and literary experience of what the countryside represents.[55] The key feature of an explicitly taxonomized and Romanized landscape was its repetitive, sequential quality. All roads led to Rome in a more than literal sense: new urban foundations, a result partly of Rome's military success, altered Italy's geopolitics. Conceptually and structurally these new towns signalled 'Rome' by representing the idea of Roman urbanism in its purest form, and

---

[49] Lucr. 5.931–52. See Leach 1988: 122–43.

[50] A glimmer of humane consciousness flickers at Lucr. 5.948–9 (the woodland nymphs' appearance hints at more meaningful future engagement with the environment).

[51] Lucr. 5.955, 990–8.

[52] Lucr. 5.1028–55.

[53] We return to this in Chapter VI. On (the implications of) viewing humans as the exception to Nature, see Peterson 2001: 28–50.

[54] See e.g. Stamper 2005: 49–67, 105–29; Wallace-Hadrill 2008: 73–210.

[55] For a range of approaches, see Purcell 1987b, 1995; Rich and Wallace-Hadrill 1991; Ando 2002; Foxhall, Jones, and Forbes 2007; Wylie 2007: 139–86.

rolling it out across Italy (and the empire).[56] Ideological, idealizing topography and political geography therefore intersect with a physical landscape that through the fourth and third centuries saw elite focus shift from working the country estate to jockeying for urban power, and an increasing opening up of the land to tenure by smallholders and tenants.

Aristocratic nail-biting about land use, common in the literature of the late Republic, reflects socio-political shifts already in progress two or three centuries earlier. Varro's *On Country Matters* keys into this when his characters cite the long-ago agrarian legislation (367 BCE) which made it (theoretically at least) more possible for plebeian families to hold land.[57] In the world of Cato's old age, Italian communities' interest in participating in the benefits of Rome's imperial project suggested a rural to Roman – and urban – drift in focus. This, meshed with the military repercussions of imperialism at home (in the shape of Hannibal's Italian campaigns in particular), brought about a conceptual shift in core Roman identity: the contemporary world was recast in conservative elite discourse as having lost touch with its roots. After the Social War's bloody drama of realignment between Roman and Italian peoples, the ensuing century saw a scramble to explain in writing what had happened, making political crisis the fallout from a disinclination to view the countryside as a source of food and produce, and a supposedly new preference for commercial gain and a consumer lifestyle.[58]

Taking Cato's pessimism at face value would therefore be a mistake, in particular his rhetoric of a 'lost generation'. Rosenstein argues that, even during and after the Hannibalic war, the effects of conscription on agriculture were less straightforwardly a drain on manpower than has traditionally been thought, and in fact may have helped make space for more small farms to prosper.[59] The artificially nostalgic quality to literary landscapes of the first century BCE also

[56] Morley 1997; Attema 2005 (early urbanization). In brief, see Purcell 2007: 191–4. Gruet 2006: 63–83 discusses Roma Quadrata, street grids, and the reality of Rome. Rome, of course, was *not* laid out on a grid.

[57] Varro, *Rust.* 1.2. On the agrarian laws, see Gargola 1995: 129–46. More generally, on the state land known as *ager publicus*, see Rathbone 2003; Roselaar 2008.

[58] For background, see Lomas 2004, and von Ungern-Sternberg 2004.

[59] Rosenstein 2004: 20–2. See also e.g. Rich 1993, Cornell 1996. On demography and landscape, see de Ligt and Northwood 2008. On farm size and ownership, see K. D. White 1967. Rousseau 2008: 229, 230 presents possible reconstructions of two villa types (one quite modest, one luxury) in the context of the wider debate on what constitutes appropriate reconstruction activities on archaeological sites.

benefits from the persuasive argument, made concisely by Terrenato, that the (luxury) villafication of the Italian countryside did not gather pace until the years after the Social War.[60] Despite Cato's reactionary anxieties, lavish country estates were not devouring the agricultural landscape until rather later, and even then, such villas were always part of a landscape of production – at once farms and manufactories, increasingly part of a surplus economy linking city and countryside rather than a novel intervention in how the land was worked. Literary discourse, a product of elite concerns, may have been talking up a crisis in agricultural landscapes as part of a wider political debate about whether traditional Roman values continued to be fit for purpose. As Wallace-Hadrill pithily sums up, the Roman symbolism of the villa is what is primarily on display in literary texts, and this symbolic value is at the heart of 'the cultural polarities of town and country and of Greek and Roman'.[61]

We might therefore suspect that the major transition in viewing the Italian countryside as a venue for *labor* or *otium* is conceptual: from the first century BCE onwards, expansive villas were increasingly zoned *intellectually* as landscapes of cultured *otium* and self-display. Ploughing the 'happy fields', manufacturing, and laborious cultivation, all of which continued in the background (and on less prestigious properties), formed the white noise against which elite interrogation of what landscape represented (or symbolized) could develop. Indeed, as we will see in Chapter V, a good site for an *otium* villa is not necessarily in sync with what agricultural production (or year-round occupation) requires.

---

[60] 2007: 144–5; Terrenato also summarizes the current state of the debate. See also Kehoe 2007: 553–5.

[61] Wallace-Hadrill 1998b: 43.

IV LANDSCAPE: TIME AND MOTION

Gardening is not about those mythical 'green fingers'. Gardeners know that the plants, the trees, the staff, and the grounds *are* the identity they create for themselves by doing every single thing that can be done, over and over, as the year wheels about.[1]

We have already thought about how Golden Age imagery influences understanding of what landscape should be about, and we will return later to issues of chronology and temporality. Here, we start with some strategies for reading landscape as a sequence of places that can be combined to tell a story. One definition of space makes it what we experience by moving through a series of places, which we connect up into patterns by picking particular routes to follow.[2] Using this model, landscape stories invite us to move into and around them, offering different 'ways of going out and coming back in', depending on how we map our route.[3] Following the narrative flow through a landscape takes time.[4] Time, however, is relative – and culturally constructed; depending on context and terminology, time can move at different speeds and follow different logics.[5] Bakhtin's **chronotope** is helpful here. Using the natural environment to create a structure for understanding how time passes gives meaning and order to the passage of the year. For agricultural communities, it was a matter of life and death: studding the calendar with legends and myths closely linked to places, seasons, and appropriate activities was one way to ensure that good and bad ways of doing things were remembered over

[1] Henderson 2004b: 19 (discussing Sen. *Ep.* 12).
[2] See de Certeau 1984: 127; cf. Augé 1995: 85–6. On chronology and archaeological narratives, see A. M. Pollard 2009. For movement through a landscape in time, see Conan 2003a.
[3] De Certeau 1984: 106. Useful analogies (on the relationship between urban space, social organization, and intellectual structure) emerge from Hillier 2003a and 2003b.
[4] For time as 'placial', see Casey 1993: 9–13; this phenomenological approach, tracing its roots to pre-Socratic philosophy, states that everything in existence has a 'place', and the 'place world' exists in time as perceived by humans (e.g. the terms 'before' and 'after' relate to 'in front' and 'behind'). V. Evans 2004 connects this up with language use. Ricoeur 1984/5/8 (three large volumes) works towards an analysis of the subtly open-ended conversations between author, text, and reader that generate acceptable participatory narratives and shared, acculturated versions of how to 'tell' the time.
[5] See e.g. Cox and Forshaw 2009. Feeney 2007: 7–42, 138–42 introduces the practical and conceptual issues for Rome.

time.[6] Calendars therefore engage in a complex dialogue with religious and cultural assumptions, and they also respond to scientific advances in measuring the passage of time.[7]

When we gaze upon any landscape – physical, literary, or representational – we are plotting space with reference to time. We progress through a landscape's topographical elements (hill, tree, stream, temple) by tagging them, and then connecting up the tags in a way that satisfies our preferred interpretation or route. We can also term this 'marking up' a landscape. This can be intensely personal (linked meaningfully to individual desires, fears, and experiences) and can also plug into a society's collective myths, stereotypes, and concerns (ruins: romantic, frightening?; a patchwork of small, irregular, hedged fields: quaint, inefficient?; a canal: boating holidays, freight?). In this way, drawing on Lynch's analysis of urban form, we see that individual landscape elements change depending on how they are connected up; we plot their relative positions within a frame (the edges of the landscape as they relate to our points of view), and size up how and how long it might take to account for them, to move between them, and even the different perspectives that strolling along a path, into a valley, or through a gate could open up.[8]

This is **narratology** and, drawing on de Certeau's important analysis of how space gains meaning as a network of time, place, and stories, a few examples might work as follows: the shady plane tree encourages the viewer or passer-by to move towards it, and away from the midday sun; the regimented vineyard encourages a linear gaze along its lines, and invites us to imagine seasonal ripening of the grapes and their eventual harvest, and pressing and ageing elsewhere on the estate. A

---

[6] See Rüpke 2004: 32–4. Summing up the Roman calendar tags, see Webography: Nova Roma, and *Rogue Classicism*'s 'This Day in Ancient History' section; more discursively, see 'Early Roman Calendar'.

[7] The Western (Gregorian) calendar adapted the Julian calendar (45 BCE), reframing the year in terms of Christian concepts and temporal cycles. Other religions (e.g. Judaism, Islam) and cultures (e.g. China) count time differently. Greenwich Mean Time (GMT) – Greenwich gained the Prime Meridian in 1851 – recalls a time when Britain dominated the globe. Echoing Imperial Rome's standardization of the calendar, the original division of the world into twenty-four time zones was the British empire's response to increasing globalization. Modern systems continue to refine chronology: Universal Time (and its variants, e.g. UT1), which replaced GMT, is sidereal (measuring the rotation of the stars) rather than solar. International Atomic Time (TAI) takes the average of a set number of atomic clocks (measuring the microwaves emitted by electrons). Co-ordinated Universal Time synchronizes TAI with UT1 so that the perceptual experience of time (the diurnal cycle) matches the most accurate standards of measurement. Leap seconds (rather than leap days, seasonal change, festivals, or intercalation) are now what keep things in sync.

[8] Lynch 1960: 96–9, 106–7.

surging river suggests its whole course, from mountain source to sea, while also evoking the god of its source, and associated festivals.[9] The time taken to 'read' a landscape therefore includes how long one needs to explore it and to make sense of it. Cognitive linguistic approaches will add an extra dimension here, but we can also draw on space-syntax terminology. We now see how storytelling and its temporality (time passing within a 'story' and the time taken to read or tell a story) is central to **way-finding** through 'fat space'. A combination of memory and experience, plus a landscape's signs, routes, and **axial lines**, enable us to make meaningful connections between landmarks, nodes, and **isovists**.[10]

Parsing a landscape: Virgil and Statius

If we treat space as a form of discourse, then we can analyse it in linguistic terms.[11] In its most basic sense, parsing a landscape means identifying its topographical features (vocabulary) and interpreting them relationally (syntax).[12] As Gombrich influentially commented, 'All thinking is sorting, classifying. All perceiving relates to expectations and therefore to comparisons.'[13] More specifically, embedded within language is a relationship between grammatical case and movement that specifies how we react cognitively to space as we verbally define or respond to it. For texts or sites composed or interpreted in an inflected language such as Latin, syntax and semiotics are particularly closely linked because of the flexibility of word order.[14] Cognitive linguistic terminology helps us see how the process of connecting up sites and vistas into meaningful and complex isovist space is rooted in the structures of language and the linguistic choices made by authors and readers.[15] Language and its mental spaces determine how landscape operates via a range of symbols within a semiotic system: we understand landscape by recognizing its components and ordering

---

[9] De Certeau 1984: 115–30. On narratology, see Bal 1985; also Barthes 1986; J. Potter 1996. On geographic epistemology, see Lowenthal 1961. On narratology and semiotic chains of association, see Barthes 1967. On visual semiotics, see Saint-Martin 1990.

[10] On way-finding, see Lynch 1960: 4, 46–90; a useful recent collection is Golledge 1999.

[11] See Werth 1999 for this approach.

[12] Testing space-syntax theory on Rome, see von Stackelberg 2009: 54–9; as applied to Pompeii, see Grahame 2000.

[13] Gombrich 1960: 254.

[14] See Short 2008: 106–10. This article tackles the complexities and is well worth the effort.

[15] Cf. Thoreau 2004: 110, attempting to define the Concord river.

them in ways that make sense.[16] When we recognize a topographic entity as water, if it is wide, flowing water, we refine this interpretation by terming it a river; we understand that rivers flow downhill. Downhill means a sloping scene; by following the course of the river in either direction we are 'moving' up or down. Furthermore, returning to Latin we know that, syntactically, our river is located in space (the ablative or locative case), and also flows away from one place (the ablative) and towards another (the accusative).[17] This approach overlaps with the terminology of cultural memory, which similarly relies on shared linguistic structures generated by and productive of agreed meanings for particular verbal signs.

Virgil's *Aeneid* offers one of the most famous examples of a temporally complex landscape when the Greek émigré Evander, returning from the Ara Maxima, takes the newcomer Aeneas on a tour of the site that will one day be Rome.[18] Key verbs introducing this passage are *refero* (return, 8.307), *eo* (go, 8.307), *ingredior* (walk along, 8.309), and *miror* (marvel at, 8.310). Evander enriches the space they traverse with stories that conjure up vistas.[19] An intricate collection of chronological and spatial ideas is in play, and these are best illustrated by plotting the story using Figure 5. The route, however, remains surprisingly difficult to visualize. Evander's back-to-the-future lecture tour of the future site of Rome configures space as a synchronous sequence of tagged landmarks: a hypertext. Moving towards, pointing to, and hovering at each site brings up additional resources for reading the topography. Evander's toponyms are at once pre-Roman (from

---

[16] Lynch 1960: 83–90, 95–105; Grahame 2000: 3–4, 24–8; Conan 2003b: 288. Ricoeur 1977 is unavoidable on metaphor and identity; for our purposes (metaphor and the analysis of space), approaches presented by Lakoff and Johnson 2003 are particularly useful.

[17] This bare-bones explanation picks out prepositions governing specific cases that denote or connote movement and location, e.g. *a/ab* (+abl.), *ad* (+abl.), *de* (+abl.), *in* (+acc./abl.), *per* (+acc.), *ex* (+abl.). We can also factor in verbs followed by the dative, e.g. *appropinquo* (I approach); ablative of place from or place where; and locative.

[18] Verg. *Aen* 8.337–69. This passage has a large bibliography; for discussion and references, see e.g. Hardie 1992; Zetzel 1997; Ando 2002; Papaioannou 2003; Reed 2007: 129–47 (part of a study of cities in the *Aeneid*). Witek 2006's detailed examination of landscape in Virgil is not available in translation. Alden Smith 2005 focuses on vision in the *Aeneid*. On the semiotic richness of Roman scenography, and suggestions for further reading, see e.g. C. Edwards 1996; Lowrie 2003; Larmour and Spencer 2007a.

[19] Evander is described as '*Romanae conditor arcis*' (*Aen.* 8.313), which is usually translated as 'founder of the Roman citadel'. *OLD s.v. conditor*: 2–4 gives 'originator (of a practice)', 'author', and 'organizer'. Hence we have additional nuances configuring Evander (the 'good man') as creator, scripter, and planner of what follows. Aeneas' understanding of the story is inevitably different to that of an ideal reader.

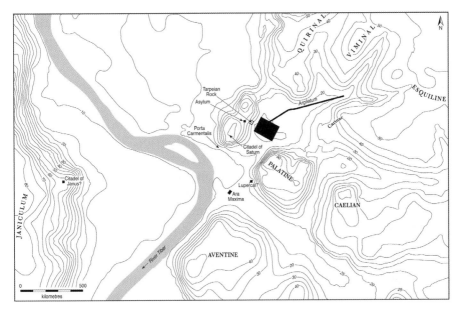

Figure 5 Evander's tour of 'future' Rome (Verg. *Aen.* 8).

Evander and Aeneas' point of view the city does not yet exist), and
ur-Roman (resonant of the legendary past, in Virgil's city).

The tour proper starts at the spot that we learn 'the Romans' (re)
call by the name Porta Carmentalis.[20] Naming this site orients the
group (and ourselves as audience) to face it. Behind us is what will be
the Forum Boarium, and the temples of Fortuna and Mater Matuta.
Within the *Aeneid*'s narrative present, however, neither 'the Romans'
nor their/our *future* toponyms exist; this interjection is offered by
the narrator. By marking up Evander's tour with anachronistic sites,
Virgil implies that Roman toponyms are autochthonic and inevitable:
intrinsic to and inextricably embedded within this space. The pre-
Roman pastoral landscape's innate qualities are already primed for
tagging by Evander and Virgil. They make it inevitable that, one
day, *bona fide* citizens will become fully Roman by inhabiting the
site that has always been waiting for them. Moreover, as the poem
makes clear, this tour is the nearest thing to a stroll around Rome
that Aeneas ever gets.[21] Viewers are encouraged to perceive the scene

[20] '*Carmentalem Romani nomine portam / quam memorant*' (Verg. *Aen* 8.338–9).
[21] On reciprocal gazes (Aeneas' arrival and interest guarantees Rome's foundation; walking
around the pre-Roman site embeds Aeneas ideologically and figuratively in a city he will never
see), see e.g. Merleau-Ponty 1964 (and, for context, Jay 1993); cf. Varela, Thompson, and Rosch

as three overlapping isovists: the pastoral hills, woods, and river; the selected prefigured urban landmarks of Rome; and the totality of the city as experienced by each of the poem's audiences. Facing the Porta Carmentalis, however, makes impossible the uninterrupted transition to the next site as scripted: '*from here*, a vast grove...' ('*hinc lucum ingentem*...').[22]

This next site, the grove tagged as the Asylum, highlights the tension between narrative and experiential space. The Asylum is yet to be founded (by Aeneas' descendant, Romulus) and, straddling the Capitoline peaks, its natural depression should be invisible from the Porta Carmentalis, below and south-west of the hill.[23] The lack of a verb of movement to configure the transition between sites encodes the group as rotating on the spot (taking in a series of vistas rather than walking from one site to the next), yet '*hinc*' can imply movement as well as directionality, despite no localized specification of a new stop on the tour. This ambiguity places our group simultaneously (still) at the Porta Carmentalis and also somewhere (else) with a sightline on the Asylum (perhaps drifting around the Velabrum; see Figure 3, no. 52). The compression of the scripting offers one solution. Focusing on what Evander does, we see that he both *points out* and *calls attention to* ('*monstrat*', 8.337) the Porta Carmentalis, with the same verb doing duty for how he presents the Asylum. Hence the emphasis is on gestural axes and conceptual isovists rather than uninterrupted sightlines or proximity.

This interpretation gains weight when we see that the next tagged site, again dependent on *monstro*, is the Lupercal. The transition here is managed solely with '*et*' (and), suggesting the group rotating a further ninety degrees or so clockwise to gaze back towards the Palatine.[24] Virgil embeds movement of a different sort in the topographic mark-up here: the Lupercal is named for (the wolf-god) Lycaean Pan in Parrhasian (that is, Arcadian, 'exile') fashion. The link to Romulus connects Greece to the eventual city foundation, long after Aeneas. So, gazing at the Lupercal, the isovist expands imaginatively to take in a god-haunted domain in Greek Arcadia, adding that touch of exotic wilderness to the (contemporary) city centre.

1991: 241: 'a path exists only in walking'. Royo and Gruet 2008: 382–91 survey Rome along lines that Merleau-Ponty might recognize.

[22] Verg. *Aen* 8.342.

[23] '*Rettulit*', 'Romulus founded...' (*Aen* 8.343); the perfect tense adds chronological complexity.

[24] Verg. *Aen* 8.343–4.

The next site presents a conflict. It appears to follow seamlessly by reusing the verb *monstro*, but the formal transition suggests a double-take: '*nec non et...*' ('and moreover'), with the double negative requiring a moment's thought.[25] This signals a halt to the clockwise sweep of Evander's tour, which is confirmed when we find that the Argiletum is the next stop. This (then) wooded site, north-east of what will become the Forum, requires the group to swing around roughly forty-five degrees anticlockwise from the Lupercal. This reverse rotational momentum then continues as Evander leads (*duco*) them from here ('*hinc*') back to what will eventually be the Tarpeian 'seat' and (*et*) the Capitol (the two sites are presented as a unit, depending on the verb *duco*). Chronological friction is highlighted by the narrator's focalization in the next line: the Capitol is golden *now*, but *then* bristling with woodland thickets; 'now' must mean in Virgil's city.[26]

Almost all of the many senses of *duco* imply actual movement through space, but one significant exception that keeps us guessing is the sense 'spin a yarn' or 'compose'.[27] The ambiguity in *duco* suggests Evander as the scripter of the scene rather than as the enthusiastic cicerone, tramping the sites; yet the relatively lengthy description (8.347–54) creates a density of space in these lines that could suggest time taken scrambling through the undergrowth, as well as time needed to come to an understanding of the complex site. The complexity is underlined when we meet the next transition term. 'What's more' ('*praeterea*', 8.355) implies that our isovist is being semiotically enriched rather than topographically redefined. What transpires is that the Capitol is redesignated as a ruinous town, twinned with the now (from Evander's point of view) ruined citadel of Janus (the Janiculum, across the Tiber).[28]

If Evander is lecturing a tour party on the Capitol (suggested by *duco*, meaning to escort, lead, or move), Virgil's deployment of *hic* (this, here) in the following lines is idiosyncratic. The two landmarks featured next (the citadels of Saturn – that is, the Capitol – and Janus, on the Janiculum) are relationally connected using *hic* (8.355, 357). This **deictic** conjures up a performative gesture on Evander's

---

[25] Ibid., 8.345.

[26] 'Now'/'then' terminology emphasizes that the mark-up here is squarely in the narratorial voice: '*aurea nunc, olim siluestribus horrida dumis*' (*Aen* 8.348).

[27] *OLD* sense twenty-three (of thirty). See e.g. Prop. 4.6.13; Ov. *Met.* 1.4.

[28] On ruins and Roman identity, see Fowler 2000; Spencer 2005. On Janus' Hill, see Grimal 1945.

part – an arm sweeping demonstratively between two sites (here... and here...) spatially removed from (or equally adjacent to) the tour party. This setup works far better in phenomenological terms for an audience down near the Porta Carmentalis (with a sightline on the two citadels) than up on the Capitol itself or even at the Tarpeian Rock, and the next line seems to encourage us to imagine the group back down somewhere in the vicinity of the Porta Carmentalis.[29] We are thus implicitly encouraged either to fill in an unscripted phase in the tour (where the group treks back down from the Capitol to the low ground), or to read *duco* as primarily about storytelling rather than physically leading.

Referring back to Figure 5, we find further support for a primarily static tour when we examine the next transition, taking the group to a Palatine site: 'amidst such conversation they were making tracks [*subibant*] to the house of modest Evander' (8.359–60). This transition phase, closely linked to some leisurely sightseeing ('*uidebant*', they were looking, 8.360) concludes the excursion and takes us back ('*subibant*') to our last unambiguous verb of movement ('*progredior*', see 8.337). No mention is made of a scramble down from the Capitol (no roads yet), and the intuitive response suggests that a stroll back to Evander's place from the (future) Porta Carmentalis (or perhaps the Velabrum) is what rounds off the tour. Instead of emphasizing physical movement through space, this reading finds that sketchy description blending with reminiscence and imaginative visualization generates an evocative but fragmentary and imprecise landscape. By downplaying real-time movement, Virgil seems to bring the future city's hotspots directly to 'us' (as readers), providing 'us' (and Aeneas) with the need-to-know lowdown.

Movement can be encoded to play a part in texts in other ways too: letters are envoys, travelling the roads of Italy, instantiating dialogue between author and addressee and tying individuals, families, and communities together. Tacitly, the conversational qualities of epistles are underpinned by the unspoken delights and discomforts of travel as they wend their way between the correspondents. In the speed or distressed state of their imagined delivery we might assume that a further layer of landscaping is overlaid – the human response to infrastructural factors such as roads, the relationship between travel across a weather-beaten landscape, seasonal patterns of movement

---

[29] Verg. *Aen* 8.357–8.

such as transhumance, and Roman pride in the ability to move traffic briskly.[30] Jumping forward just over a century from Virgil, we find another example of a text generated by and also redefining movement, but with particular reference to roads, in Statius' *Siluae* 4.3, praising and describing the Via Domitiana (see Figure 2). This long, hendecasyllabic poem (at 163 lines, by far the longest in *Siluae* 4) takes the wayfarer (*uiator*) down through Campania, following Domitian's new highway completed in 95 CE.[31] Seven key lines close the introductory section:

> hic segnes populi uias grauatus
> et campos iter omne detinentes
> longos eximit ambitus nouoque
> iniectu solidat graues harenas,
> gaudens Euboicae domum Sibyllae
> Gauranosque sinus et aestuantes
> septem montibus admouere Baias.   Stat. *Silv.* 4.3.20–6

this man [Domitian] – frustrated by highways holding people up
and plains that make every journey a delay –
banishes long, meandering routes and with new
laid surface stabilizes the heavy sands,
delighting that the home of the Euboean Sibyl
and the bays of Gaurus and sweltering
Baiae too, he's shifting a little closer to the Seven Hills.

This new route, as an itinerary, collapses time and space while also (at some length, and with some meanders of its own) cataloguing a trip south to where Rome meets Magna Graecia's northern zone of influence.[32] Until 'now', travel south has been a constant struggle against an obdurate landscape and changing geopolitical needs: now, if one leaves the Tiber at dawn one can be sailing the Lucrine Lake at twilight. This is not simply a domestic matter, since it also

---

[30] Hor. *Sat.* 1.5 recounts a trip through the Pontine Marshes to Feronia by canal, with a sleepless night tormented by midges and the croaking of frogs (see Welch 2008). On low-tech travel and local networks see, briefly, Dench 2005: 190. On transhumance, see Garnsey 2000: 689–91; on movement more generally, see Scheidel 2004.

[31] The new *Via* cut the journey time between Rome and Naples by splitting from the Via Appia where it turned inland towards Capua. Coleman 1988 provides an excellent, detailed commentary on this poem. See also Newlands 2002: 284–325; Smolenaars 2006. Cf. Hor. *Sat.* 1.5.

[32] Cf. Hor. *Sat.* 1.5. The structure is broadly tripartite: terrain/construction; eulogy of Domitian as road- and bridge-builder (spoken by the river god Volturnus; description of the monumental arch marking where this road leaves the Via Appia); a mythologizing and historicizing eulogy of Domitian, spoken by the Cumaean Sibyl.

opens up Rome to a new superhighway from the east;[33] semantically, however, the focus remains on Rome, and a Roman point of view is being addressed whereby other parts of the route always operate relationally. The benefits come when places that one might want to visit from Rome take less time to reach, or to travel (back) from. Statius' estimate of the new journey time of one day seems optimistic, but the reconceptualization of Baiae, for example, as a day from Rome transforms it from a getaway to a suburb: Rome-on-Sea. Baiae's fleshpots are now accessible, in theory at least, to those who also wish actively to participate in the *res publica*.

As a sense unit, this passage connects the main man, Domitian, directly to the Seven Hills. By naming evocative sites around the new route's southern terminus, and dismissing the whole interim landscape as a now-vanished series of detours and hindrances, Statius makes evident how modern technocracy has redefined Italy spatially and relationally.[34] There is no longer any reason to note the towns or places *en route* because the new streamlined way-finding process has erased their landmark status, and bypassed many communities. Traditionally, the parts of roads closest to these and other urban settlements were lined with tombs. We still see evidence of this on the Via Appia (as it leaves Rome) and outside ancient Pompeii.[35] A modern comparison could be drawn between the high density of tombs at strategic sites – in effect advertising family history – and the billboards and promotional hoardings that colour contemporary high-traffic areas.[36] Perhaps the speed of Domitian's new superhighway will have the effect (in Statius' poem at least) of making these building blocks of shared memory unavailable and thereby implying one more way in which movement through landscape and cultural identity are intertwined.[37]

---

[33] See Stat. *Silv.* 4.3.36–7, 4.3.107–10, 4.3.112–13. Statius speaks of 'easterners' coming by sea to Puteoli, cutting out a big chunk of slow road travel.

[34] See Pavlovskis 1973.

[35] See Webography: 'Street of Tombs'.

[36] See Webography: *Awesome Billboards and Outdoor Advertising*; *Extraordinary and Attractive Billboards*.

[37] On tombs and roads, see e.g. Purcell 1987a; Koortbojian 1996; Gowing 2005: 13–15. Recall Chapter I (on cultural memory). Huyssen 2003 explores the relationship between cultural identity and traumatic urban redevelopment (e.g. the fall of the Berlin Wall; 9/11).

Et in Arcadia ego: difference and repetition in Varro and Ovid

Habit is the foundation of time, the moving soil occupied by the passing present.[38]

Another kind of chronology, the repetitive process of working the land, exploits philosophical tropes – principally Stoic – that Foucault defines as 'care' or 'cultivation' of the self.[39] Each iteration of ploughing, sowing, and harvesting in the farming year is at once a new act, and an echo of and riff upon previous acts in the sequence, rooted in a specific sense of place. Constancy of place helps 'promote the highly reassuring conservative illusion that nothing fundamental has really changed'.[40] This cyclical quality hints at the hermeneutics of reception (farming needs to remember, respond to, and develop agricultural lore; Rome's farming manuals drew heavily on Greek knowledge).[41] Thus, when Varro has a stab at rationalizing the historical connection between planting schemes, the Italian countryside, and calendars in the late Republic (*Rust.* 1.27–8) he is also flagging up farming and gardening as key **ontological** activities for quizzing how Roman epistemology and Italy's landscapes combine to generate Roman perception of time. He is simultaneously alluding to and reinventing the hermeneutics of Rome's reception of 'Greek' paradigms of time, familiar from Hesiod.[42]

Writing about the relationship between history and the measurement of time, Feeney sums up:

The horizons of Roman time were progressively extended, reaching backwards to Troy and sideways to assimilate the synchronistic time systems that the Greeks had devised as an indispensable part of their own contentious historical sensibilities; further, key

---

[38] Deleuze 2004: 101. This difficult and at times oblique book – first published in 1968 – has proved hugely influential. It attempts to unpack and analyse the relationship between difference and unified identity by way of some of the giants of Western philosophy (from Aristotle all the way through to Nietzsche, Kierkegaard, Kant, and Hegel). For a clear introduction, see J. Williams 2003.

[39] Foucault 1988: 43, 45–8, 67. In general terms, for Roman gardens, see von Stackelberg 2009: 62–4. On the mutually sustaining interplay between *historia* and *memoria* in Roman culture, see e.g. Gowing 2005, 7–13 (in the wake of Halbwachs 1992).

[40] Zerubavel 2003: 41.

[41] This is 'complex repetition', Deleuze 2004: xviii, 368. See also Deleuze 2004: 96–7 (how this operates in the visual and perceptual fields). On the knowledge base for Roman farming, K. D. White 1973 is a good starting point.

[42] E.g. Hes. *Op.* 383–669, 765–828, cited by Varro, *Rust.* 1.1.9, as part of a lengthy catalogue of Greek agricultural classics.

transitional moments in Greek mythology became a tool for the Romans to use in order to reflect on their status as an imperial people, guilty masters of nature and of technology.[43]

This makes clear the sheer complexity of the idea of time and its measurement at Rome. Also at stake here is the close relationship between what Varro terms 'natural' (that is, in effect, seasonal and inevitable) and 'civil' (that is, contingent) urban timeframes.[44] As Cancik suggests:

Sacred landscape is a constellation of natural phenomena constituted as a meaningful system by means of artificial and religious signs, by telling names and etiological stories fixed to certain places, and by rituals which actualize the space.[45]

Varro is an interesting test case – his first account of the calendar (in his study of the Latin language, *De lingua latina*) was followed, almost a decade later, by *De re rustica* (in the form of a series of debates about the nature of farming and country life). As Feeney puts it, 'When Varro talks [*Rust.* 1]…about the divisions of the year and their relationship with agriculture and nature we are, all of a sudden, in a completely different world' – the world of Caesar's seasons.[46]

The lead-in to the debate on measuring time in Varro saw a group of punningly named friends awaiting the arrival of the sacristan at the temple of Tellus (the Earth) in Rome: Agrius (Mr Fallowfield), Fundanius (Mr Farmish), and Scrofa (Mr Porker).[47] Clearly, anyone planning a landscaping project must know that cultivation involves knowing the cycles (seasonal, annual) and understanding **teleology** (how plants mature). This is the same for pleasure gardens, small plots, and farmland alike.

Porker's description of solar and lunar schemes makes the celestial bodies control the kinds of agricultural time available to mankind. Mr Sucker (C. Licinius *Stolo*) then interjects, complicating matters by suggesting that agriculture need not *follow* the seasons but as a way of life can instead help to make the seasons work for the educated and

---

[43] Feeney 2007: 138.

[44] Varro, *Ling.* 6.12 – probably composed before Caesar's calendar reform, though possibly published shortly after the new calendar. See Feeney 2007: 202–9. Cf. Plin. *HN* 18.205 on the problem of over-reliance on compartmentalized chronological systems: a blend of natural and civil is what's needed, but subject to the common-sense proviso that the weather will never fit itself to fixed dates.

[45] Cancik 1985–6: 253.

[46] Feeney 2007: 200.

[47] Varro, *Rust.* 1.26.

skilful farmer, who actively identifies the growth cycles of different crops and plants accordingly for maximum productivity. Each field will be, as it were, part Spring, part Summer, part Autumn, part Winter, depending on what crop is sown, with each moving through its own process of ripening to maturity and harvest according to its own biorhythms but also to suit the farmer's order.[48] Sucker's alternative calendrical scheme is broadly complementary to the imperatives of heavenly calendars, but is based around human know-how and contingency: the ripening to maturity and consumption of in-demand produce.

In Varro's discussion, every way of measuring the year is tied to farming but, as Kronenberg observes, this array of calendars highlights how circumscribed the farmer's many and varied attempts to impose order on 'the haphazard world of nature' are, and how, ultimately, mankind is alone in the struggle to make practical and productive sense of the passage of time, since 'the gods never helpfully intervene' to sort things out.[49] This concern with identifying and setting limits to cycles, and in particular with articulating differences between them and specifying their internal logics, encourages readers to recognize 'the operations of power, and the tensions and conflicts those operations generate'.[50] Getting calendars right, and choosing the appropriate scheme for the task at hand, can be a matter of life and death.

Varro's second book takes Pompey's campaign against the pirates in the Mediterranean (60s BCE) as its backdrop. Notionally in conversation with provincial farmers, 'Varro' recounts a quasi-philosophical myth of ages, tracing agriculture and animal husbandry alike back through time to the remotest (and Greek) past, via obvious suspects such as the philosophers Thales and Pythagoras; 'Varro' is in fact greeted Homerically as 'ποιμένα λαῶν' (shepherd of the people), connecting a pastoral pre-Roman world to the big names of Trojan epic, and making Varro (and his farming manual) a Homerically flavoured guide for configuring a new world.[51] This leads eventually to a whimsical account of the founding of Rome by shepherds, and the consequences

---

[48] Ibid., 1.29, 1.37.4. See also 1.41.1 (the vagaries of fig-growing); 1.45 (each plant has its own internal calendar); and 1.46 (the leaves of some trees are natural seasonal markers, twisting over at the summer solstice).

[49] Kronenberg 2009: 91.

[50] Cubitt 2007: 224.

[51] Varro, *Rust.* 2.1.3–5, 2.5.1.

of this vision of Rome's pre-history and inception for the operation of Roman time.[52]

The significance of Rome's past (and in particular its foundation stories) in the cultural production of the late Republic has featured in every chapter thus far. Varro's synthesis of agriculture, pastoralism, and history shows just how tight the connections are between the practicalities of marking time and the consequences of chronological and calendrical choices, particularly when the Roman calendar itself was being radically overhauled. In this context we can conclude with one other chronologically focused landscape, taken from Ovid's calendar poem (*Fasti*), commenced in the early years CE.[53]

Ovid's lengthy opening entry tackles the month's titular god, Janus, who manifests himself to explain why he has two faces. Janus is the gatekeeper to the year; he completes the old year and ushers in the new one, but also describes himself as controller of the natural environment:

> '*Quicquid ubique uides, caelum, mare, nubile, terras,*
> *omnia sunt nostra clausa patentque manu.*'   Ov. *Fast.* 1.115–116

> 'On whatever and wherever your gaze falls – on sky, sea, cloud, earth –
> all these things are closed and opened by my hand.'

Quickly, Janus and the narrator tackle why the year came to start in January, a dead time agriculturally, rather than in the traditional month, March.[54] Janus' reply points up a friction between different chronological models that we saw explored by Varro. As Feeney comments, Ovid

knows…that the controlling power of the grid falls short of controlling nature, or of ultimate success in tracking its day-to-day unpredictability. The inherent arbitrariness of the human plotting of time is an important theme… *Natural* time…is not arranged by human agency through the year but is indivisibly continuous… The flow of time and the human grid can never finally be one and the same.[55]

The year begins, Janus states tersely, when the sun is reborn after midwinter.[56] In shifting the New Year from March to January, Janus

---

[52] Ibid., 2.1.6–9, 9–10.

[53] Wallace-Hadrill 2005 usefully connects up Ov. *Met.* and *Fast.*

[54] Ov. *Fast.* 1.149–50.

[55] Feeney 2007: 203, emphasis original. Cf. Berns 1976 on Lucretius.

[56] Ov. *Fast.* 1.163–4.

makes the sun-god Apollo's return provide one mythic rationale for setting aside the intuitive, practice-based, seasonal calendar, despite a lingering preference for that traditional agricultural scheme.[57] As we read on through the *Fasti*, on reaching March the issue is reopened. Here our guide revisits and resists the traditional preference for using agriculture as the reason for a March new year. He strips away the agricultural explanation previously offered, instead presenting a pre-existing political rationale: Romulus gave Mars's month the honour of ushering in the year to emphasize his importance; reflecting the hard work of farmers is aetiologically sidelined.[58] March, this calendar entry suggests, was just as much a political choice as January. This inbuilt contingency in how time was measured and marked shows the calendar flexing in tune with cultural and ideological shifts.[59]

One further mark-up is also taking place, one that we have met already in Varro and Virgil: the translation of Greek knowledge into Roman operating systems. Here in *Fasti* 3 we also learn that early Romans were, the story goes, incapable of reading the stars, unlike the Greeks, who made the constellations tell a tale that made time pass meaningfully as the year turned. Romans, Ovid suggests, traditionally depended on 'foreign' wisdom to make sense of how their environment worked.[60] Telling the time using these sidereal stories explained, reinforced, and universalized a sense of pan-Mediterranean Hellenism that Rome's first citizens could not match, either scientifically or as an embryonic political community. As Feeney reminds us, Greek continued to be the language of enquiry even in Augustan Rome – the *horologium* (sundial), a feature of the Campus Martius, was marked up in Greek.[61]

As we now move on to detailed case studies in Chapters V and VI, we will see how Romans continue to turn to Greece for raw material.

---

[57] Ibid., 1.151–60.

[58] Ibid., 3.97–8, 79–104, 135–66. On why the Romans started their year when they (variously) did, see Feeney 2007: 204–5.

[59] We also see it at work in the festal calendar, e.g. Ov. *Fast.* 1.657–62. See Beard 1987 (seminal discussion).

[60] Ov. *Fast.* 3.105–12.

[61] Feeney 2007: 206.

V ITALY AND THE VILLA ESTATE, OR, OF CABBAGES AND KINGS

Luxury villas and working farms are crucial to Roman interest in what constitutes landscape, and they form the backdrop for this *Survey*'s final two chapters. By the mid-first century BCE, lavishly designed and decorated villas represented not just a source of revenue qualifying their wealthy and educated owners for entering public life, but also an alternative performance venue to the traditional urban sites for political debate – Senate and Forum. Relationship with and management of land became a way of 'defining what it meant to be a member of the Roman elite, in excluding outsiders from this powerful and privileged group and in controlling insiders'.[1]

As archaeological evidence makes clear, the lifestyles and value judgements explored by this chapter's authors were also grounded in recognizable reality.[2] Some part of every villa was – however little the evidence sometimes reflects this – a working landscape, but luxury villas also harnessed the delights of nature and embellished them with works of art and architecture that evoked Rome's Mediterranean empire. Statues of Pan or busts of Socrates gained new, Roman meaning from the commercial (and political) reality of their acquisition and the domestic and public contexts for their niches and colonnades. In turn, they enhanced a wider idea of landscape as a nexus of luxury, display, power, production, and cultivation. Landscape, therefore, could symbolize a uniquely and traditionally Roman attribute: a space combining agriculture, imperialism, and citizenship. How a man inhabited and developed his luxury villas and working estates alike, the qualities they represented, and the activities they staged added up to a portrait of the citizen; in learning how best to work the land harmoniously, one might achieve 'Romanness'.[3]

---

[1] C. Edwards 1993: 12. On being a 'good' Roman, see C. Edwards 1993: 1–4, 141–9.

[2] On the villa at Setttefinestre (approx. 140 km north-west of Rome), often cited as an example, see Carandini 1985 i.101–88, ii.253–6, 257–60. For the overview, see T. W. Potter 1987: 9–10, 106–10; and Perkins 2000: 186–92.

[3] Agache 2008: 18, n. 9. To access the debate, see C. Edwards 1993: 150–72; Wiseman 1994; and Wallace-Hadrill 1998b. For the villa in context, consult Purcell 1995. For what 'villa' means, see J. T. Smith 1997: 10–11. For a range of additional approaches to villas and their social landscapes, see e.g. Canter 1939 (strongly of the view that Rome invented the villa); D'Arms

This chapter samples landscapes from a range of authors who describe and scrutinize villa life. Analysing these literary scenes provides detailed context for Chapter VI, where our frame of reference embraces landscape frescoes and real sites. Here, I have selected sample texts designed to encourage further thinking, taking you beyond this *Survey*'s scope, about how landscape discourse develops in conversation with different agendas associated with habitation and belonging. What follows, therefore, is a series of jumping-off points rather than the whole story.

V.1 Philosophical landscapes: Cicero, *loca*, and *imagines*

'illo loco libentissime soleo uti, siue quid mecum ipse cogito, siue aliquid scribo aut lego.'

Cic. *Leg.* 2.1[4]

[discussing an island on the River Fibrenus at his place in Arpinum] 'That's the place where passing the time is most fun – whether thinking something through for myself, or writing something, or reading.'

Vividly present across his varied literary works, delightful and elegant country estates provide Cicero with an ideal backdrop for tackling weighty political and philosophical topics, showcasing how and why landscape enriches and nuances Roman models of identity rather than solely filling the coffers, or merely presenting traditionalists with evidence of a decline in morals.[5] This makes Cicero a perfect starting point. In the wake of his return from exile (57 BCE), his country estates became places where power and culture could be negotiated behind the scenes of public life. As observed by Grimal, Cicero's ongoing fascination with shopping for the ideal estate (*horti*) points up a crucial subtext: underlying his many stratagems and attempts to prescribe and obtain the perfect parkland is an awareness of the importance of owning and inhabiting a landscape given meaning and form by acculturated points of reference – and with which the Roman landowner could engage empathetically.[6]

1970; Littlewood 1987; Purcell 1987b, 1995; Mielsch 1987; J. W. Mayer 2005; Moormann 2007; Mattusch 2008.

   [4] Cf. Cic. *Att.* 12.15, 13.16.

   [5] See Cic. *Att.* 1.4.3: 'a splendid library is more valuable than farmland'.

   [6] Grimal 1984: 360–1 (cf. Davies 1971: 162–5). See e.g. Cic. *Att.* 12.19.1, 12.21.2, 12.22.3, 12.25.2, 12.38a. Giesecke 2001 tackles the 'ideal' villa. There was a bustle of interest in Cicero's

This nexus colours Cicero's acquisitive urges and his often movingly expressed determination to immortalize his dead daughter, Tullia, in a landscape-park setting.[7] Although the garden-tomb project for Tullia came to nothing, this connection between mourning, retreat, and landscape parks was not simply a Ciceronian quirk; 150 years or so later, Pliny commented disapprovingly on one Regulus' inappropriate retreat to his immense Transtiberine *horti*. There, under Rome's gaze and amid colonnades and along statue-lined river banks, he paraded his mourning for his son.[8] Cicero's association of landscaped gardens with nostalgia and loss thus fits into a recognizably Roman scheme whereby memory, memorialization, and history are enshrined in a quasi-natural scenography.

Personal and political considerations combine in Alcock's discussion of Roman 'Grand Tours' to Athens – here we see another facet of how landscapes become ethnoscapes. Athens as a whole represented 'a kind of museum, a collection of monuments and images to be selectively rummaged through'.[9] Taking this a little further, the scenography of subaltern 'Greece' presented wealthy, aspirant Roman tourists with a cultural hypermarket where they could accessorize their experience, off the peg, with all the signifiers of artistic, literary, and intellectual enlightenment. Alcock centres this on Cicero's *De finibus*, where a selection of Rome's gilded youth find that their experience of place in Athens plugs directly into their emotional, even ethical, engagement with the individuals most closely associated with it.[10] The landscapes of the Academy, for these young men strolling through them, are so intertwined with Plato that they evoke a simulacrum of him; for Romans with enough cash, such cultural touchstones could be brought home to keep the scenographic vibe alive.[11]

Tusculan villa in the early twentieth century (see McCracken 1935).

[7] E.g. Cic. *Att.* 12.18.1, 13.1.2, 13.29. On Tullia's memorial, see Verzár-Bass 1998: 401–6; Erasmo 2008: 176–7. On villas and tombs, see Bodel 1997: 18–26; Griesbach 2005. On garden tombs, see Jashemski 1979: 141–53; Grimal 1984: 322–3; Littlewood 1987: 12–13; Purcell 1987a, 1996a: 123–5. Bodel 1994 looks at some of the practical considerations.

[8] Plin. *Ep.* 4.2.5. Boatwright 1998: 77–81 shows how over-extravagant gardens connoted effeminacy.

[9] Alcock 2002: 67.

[10] Cic. *Fin.* 5.1.1–2. Composed in the mid-40s BCE, but set in 79. See Vasaly 1993: 26–33.

[11] Cf. Cic. *Att.* 6.1.26; *Leg.* 2.4. See in particular Alcock 1993: 178–80. On the interface between Greek and Roman art in this context, see Bergmann 1995a; Kuttner 1995, 1999a; Wallace-Hadrill 1998a. Miles 2008 opens up some big issues for consumer tourism. Cicero and Atticus frequently discuss *objets* required for houses and estates (e.g. *Att.* 1.4.3, 1.5.7, 1.6.2, 1.7, 1.10.3–4). On the marvellous celestial globe captured from Syracuse (212 BCE), see Cic. *Rep.* 1.21–2.

Cicero's dialogue *De oratore* (composed during the 50s BCE) shows how this plays out back home.[12] The scene is set during a political crisis. It is 91 BCE, just before the death of L. Licinius Crassus (famous for attempting to deny full Roman citizenship to anyone who had ever wangled citizen privileges) and the murder of L. Drusus – whose attempts to regain the upper hand for the Senate were to have included agrarian reform and an extension of Roman citizenship throughout Italy. This context (and Crassus' part in the debate) emphasize that we are on the eve of the Social War – even though the dialogue cannot acknowledge it.

To get some productive distance from Rome, the major players, Crassus and M. Antonius, together with Q. Mucius Scaevola and the youngsters C. Cotta and P. Sulpicius, make their way out from the city to Crassus' Tusculan villa.[13] The preliminary scenography likens 'Crassus' to Socrates under his plane tree (in the *Phaedrus*), and Cicero's group, following a stroll in the garden, self-consciously make just such a tree their shady canopy as they recline on cushions to discuss oratory and its importance to state and society.[14] Plane trees crop up again and again as we continue our *Survey*.[15] The *maiores* on parade here are primarily emblematic elder statesmen, part of a quintessentially Roman historical pageant set at a moment just before the world changed.[16] They find themselves rethinking what being Roman means as they debate the rationale for empire-building and their borrowings from the new provinces. Redeploying Greekness as a kind of **palimpsest** for Roman use performs a service to both cultures: actively overlaying Greek cultural achievements with Roman *mores* and authority sets a practical Roman agenda. This shows how new imperialists can imagine themselves to be enriching the Mediterranean experience by grafting the best from provincial cultures onto Roman pragmatism.

---

[12] Key sections: Cic. *De or.* 1.7, 28; 2.20; 3.18. Fantham 2004 sets this dialogue in context. Cf. Cicero's landscape scenography at e.g. Cic. *Rep.* 1.14, 18 (another state-of-the-nation debate: composed in the 50s BCE; dramatic date 129 BCE; set in the 'younger' Scipio Africanus' suburban promenades and porticoes; cf. Cic. *Amic.* 7.25); Cic. *Acad.* 1.1–2 (at Varro's Cumaean villa), 2.9 (at Hortensius' villa at Bauli).

[13] *De or.* 1.24–9.

[14] Ibid., 1.28. See Görler 1988. On walking, see Corbeill 2002 (on the late Republic) and Fontana-Giusti 2007: 259 (looks specifically at Cicero). From here on, single quote marks indicate real, named characters given speaking roles.

[15] Henderson 2004b keeps returning to them (discussing Seneca) in ways that make sense of Roman usage.

[16] Fantham 2004: 26–48 sums up the significance, in the 50s BCE, of choosing Crassus and Antonius as *maiores*.

As the group strolls in leisurely fashion around Crassus' grounds, 'Scaevola' asks 'Crassus': why don't they imitate the Socrates of Plato's *Phaedrus*? Playing at this specific version of Socrates nudges Cicero's audience to think through their own positionality vis-à-vis the unfolding scene. Almost a kind of **prosopopoeia,** this processing of landscape also benefits from consideration in cognitive linguistic terms as a 'conceptual metaphor', what Short defines as

a fundamental cognitive process through which human beings conceptualize the world and their experience of it... the systematic projection of cognitive structures from one domain of experience to another that allow humans to get a better handle on certain concepts by understanding them in terms of other.[17]

The imaginative slippage between characters in a Roman drama, and the second-generation fiction of Plato's Socrates as they know him, is tied here to the landscape evoked by Cicero as being just like (to the extent that 'Scaevola' makes the connection) Socrates' day trip. The parkland scene is both supremely natural (a plane tree and a brook) and quintessentially artificial (ditto, tagged using the topoi of a Platonic *locus amoenus*); moreover, it is a specifically Roman reinvention (by Crassus, the owner, and by Cicero, the author) of a famously evocative and influential Greek 'realandimagined' landscape (as we saw in *De finibus*, above).[18] The plane tree that kick-starts Socrates' Roman renaissance is a curious motif, frequently signalling a deadly combination of sterility and luxury.[19]

The role of Cicero's ideal orator is to be the ultimate statesman, closely involved in both the theory and practice of government. His scenography here deploys symbolic landscape features and points of reference, foreign and familiar, to give reality to the forces of cultural memory – forces also tapped into by his choice of key characters and the pivotal historicity of this moment. In this way, Cicero connects his personal position (a returned exile, spending much of his time in his villas developing a philosophical system for Rome) to a fracture that he identifies in the political landscape – this position is surprisingly similar to that identified by Olick writing on the twenty-first century's 'memory boom': 'memory is now a matter of explicit signs, not of implicit meanings. Our only recourse has been to represent and invent

---

[17] Short 2008: 112.
[18] Terminology from Soja 1996: 11.
[19] On the sterile plane, see Plin. *HN* 12.3–6. See also Verg. *G.* 2.70; Hor. *Carm.* 2.15.4.

what we can no longer spontaneously experience.'[20] Rome's Forum and Senate are no longer, even in 91 BCE, or even for these fictionalized characters ('Crassus' and 'Antonius'), the ideal venues for shaping core values and politics that elite nostalgia at least imagined them to have been. Refounding Rome as a collective of ideal statesmen seems here to mean going back (and out) to the rustic beginnings of a city that developed from a primitive pastoral and then agricultural landscape. Cicero's agenda-setting *De republica* plays with the same ideas: Romulus and Remus were brought up on a diet of farm labour and rural customs, and sowed the new Commonwealth just as a farmer plants his fields.[21]

The landscape setting in *De legibus* (set in the late 50s BCE) has some similar features: it opens on Cicero's family estate at Arpinum, and the *dramatis personae* comprise 'Cicero', his brother, 'Quintus', and his close friend, T. Pomponius 'Atticus'.[22] Plunging us *in medias res*, 'Atticus' spots a grove and a tree known as Marius' oak, a local landmark familiar because it features in Cicero's epic on his fellow-countryman, *Marius*. 'Quintus' makes a direct connection between what the oak means in its landscape and the words and form in which it becomes a literary feature.[23] This reminds us that Romans also recognized textual qualities in landscape, but also hints that 'at its most intense, the boundaries between person and place, or between the self and the landscape, dissolve altogether'.[24] As at Crassus' country place, this group of citizens finds that strolling in the grounds of an estate facilitates structured conversation with a practical end, and they too decide eventually to find a pleasant open-air spot to sit.[25] Relaxing on an island in the River Fibrenus, 'Cicero' comments that this spot is hugely conducive to intellectual activity, and he uses it often as a philosophical laboratory.[26] 'Atticus' makes the riposte that artificial parklands are laughably inferior to the kind of 'natural' scene spread before them, but we may sense that this supposedly untouched landscape is in fact an ideal example of **hyperreality**:

[20] Olick 2003: 3.

[21] Cic. *Rep.* 2.4–5.

[22] For a round up of Cicero's estates, see Littlewood 1987: 11–13. On Arpinum (approx. 100 km south-east of Rome) in the late Republic, see Farney 2007: 47–9.

[23] Cic. *Leg.* 1.1–2. Cf. Thrift 2004 on space and 'affect'.

[24] Ingold 2000: 56. The well-known discussion developed in Bachelard 1994 is sympathetic to this approach.

[25] Cic. *Leg.* 2.1–2 (and 1.14, 15); see also Cic. *Rep.* 1.18.

[26] Cf. Cic. *Q Fr.* 3.1.5 (contrasting villas as sites of philosophy or luxury).

'Ductus uero aquarum, quos isti Nilos et Euripos uocant, quis non cum haec uideat inriserit?
Itaque ut tu paulo ante de lege et de iure disserens ad naturam referebas omnia, sic in his
ipsis rebus, quae ad requietem animi delectationemque quaeruntur, natura dominatur. Quare
antea mirabar – nihil enim his in locis nisi saxa et montis cogitabam, itaque ut facerem et
narrationibus inducebar tuis et uersibus –, sed mirabar ut dixi, te tam ualde hoc loco delectari.
Nunc contra miror te cum Roma absis usquam potius esse.'   Cic. *Leg.* 2.2

[Atticus:] 'Indeed, those water conduits which some call "Nile" or "Euripus", who
could not find them a joke when he sees this place? Just as you, a while ago when
speaking about law and justice, referred everything back to nature, so in this case when
seeking intellectual refreshment and delight, nature wins out. I used to wonder why –
for I thought there was nothing here except rocks and mountains, a conclusion I drew
from your speeches and verses – but as I said, I wondered that this place gave you such
delight. Now however I wonder why when you are not in Rome you are anywhere else.'

Jenkyns' face-value reading ('into his praise of an exceptional
landscape, Cicero slips what is in effect praise of ordinary landscape –
or all landscape, wherever it may be') sets things up.[27] Farrell helps us
to dig deeper: the debate cued up by 'Atticus' (nature versus culture)
deploys ekphrasis to show how the right sort of landscape (here, one
with authentic features rather than foreign-import mark-up) promotes
particular cultural activities, and how the points of reference imposed
upon particular spaces and vistas ('Rome', here, is a species of 'foreign',
a point of reference for the Egyptian 'Nile' and 'Euripus') offer a
commentary on Roman identity.[28] This also takes us back to the term
'ethnoscape'. 'Atticus' observes that, knowing this as the landscape
where his great friend was born, he now feels emotionally engaged
and personally involved with the place. Without this knowledge, it was
only a craggy nowhere, or merely a charming spot. Now it is, as we
saw in Chapter III, a second homeland.[29] Marking up a landscape
with personal and communal memories, and enriching it with cultural
allusion, makes a huge difference to how 'Atticus' and Cicero's wider
audience understand and respond to it.

A feature termed the *rostrum* (ship's beak), at the tip of the island,
divides the Fibrenus before it joins the larger River Liris. This draws in
Rome's *Rostra* (speaker's podium) in the Forum, but the ship-shaped
island also suggests Rome's Tiber Island, and this is where the debate
seems to lead.[30] Rather than pressing ahead with the wordplay that

[27] Jenkyns 1998: 94.
[28] Farrell 2001: 22–4; see also Chapter V.6 for *euripus*.
[29] Cic. *Leg.* 1.3, 2.4, 5.
[30] The recent Tiber bridges (Pons Fabricius and, possibly under construction, Pons Cestius
[see Figure 3]) were matched by restoration of Aesculapius' temple and the shaping of Tiber

brings the Forum flickering into view, 'Atticus' instead highlights the island's suburban landscape qualities, evoking the fashionable world of the Tiber-side *Horti*: the island is just right for a (Greek) palaestra – the porticoed building form adopted enthusiastically in Roman public and domestic architecture.[31] Cicero's Arpinum-on-Tiber is 'like' the estates that thronged the Tiber's banks, while its *rostrum* adds a political and Roman gloss to the debates that it stages. Drawing the Tiber into the frame evokes the luxury riverside villas with their portico gardens, and the river's vital role in Roman economic life as a focus for shipping, economics, and trade. Tiber Island, gaining increasing significance as a focus for cross-river traffic, also overlooked the commercial and newly developing entertainment and ceremonial sites of the Campus Martius and its porticoes.

Tiber Island and the *Rostra* make for two specific add-ons, enriching the experience of Cicero's estate, but the scenography makes one further connection between Rome and Arpinum. The Fibrenus' confluence with the Liris and its subsequent name-change are just like adoption into a patrician family (*Leg.* 2.6). By evoking the physical Tiber, and gaining new patrician status by changing its name, the Fibrenus helps to realign Arpinate identity in a literal, figurative, and genealogical network that links Cicero's home turf to Rome.[32]

V.2 Varro's exopolis: landscape and Italy

...a simulacrum: an exact copy of a city that has never existed...a simulated country-city-state of mind that is infused with and diffuses ever-encompassing hyperrealities.[33]

...from at least the first half of the first century B.C. house, garden, agricultural land (the *villa*), and even sea and surrounding countryside were regarded not as discrete units but as an aesthetically integral entity.[34]

Island's south-east end into the form of a ship's prow. See Haselberger, Romano, and Dumser 2002: 149.

[31] Cf. Cic. *De or.* 2.12, 20–1. Adams 2008: 31–5 discusses the archaeology of suburban villas. On architectural change at Rome, see Wallace-Hadrill 2008: 170–90 (public), 190–208 (domestic).

[32] Farrell 2001: 23–4 discusses the implications concisely as part of a wider debate about language and identity. Jenkyns 1998: 93–4 prefers to read this as a straightforward example of Ciceronian pride in ancestral estates.

[33] Soja 1996: 19.

[34] Littlewood 1987: 9.

Perhaps surprisingly, Varro's *De re rustica* makes Italy's productive land first and foremost a function of aesthetics, genre, **dialectic**, and *otium*. Looking back to Chapter III, we recall that this is not a world where hard graft is to the fore. Here, the villa farm is a paradigm; it works as a device for exploring what being Roman is all about. Varro's imaginative interest focuses on the moral implications of big estates, not on composing a manual for smallholders, and this leads to some unexpected twists: for example, book 1 is notionally addressed to the narrator's much younger wife, Mrs Farmery (Fundania).[35] Using a female addressee, Varro rewrites Rome's macho agricultural identity – the whole creaky tradition defining Romans as citizen-farmer-warriors – for a land-owning Everywoman expecting, at every moment, her aged husband's death. The farmed countryside in book 1 becomes a set against which Varro can scrutinize a range of citizen personas, but also works as a stage for exploring some highly significant socio-cultural shifts. Green neatly sums up the implications of Fundania's speaking-name:

She is Fundania, and she has just bought a *fundus*, an estate. We must not forget, however, that *fundus* also means the ground, the foundation of a thing. The verb *fundo*, 'to establish, fix, confirm' (LSJ s.v. 2.II) is used particularly of the foundation of the city and the power of Rome. Rome, in Varro's view, never could be separated from the farmers who were its true founders, or from the land, its true foundation.[36]

The idea of Rome as a city that serves and depends upon its agricultural hinterland – a development of the 'consumer city' model – is complicated by this linguistic playfulness, re-imagining Cato's Farmer Rome as Woman and emphasizing a generational shift in expectation of what landholding signifies.[37] By no stretch of the imagination will Mrs Farmery herself be ploughing, tending sheep, or harvesting produce. Deploying gender in this way, at the beginning, suggests a new world order when compared to Cato's setup. Representing Generation X, Mrs Farmery could symbolize shifting values linked to changing patterns of labour, land use, and ownership. Making this agenda into a trajectory of decline would slot neatly into reactionary elite ideology, and read this way Varro could be presenting a narrative of falling standards, abandoning formerly shared, securely identifiable,

[35] For 'Mrs Farmery', see Henderson 2002a: 131.
[36] Green 1997: 447.
[37] Recall discussion of Cato in Chapters 1 and 3. For discussions of the 'consumer city', see Laurence 1997 and Morley 1997; Witcher 2005 problematizes it.

and containable tags modelling citizen identity. The farmer is no longer necessarily a soldier in Rome's army, and may be an absentee landlord, farming by proxy and spending his time on political, legal, or financial intrigues, and in the city. Rural landscapes, in this pessimistic view, no longer present an imagined straightforward genealogical map whereby individual families have positive, perhaps unspoken, but perceived ancestral connections to specific places.[38]

Decoding the relationship between the apocalyptic 'change' in the landscape characterized in such conservative elite rhetoric, and the reality of incremental natural change, is hard. Rather than finding bitter-sweet nostalgia for a lifestyle under threat, as outlined above, we might instead read Varro's *De re rustica* as placing traditionalists' fears in sharp relief by scrutinizing them from a range of perspectives. Like Cato's *De agricultura* in the previous century, Varro represents the farmed countryside and its landscapes as business propositions serving individual owners' ends, rather than primarily as documents of family history, but he is also strongly interested in a villascape's autobiographical qualities – the landscapes of a villa will, we increasingly come to see, tell on their owner. Varro's combination of sampled farming pragmatics with discussion of 'good' and 'bad' luxury villas, and their relationship to their wider landscapes, points up interesting frictions between real-world aspirations and the anxieties of reactionary commentators. This interpretation works well for Kronenberg, who argues that Varro was pricking the bubble of Roman hypocrisy: showing up as fantasy the virtues of the citizen-farmer-*paterfamilias*.[39]

The verb *colo*, significant in Varro's introduction, denotes the characteristic activity of agriculture and thereby of the Italian condition.[40] *Colo* indicates a process of refining or refashioning something already intrinsically present, but also implies worship, habitation, and attentiveness. So from the start we see that how one goes about farming and approaches the land will have complicated implications. *De re rustica* 1 takes place at the recently restored temple of Tellus at Rome (probably on the Carinae), setting events in a recognizably Roman, urban, and religious but relatively low-key and agriculturally

---

[38] Farney 2007: 5–11, 26–34 sums up on this nexus. Cf. Cicero Junior's humorous comments to Tiro on his transformation from *urbanus* to *rusticus* and its knock-on effects on his lifestyle (*Fam.* 16.21.7). On austerity as a cultural norm, see Dench 1996, 1998. Cf. Varro, *Rust.* 1.2, 4; 3 (and see Kronenberg 2009: 108–29).

[39] Kronenberg 2009: 74.

[40] Varro, *Rust.* 1.1.2, 4 (see Chapter I).

resonant landscape (see Figure 3). The action unfolds as a group of Everymen ('Varro' included) gather at the invitation of Tellus' *aedituus* (sacristan, or caretaker). While awaiting him, they mull over the state of affairs in the countryside. The occasion (the January festival of Sementiuae, or Sowing) emphasizes interconnections between city and country – and thereby potential differences and tensions – and we learn that Tellus' temple locates us in the world of an alternative, rural pantheon of twelve: the farmers' gods.[41]

This winter sowing festival looks forward to the harvest from the bleak days of January, and falling as it does in the period of quiet before the 'old' Roman new year (March) it suggests a time for taking stock and also perhaps for planning change and addressing urgent issues of maintenance. Apparently at a loose end, the group turn their attention to a fresco of Italy on the temple wall, and then to dialogue.[42] This opening cues up the text's interest in representation (or appearance) and dialectic. As we saw in Chapter IV, speaking names define these characters as 'farmers', yet none of them are actively farming because they are currently in Rome for the elections.[43] This puts the relationship between farming and political landscapes into the frame. Setting the scene at Tellus' temple puts the soil itself on the agenda, and reminds readers that Tellus gazes magisterially across one of Rome's most densely populous areas (the Subura) and towards its political and patriotic heart, the Forum and Capitoline (and Palatine). The land at issue here, however, is *Italia*, not *Roma*, the political implications of which could not have been lost on an original audience:

The continued importance – in an undoubtedly changed universe – of a sense of variegation, regionality, and the specifics of local identities, should make us hesitate before reading as simply descriptive the monolithic concepts we find in literature, such as the highly emotive, and sometimes politically effective *tota Italia*. We should, instead, read such expressions as efforts to create a shape for new realities, perceived or desired.[44]

---

[41] Feeney 1998: 133–6 discusses the relationship between rusticity, religion, and nostalgia; see also Leach 1980, 1998. Rathbone 2008 considers what might have been closer to the smallholder's reality than Varro (or Cato) would like to admit.

[42] Varro, *Rust.* 1.2.1.

[43] All the characters (except 'Varro') in this first gathering have names derived from either *ager* or *fundus*. An extra joke (spotted by one of CUP's anonymous readers): the first ever 'Varro' victoriously lifted this nickname from an Illyrian he defeated (see Maltby 1991: 630). Might this make our 'Varro' into Mr Roman Hero?

[44] Dench 2005: 178. Isayev 2007 contextualizes recent thinking on regionality and Romanness.

Dench's warning is important when examining Varro's redrafting of Italian landscapes in terms of Rome's physical but also conceptual reorganization of the peninsula – making an 'organic whole, sometimes even a body, an ordered composite with variegated parts', designed in part at least to add value to Roman prominence.[45]

Cum consedissemus, Agrasius, 'Vos, qui multas perambulastis terras, ecquam cultiorem Italia uidistis?' inquit. 'Ego uero', Agrius, 'nullam arbitror esse quae tam tota sit culta.'
Varro, Rust. 1.2.3

When we had seated ourselves, Fielder said: 'You who have made your way though many lands, have you seen anywhere *more cultivated* than Italy?' 'For my part', said Fallowfield, 'I think that no land is so wholly *cultivated.*'

Here, Fielder and Fallowfield make clear that Italy's characteristic quality is cultivation, probably in every sense. The peninsula's accession to the top spot in the world rankings of best places to live leads Fallowfield to turn his hand to global taxonomy, starting with Hellenistic advances in geography and global categorization on a grand scale to show how inevitable this conclusion is. The companions' perusal of the utopian 'Italy' depicted on Tellus' wall shows how inconveniently diverse Italian local identities disappear once their landscapes are rezoned as Rome, from a Roman perspective, and regions are redefined in terms of quintessential crops rather than as unique ethnoscapes: Falernum becomes a sea of vines, Campania waves of spelt.[46] Eventually, such examples are trumped by some dramatic totalizing perspectives regenerating *Italia* implicitly as an ethnically unified whole, a 'Rome' greater than the sum of its parts.

We have already noted how the relationship between ethnicity, identity, and the landscapes of Italy was a conventionally hot topic: subscribing to a particular ethnoscape meant signing up to a particular version of citizen or non-citizen identity. Many Italians were only newly minted Roman citizens, and some ambivalence must have attended their early participation as partners in Rome's empire.[47]

---

[45] Dench 2005: 191. Anthropomorphizing Italy recurs in Columella (see the next section of this chapter). Kronenberg 2009: 88–9 argues strongly that Varro is sending Cicero up; contrast Bloomer 1997: 53–5.

[46] Varro, *Rust.* 1.2.3–4, 6. R. Evans 2003 introduces and discusses Roman Utopianism concisely (for case studies, see R. Evans 2008); more generally, see DuBois 2006.

[47] Farney 2007: 1–5.

'Non arboribus consita Italia, ut tota pomarium uideatur? An Phrygia magis uitibus cooperta,
quam Homerus appellat ἀμπελόεσσαν, quam haec? Aut tritico Argos, quod idem poeta
πολύπυρον?'   Varro, *Rust.* 1.2.6–7

'Has Italy not become so planted with trees that the whole seems to be an orchard?
And is Phrygia more covered with vines than this country, though Homer calls it "vine-
clad"? Or Argos, with wheat, though the same poet calls it "wheat-rich"?'

These words preface a citation of Cato's *Origines* (now mostly lost),
and showcase a process of intertextual redefinition.[48] Farmish here
displays his familiarity with Greek, with Homer, and with how
Italy relates to Greek agriscapes. Literary allusion shows that to
conceptualize Italy's agricultural fertility is (for the educated, wealthy,
Romano-centric landholder) to root around in pan-Mediterranean
Greek semiotics, not local Italian agenda. Written out, here, is any
sense of valuing localized strangeness in indigenous Italian cultures,
cohabiting in their own sacred and historicized landscapes complete
with quirky deities and unintelligible ritual. Italy is instead most
vividly itself when compared to Greece. This argument is brought up
short by Farmish's next comment: agriculture means bulk produce.
Picenum and Faventia, two areas mentioned, are clearly conceived here
as commercial success stories for Roman Italy rather than quaintly
romantic collections of local smallholdings, or cultural hotspots for
Hellenism.[49] Farmish thus makes ultra-traditional Cato's account of
Italian townships and territories a backdrop for remapping Italy in
terms of contemporary ideas of agribusiness. Varro, meanwhile, subtly
confronts his readers with the mercantile reality behind the misty-
eyed traditionalism behind the intellectual posturing, and the détente
between layers of (post)colonial intervention in the peninsula's landscapes. It's only *otium* (the first word of *De re rustica*) that gives Varro
the time and mental space to scrutinize good (thoughtful, cooperative,
productive) and bad (underproductive, wasteful, disengaged) uses of
the landscape, and to try to show how excessive pursuit of wealth and
power connects up with excessive expenditure on luxury and display
in a morally grey area.

---

[48] On Cato, *Orig.*, see Sciarrino 2004; Walter 2004: 274–96. Cf. Thoreau 1906: 229, making
a nexus of history, flourishing statehood, and generations of falling, rotting forests guaranteeing
fertility. Greece, Rome, and England prospered, he comments, while their soils were allowed to
regenerate in this way.

[49] Compare the 'reality' of small-scale farming: see e.g. Ando 2002, Gualtieri 2008, Rathbone
2008, Witcher 2008. Farney 2007: 244 sums up on Roman rationalization of multi-ethnic
foundation stories.

Cato's account of Roman agriculture was probably already anachronistic in second-century BCE Rome, but as a touchstone for the *mos maiorum* he was perfect for Varro's purposes. The collision between traditional Roman canniness, newly available luxury goods and increasing consumerism, and an aestheticization of landscape marked up in conventionally Greek terms, is economically portrayed here. Cato's *Origines* focused on the foundation of the Italian towns, centring on Rome itself. 'Varro' and his gang, getting together for Sementiuae, provide a formal echo of Cato's text because this is not just a sowing festival but specifically a fertility festival associated with Italian country villages and rural settlements.

Varro's opening sections prime us for a sophisticated and polyphonic account of country matters, and one in which cultural relativity is to the fore.[50] Patterns of land ownership are changing, but we also see how these changes should not be used as a way of decrying the evils of modern life: Fundania, *like her father*, but a girl – and so perhaps not educated in the wider, Greek-glossed citizen sense of what landscape means – wants to enjoy a profit.[51] Like Cato's, this landscape is an inherently productive and fertile aspect of the *patrimonium*, encouraging cultivation and human intervention. But these citizens are also different from Cato and foreign to the world in which he grew up; they are products of an era in which a good education was much more self-evidently also an education in Greekness, an education which prioritized self-conscious display of erudition and facility with rhetorical strategies, emphasized skills of literary composition and intellectual adroitness, and encouraged Romans to exploit Greece as cultural capital.

These opening moves also suggest that Varro encourages practical consideration of how Roman identity works. We can tackle this via Farmish's comments when he observes two acquaintances ('Sucker' and 'Porker') approaching.[52] Farmish himself plays on their names, reminding readers to get thinking about semiotics (famous names connecting to key moments in collective memory) and to be alert to the connection between names, sites, and politics. These names also put criteria and contexts for parcelling up the countryside into the

---

[50] Kronenberg 2009: 91 puts this even more strongly, making Varro's game to send up and satirize 'expert knowledge and intellectual culture' and 'the excessive pedantry of the dialogue participants'.

[51] Who wouldn't want to make a profit? (Varro, *Rust.* 1.2.8).

[52] Ibid., 1.2.9–10. C. Licinius Stolo (Sucker) and Cn. Tremelius Scrofa (Porker) are real names, chosen for effect.

mix: in particular, the continuing fallout from the agrarian reforms proposed by the Gracchi in the late second century, and the impact of Italian unification and veteran resettlement on patterns of landholding in this era. Farmish outlines how one ancestral 'Sucker' regulated how much land a Roman could own, how another was first to address the people legislatively in the Forum's 'Seven Iugera' (defining the Forum by the notional size of a farm plot), and how this 'Sucker' in turn has made good on the family name by digging out every sucker from his orchard. 'Porker' served on Caesar's commission that parcelled out land in Campania (59 BCE) and was, we learn, similarly famed for his excellent agricultural skills and delightful farmscapes. Farming, family (names), landholding, and politics are intimately connected.

Cato, despite his conservative persona, still picked up on the Hellenistic Zeitgeist enough to write on 'origins'; over a century later, Varro now turns the table on Cato by rewriting 'origins' in Roman terms as ancestral roots – the farm (*fundus*), rather than the villages and towns catalogued by Cato, is the foundation (*fundus*) of Italy.[53] In this version, marrying aesthetics to practical cultivation with an eye to long-term development is what makes a landscape excellent. Properly focused *cultus* (exemplified by 'Porker'), connoting cultivation of crops *and* intellectual faculties, trumps the estates of men whose 'regal' farming style harks back to the wrong era in Roman history.

'Good' *cultus* can link Rome and Italy, city and country, in a reciprocal dialogue involving production, organization, and consumption, but things can also go wrong. Significantly, a fruit market on the Sacra Via is described as the *image* of 'Porker's' orchard ('*pomarii...imago*', *Rust.* 1.2.10). This vision suggests that Rome struggles to offer something distinctive to Italy, and gets by on packaging and reselling consumables and a fantasy lifestyle of rustic authenticity. One result of such a reading would be to redefine Roman success or failure as a reflection (*imago*) of the health and vitality of a unified Italy's landscapes of production. In these terms, Rome as a complex city-and-empire represents what Soja terms 'the paradigmatic Exopolis, a simulated country-city-state of mind that is infused with and diffuses ever-encompassing ideological hyperrealities', a place where 'the real and the imagined, fact and fiction, become spectacularly confused'.[54]

---

[53] See Kronenberg 2009: 109.
[54] Soja 1996: 19.

Describing 'Porker's' *'oporotheca'* ('fruit gallery': a loan word from Greek), Varro transliterates ὀπωροθήκη so that the display sounds Greek but looks Latin. Getting the point means recognizing the **code-switching** and knowing where the word's roots are.[55] Close juxtaposition with *pinacotheca* ('art gallery' – a more common Greek loan word) further underlines how Roman command of agriculture can be compromised so that spectacle (*spectaculum*, 1.2.10) rather than flavour or quality of produce is what defines (even) the well-run and profitable farm. The difficulty in making a landscape useful, beautiful, and productive, in Roman terms, is then replayed when working the land is defined as both *ars* (art) and *scientia* (expert knowledge), developed through a series of correlations between beauty, appearance, productivity, and price.[56] The just-Greek-enough (or maybe a little too Greek) picture gallery of fruit (*oporotheca*) provides the setting for smart dinner parties – just like those painted on the walls in real 'luxury' dining rooms. This should be an ideal chance to show *natura* and *ars* cooperating but, as 'Sucker' observes, some people cut out *natura*'s direct collaboration altogether. They create these scenes of rustic plenty by buying the fruit in Rome and importing it back to the country, disconnecting it from its original landscape context, as a decorative feature for their dinner parties and visual displays.

The pessimism of this extreme vision of a contaminated relationship between city and countryside is hard to take seriously when we recall the (likely) reality:

Rather than envisaging the populations of metropolis and *suburbium* as antithetical (as in literary reconstructions of the élite gaze) or as competitive (as in archaeologists' focus on agricultural production for market), they are better conceived as complementary. In practice, the crowded *suburbium* formed a significant cultural, demographic, economic and political extension to the *Urbs* itself; it was a single system united through the flows of people (both dead and alive), gods, goods, food, information, money, and waste.[57]

Context also undermines Varro's (perhaps ironic) regurgitation of conventional wisdom: Roman *maiores* preferred *rustici* (countrymen)

---

[55] Varro, *Rust.* 1.59.2. On the beauty of fruit, see e.g. Cic. *Nat. D.* 2.158.

[56] Varro, *Rust.* 1.2.10, 3.1. Cf. 1.4.2 (beautiful land commands a higher price); 1.7.2 (appearance and beauty of land enhance profits – formal order connotes beauty and leads to productivity). The theme is taken to specifics at 1.23.4 (orchards and flowers, notionally commercial crops, are planted for pleasure), while *horti* devoted to flowers are designated as commercial spaces, to be located near cities (1.16.3).

[57] Witcher 2005: 135.

to city-slicker *urbani*.[58] Did typical Romans ever really prefer the self-denying virtue that conservative and elite *mores* valorized? We might wonder how different Varro's speaking characters are from the 'bad' villa dwellers who do not know the meaning of hard *labor*. These soft targets (the new townies) are lazier than those who have to work the fields and, whereas antique Romans used *labor* in the countryside to cut out the need for a (Greek) gym, we hear that modern Romans slink off to the city limits while also Hellenizing their villas as bolt holes.[59] This sounds like cliché. More pointedly, it might suggest just how ridiculously fossilized the debate had become, and perhaps in doing so it foreshadows book 3 where the Hellenizing qualities of elite villas help to define a lifestyle that enabled ethically sound withdrawal from Rome's increasingly rowdy popular politics.

Taking the *maiores*' reactionary view with a pinch of salt seems more and more necessary once we discover that one can be a 'good' landowner without inhabiting a shack and abandoning intellectual pursuits. Book 3 opens at the Villa Publica on the Campus Martius (see Figure 3), which provides the backdrop for another tellingly named group of friends.[60] 'Varro' has a companion Axius (*à la Grecque*, Axios, the 'Worthy One'), who jokily asks if they may join the flock in the aviary – a nudge to any readers still missing the punning names.[61] Here in book 3, the slippage between villa-as-farm and villa-as-luxury estate becomes most evident. Axius' conversation with 'Appius Claudius' (the augur and correspondent of Cicero – and elder brother of the infamous P. Clodius Pulcher – present for the elections that have brought the group together) leads 'Appius' to speculate on whether the civic and communal Villa Publica is not rather better, in essence, than Axius' luxury Sabine estate at Reate – also Varro's home town

---

[58] Varro, *Rust.* 2 *Praef.* 1.

[59] Ibid., *Praef.* 2–3. Book 2 is framed by Varro in conversations with Epirote ranchers while commanding the Greek fleets during Pompey's war against the Mediterranean pirates. This context (maritime tensions and the late Republic's edgy politics of coastal Latium) is the focus of Purcell 1998.

[60] Merula 'Blackbird', Pauo 'Peacock', Pica 'Magpie', and Passer 'Sparrow' are hanging out with Appius Claudius, the 'twitcher' (*Rust.* 3.2.2). Linderski 1985 discusses the background. If we date *De re rustica* to 37 BCE, then Pompey's theatre and portico had joined existing grand Hellenistic-style structures on the Campus. Further building works (e.g. Caesar's new Saepta Julia) were also emphasizing the political impact of architectural redevelopment of this zone. On the Villa Publica, see Agache 1987; Haselberger, Romano, and Dumser 2002: 273.

[61] Cf. Timon of Phlius' satiric comment that scholars made third-century-BCE Alexandria a discordant 'birdcage of the Muses' (Ath. 1.22d); this intertext re-emerges when Varro's aviary, near his 'Museum' at Casinum, is described (see below).

(see Figure 2). The Villa Publica is focused on the common interest (*res publica*), whereas Axius' villa benefits Axius alone.

Axius fights back vigorously, both in terms of the decor of the two complexes (the Villa Publica is awash with paintings and statues; his is adorned with farm implements and herdsmen) and their settings. His villa has a large acreage of farmland attached, embellished by thorough cultivation, whereas the sterile Villa Publica has neither land nor husbandry associated with it.[62] 'Appius' pushes harder: if Axius is so confident of his own property's excellence then he must be the person to define the ideal villa.[63] As the conversation develops, we learn from Blackbird that different kinds of husbandry exist on the country estate: livestock such as cattle, and small domestic and 'wild' stock animals (including boar, fish, and so on).[64] The sections that follow see the group trumping each other's stories of the vast profits to be made from the second kind of husbandry: *pastio*.[65]

The conversation talks us through three features directly associated with this kind of husbandry: the bird house (more embedded code-switching: from the Greek ὀρνιθών), the *leporarium* (literally hare warren, but *leporaria* also housed game, chickens, bees, snails, and dormice), and the fish pond (*piscina*).[66] These characteristic features developed naturally and practically from the environment rather than as signs of a designed landscape, because the land surrounding early villas was chosen with particular needs in mind. Early farmers wanted to keep poultry (needed for taking auspices – in effect, communicating with the environment) and husbanded animals to hunt (an early, but more sporting, version of domestication); then bees 'naturally' shifted their accommodation to the eaves of the first villas, and (moving towards more interventionist landscaping) freshwater ponds were dug so that fish could be transported from rivers and farmed. An intratextual allusion from Blackbird recalls alert readers to the wider issues: unlike the key features of the frugal, primitive villa, a new and paradoxical kind of authenticity characterizes contemporary luxury estates. The villa now is not properly villa-like unless its sights also transport its inhabitants and guests to Greece. What were once Latin aviaries (*auiaria*) are now, we hear, pastiche-Greek *ornithones*. This

---

[62] Varro, *Rust.* 3.2.3–6.
[63] Ibid., 3.2.7–8.
[64] Ibid., 3.2.10–13.
[65] Ibid., 3.2.14–17.
[66] Ibid., 3.3.1–5.

Hellenization is so complete that the Greek loan-word has embedded itself fully in Latin letters and so into Roman modes of expression and understanding.

How serious is this line of argument? Depending on how much irony we think Varro is laying on, Blackbird may be showcasing the absurdity of Roman claims to the villa as a characteristic way of life. There is strong evidence that villa culture was an early development in Magna Graecia rather than simply a function of Roman imperialism; Roman land use may in fact have been conscripting previous waves of Greek colonial practice to a new agenda. This disjunction between what Romans say they believe to be the uniquely Roman nature of villa culture, and the likely and perhaps obvious reality, suggests that there was a vanishingly small (even if carefully delineated) difference between the 'Hellenized' Italians of the south, the 'Latin' and other central and northern peoples, and those who were 'Roman' in the strictest sense.[67]

As for the *leporaria*, 'game preserve' best defines what Blackbird records as the norm 'now', with notionally 'wild' beasts part of the attraction. Landholders of 'our era' (3.3.10) enclose ever larger tracts of land, and land is not the only thing under pressure as a result of this new landscaping fetish. Where once landowners made do with modest ponds and country rivers, 'now' vast saltwater tanks blur the boundaries between land and sea, setting deep-sea fish aswim inland. This all dramatically ramps up the scale and semiotic scope of the contemporary villa, but also shows how much wiggle room there is for interpreting the villa's moral qualities – these are examples of 'bad' landscaping not strictly because of what they are (large and lavish) but because of how they are used and what they represent.[68]

The idea that moral worth is embedded in the definition and use of space comes into focus with the famous descriptions of decorative, luxury bird houses (*ornithones*) that follow. Blackbird kicks off with Varro's own example near Casinum (see Figure 2) and, unsurprisingly, Lucullus' Tusculan aviary features as a comparison.[69] There, we hear that Lucullus attempted to marry pleasure and profit by making a dining room/aviary (dining on birds while the next dish

---

[67] Lomas 1996: 137–46 introduces the relevant evidence (for more detail, see Lomas 1993). Assessing rural demography is problematic; on southern Italian identities, see Lomas 2000.

[68] C. Edwards 1993: 137–8 sets up key context.

[69] Varro, *Rust.* 3.4.2–3. Plutarch's biography (early second century CE) portrays Lucullus memorably as an enormously successful military commander, a bon viveur, and a collector on a grand scale.

fluttered around). This experiment failed (for reasons too obvious for words); the sensible solution, of course, would be to have painted birds (see Figures 16 and 17). Of more direct interest for us is the detailed description of the landscape surrounding his own bird house, as described by 'Varro'. His villa, he tells Axius, is enhanced by a delightful stream to which he has made a range of improvements. He has canalized it with a deep stone facing and, on account of its width, he has constructed bridges to allow access to both sides of the property. Downstream at a confluence with another river there is an island; upstream is his Musery; and along the banks that join the two sites runs a broad walkway. Where the walkway faces the farmland sits his bird house.[70]

First defined by a villa (Varro's) and a town (Casinum), the landscape's natural features (river and gorge) are harnessed to make aesthetic and commercial contributions to Varro's villa. The river is contained and controlled physically and semiotically: by bridges, by canalization, and by the watchful gaze of the Muses (from their Latinized $\mu o \upsilon \sigma \epsilon \grave{\iota} o \nu$). The 'aviary' itself is both a simulacrum (of the birds' natural environment) and a display of Varro's erudition and aesthetic sensibility. Shaped like a writing tablet, and with courtyard, *tholos* (shorthand for a domed rotunda, here complete with open colonnade), rivulets, fish ponds, and mock forests, the whole conjures up an elaborate stage set; there is even a mechanism that allows the rotunda's dome to depict day and night skies changing in real time, and to monitor the winds outside – the birds have their own Athenian Horologium! The detail encourages and thwarts attempts to map it, generating a reality effect that is in fact a kind of false precision, made more explicit when we learn that the 'aviary' transforms the birds into actor-spectators in their own show: one area replicates an actual theatre, complete with elaborate stage machinery.

Ultimately, this fake, impossible 'landscape' simulates an alternative natural order. Just like Romans, the birds' lives are structured by their environment. One reading might take Varro's creation of bird-named speaking characters, who then discuss SimCity-dwelling bird avatars, as an example of the complex insights into citizen identity made possible when a Roman has sufficient distance from the murderous

---

[70] Described at ibid., 3.5.9–17. In Sauron 1994: 135–67 the aviary becomes a model for interrogating the nature of existence. Van Buren and Kennedy 1919 provide a beautifully illustrated example of the tendency to use Varro's detail to 'reconstruct' the aviary imaginatively. Good modern summaries are provided by Green 1997: 440–2; Kronenberg 2009: 119–24.

brand of politics that *De re rustica* portrays in the contemporary *res publica*.[71]

'Appius' then leads us on to consider the 'warren'.[72] The *leporarium* can vary from the traditional (woodland warren) to the contemporary (impressive acreages where game animals roam) and more modest enclosures (snaileries, beehives, and dormouse casks). Despite the undomesticated nature of the livestock, what lives in a *leporarium* is clearly differentiated from the wrong sort of wild nature. High walls keep out wolves, weasels, and badgers; they also separate the unmanaged external natural environment from the villascape by containing such designed and maintained faux-natural features as coverts, woodland, brush, and grassland. These are also spaces for scrutinizing what makes for 'wild' and 'tamed' nature, and how different kinds of consumption are catered for: at Varro's Tusculan place, 'Appius' comments, a kind of feeding time at the zoo brought game animals to eat on cue for guests' amusement.

The famous account of Quintus Hortensius' 'Thracian' game preserve ($\theta\rho\alpha\kappa\iota\kappa\hat{\omega}\varsigma$) at Laurentum follows: a vast, walled forest of over fifty *iugera* (acres), called, in Latinized Greek, a *therotrophium*.[73] The Graeco-Latin designation points up the significance of the Laurentine coast for Roman origin mythology, and it is matched by the complex trickery of the space it encloses, where nothing is quite what it seems.[74] Hortensius presents a scaled down mimesis of a natural forest, but once enveloped in this simulacrum of wild space his dinner guests are treated to a dinner theatre that threatens to plunge them, unprepared and ill-equipped, into the midst of a wild-beast hunt. Hortensius effects this by summoning a theatrically garbed 'Orpheus', on whose musical signal the 'wild beasts' pour around them.

The spectacle reminds 'Appius' of the Circus Maximus' wild-beast hunts, emphasizing how quintessentially urban sights and pastimes, mimicking countryside conventions, in turn imaginatively reconfigure how rustic landscapes operate. This scheme redefines rural landscapes using simulated, urban versions of what it is like to roam the wild

---

[71] Green 1997: 442–5 explored this approach. Kronenberg 2009: 118 proposes Varro's aviary instead to be a symbol 'of his literary dialogue'. For murderous politics and electoral mayhem, see e.g. Varro, *Rust.* 1.69.2–3, 3.5.18.

[72] The full passage is Varro, *Rust.* 3.12.1–16.38.

[73] Ibid., 3.13.2. Q. Hortensius was a successful advocate and politician, and enormously wealthy; like Lucullus, he was also an enthusiastic art collector, and he crops up occasionally in Cicero's dialogues (his villa at Bauli provides the setting for a book of Cic. *Acad.* 2).

[74] Purcell 1998: 22 sets out the cultural and conceptual significance of this coastline.

woods, and so on.[75] Of course, we also get a hint of the frisson of danger: for the diners, a significant part of the fun must have been that they could imagine themselves back in Saturn's kingdom, a place stalked by demi-gods, where heroes confronted raw nature daily. In this respect, Hortensius' conceit (that nature answers to the call of his 'Orpheus') is as much about Golden Age fantasy and imagined visions of Latium's early landscapes and Trojan landfall as it is concerned with the practicalities of putting food on the table.

Varro then shifts us briskly from the decadent pleasures of a naughtily transgressive dinner party with Hortensius to the cliffs and mountain bases – furnished naturally with pools or streams – which he claims will make sensible landowners think practically about snaileries.[76] Nut groves, on the other hand, call to mind dormouse enclosures, which are enhanced by the construction of roomy caves as dormouse 'dwellings'.[77] These pragmatic landscape mark-ups redefine the natural world in human terms; we see this again when Varro turns to bees (similarly emblematic in Virgil's *Georgics*). Bees, the winged ones of the Muses, are by nature denizens of the flowering and uncultivated mountains.[78] Their link with the Muses recalls the bird citizens of the aviary, and analogy is important here too: bees' proverbially regulated and politicized society carves new states from wild and lonely places, rescripting them as socio-politically energized space. The superficially wilderness regions they favour are in fact filled with apian labour and warfare, and the bees' primitive politics have epic and heroic qualities that seem far removed from the tame *leporarium*. In short, bee society in the wild presents a far from straightforward analogy for the ideal political state.[79]

As it turns out, however, bees are rather amenable to swapping wild mountain heights for the comforts of the villa, so long as farmers provide the right landscape features and context to satisfy their desires (rather like the crowd at the Games, seeing key iconic sights places the community within a recognizable, albeit make-believe, home). In this way, the right cultivated landscape helps to divert bees from the conflict and ambition to which, left to their own devices and in their natural habitat, they give free rein. The good villa evokes the (here,

[75] Varro, *Rust.* 3.13.3. On death packaged as mythic spectacle in the amphitheatre, see Coleman 1990.

[76] Varro, *Rust.* 3.14.2.

[77] Ibid., 3.15.1–2.

[78] Ibid., 3.16.7.

[79] Kronenberg 2009: 92–3, 125–7.

quasi-Greek) remote, flowering mountain meadows and also the aggressive competition and violence of 'wild' bee society, but in solidly theme-park fashion it fixes them within safely cultivated confines, and in tune with nature's ground rules.[80] Varro's lab space, therefore, includes both the safari park (the bees) and Main Street, USA (the birds).

Our final trip takes us back to the fish ponds.[81] Fish ponds have a class system: freshwater *lymphae* are easily constructed by anyone, but only the elite have the resources to practise maritime fish-farming. These fashionable, artificial pools delight the eye but drain the purse, and are clearly not part of the canny landholder's operation. Hortensius used to advise that fish ponds needed a system of basins to mimic the tidal wash in order to keep their inhabitants fresh and healthy, yet we hear that this same Hortensius was so fond of his miniature private seascapes that he was reluctant to eat the fish for which they were designed. In fact he employed fishermen to harvest wild fish from the sea in order to provide his farmed 'wild' fish with food. So whereas birds and bees join the villascape in productive ways, fish encourage destructive boundary-blurring and sterile luxury. Lucullus, taking verisimilitude to an extreme, made a whole mini-Mediterranean for his sea fish at his estate near Baiae by channelling through a mountain in order to flush his prized specimens with fresh seawater in the most 'natural' fashion.[82]

We can compare a slightly later version of this, from Horace:

> *Iam pauca aratro iugera regiae*
> *moles relinquent, undique latius*
> *extenta uisentur Lucrino*
> *stagna lacu, platanusque caelebs*
>
> *euincet ulmos...*   Hor. *Carm.* 2.15.1–5

> Soon, it will be few acres for the plough, that massive
> palaces will leave. On all sides and spreading wider
> than the Lucrine lake, ponds
> will be on show, and the bachelor plane tree
>
> will muscle out the elm...

---

[80] Varro, *Rust.* 3.1.4; see also 3.16.10, 12–13.
[81] Ibid., 3.17.2–3.
[82] Ibid., 3.17.5–9. Cf. Plut. *Vit. Luc.* 39.3.

Famously, Horace plays with the cliché of characterizing Roman luxury space as overwriting land and sea alike. Since all the world is 'Rome', there is a cannibalistic quality to this description as 'Rome-space' devours itself.[83] The 'monster' villas – miniature 'states' that blur the boundaries between land and sea – make a direct connection between inappropriate landscape and a sense of ethical and political decline. Archaeological survey makes clear that mega-villas were not just a feature of literary discourse, but literary descriptions and responses do subtly shift between late first-century-BCE and first-century-CE texts.[84] By the time we reach Statius and Pliny on villa life, grandiose and high-concept schemes seem regularly to test the boundaries of feasibility, and even what an earlier generation might have called ethical decorum, without censure.[85]

Across all three books, Varro develops a series of perspectives on cultivated landscape as a zone for performing and contesting citizenship. Implicitly at least, traditional and reactionary models of Roman identity are being held up for scrutiny here, and found wanting as neat paradigms for the complex reality of contemporary villa culture and its political significance. Unlike Cato, Varro uses vividly realized and compromisingly luxurious estates as test cases for investigating what agricultural landscapes mean. He seems to suggest that getting the villascape wrong is both its own punishment and also an indication of the different value-systems in play in the mid-first century BCE. Like Cicero, Varro also turns his own country properties into laboratory space. His whimsical aviary shows one way in which being in a luxury villa could spur 'people like us' into posing important questions. Implicitly, we find that, in the right circumstances, intellectual production can be the result of experiencing a well-designed landscape appropriately. Getting the experience right means recognizing and developing a set of models for what happens next when politics and nostalgia blind citizen-landowners to the trade-offs between human and natural authority that modern farming necessitates.

---

[83] Cf. similar sentiments in *Carm.* 2.18. Chapter 1.2, above, introduces the issues and an array of examples.

[84] To understand the material remains, see Dyson 2003: 36–54. On suburban villas in context, see Adams 2008. More briefly, see Purcell 1995; Terrenato 2001; and Wallace-Hadrill 2007.

[85] Ball 1994 and 2004 locate Nero's Domus Aurea (Golden House) as one phase in the architectural development and cumulative process of reinvention that links later luxury estates and edifices to a tradition of increasingly ambitious projects. See Leach 2004: 156–85 (Neronian-era villa decor).

V.3 Columella: landscape and the body of history

Columella's lengthy mid first-century-CE treatise on agriculture (*De re rustica*) runs to twelve books, and in the process name-checks, cites, quotes, and alludes to everyone who was anyone in every corner of the field.[86] This scatter-gun approach combining prose and verse makes the landscapes he delineates intensely polyphonic.[87] At times, Columella personifies the landscape, hinting at a kind of love affair between farmer and his earthy mistress;[88] another key feature is his dense population of Italy's landscapes with literary and historical allusions. This makes him useful for exploring how cultivated landscapes operate as Roman memory banks, and as storehouses of the imagination – something we return to in Chapter VI.[89] In the process, Columella dramatizes how cultural memory and communicative memory draw on 'realandimagined' landscapes, actively in dialogue with the peoples who inhabit them.

Saepenumero ciuitatis nostrae principes audio culpantes modo agrorum infecunditatem, modo caeli per multa iam tempora noxiam frugibus intemperiem; quosdam etiam praedictas querimonias uelut ratione certa mitigantes, quod existiment ubertate nimia priori saeui defatigatum et effetum solum nequire pristina benignitate praebere mortalibus alimenta... Nec post haec reor uiolentia caeli numerus ista, sed nostro potius accidere uitio, qui rem rusticam pessimo cuique seruorum uelut carnifici noxae dedimus, quam maiorum nostrorum optimus quisque et optime tractauerat.   Columella, *Rust. Praef.* 1, 3.

Again and again I hear the leading men of our state blaming now the unfruitfulness of the fields, now the intemperance of the climate for some time past, as being harmful to crops. Some of them I hear toning down these complaints, as if using firm logic, saying that they judged the soil to be worn out and exhausted through over-production in harsh days gone by, making it unable to supply sustenance to humankind with its former benevolence... [I say that this cannot be right, since Nature does not grow old like a person.] And neither do I think that such misfortunes result from harshness of

---

[86] Far more so than Varro's fairly minimalist approach, mostly corralled into *Rust.* 1.1.7–11 (on the 'Greeks'). Varro implies that, whereas Greeks *write* about farming, Romans are its ideal practitioners; otherwise, only Cato gets a look in. In Cato's treatise a very few (far from famous) Roman 'authorities' are recruited (e.g. Minius Percennius, *Agr.* 151.1), but Greeks don't headline.

[87] For example, Columella mentions Virgil thirty times, Varro about half as many times, and Cato (*Agr.*) on twenty-one occasions. Other notable inclusions are the encyclopaedist Cornelius Celsus (multiple references), and Cicero (seven appearances). On demography and landscape in the early Imperial era, see J. R. Patterson 2006: 5–9, 25–60.

[88] In this, Columella is very much on the coat-tails of e.g. Lucr. 2.597–9; cf. Rosenmeyer 2000.

[89] Henderson 2002a: 122–5 looks into the real vs. metaphorical qualities of storehouses and larders in Columella *Rust.* 12. On other ancient authors, see e.g. Leach 1988: 74–9; McEwen 1995: 14–17.

the climate, but instead come about through our own fault. We are the ones who have handed over rural affairs to the worst of our slaves (just as if to an executioner for punishment), when our worthiest ancestors made country matters their particular care.

Columella's opening manoeuvres immediately recall Varro.[90] His moralizing segues into familiar territory: ethics and the practice of being a Roman gentleman. Early on, he harks back to a textually rich historical landscape when he tags his field of operation as 'this Latium and Saturnian land' – echoing Virgil and conjuring up an ideal kingdom for his audience only to shatter the fantasy by saying that this Italy is now forced to import to eat.[91] Why? Because the common conceit 'now' is that rural affairs are no occupation for a gentleman, the countryside no longer sets the scene for citizen endeavour, and provides no mental challenge.[92] Contemporary aristocrats, this familiarly pessimistic view suggests, (still) do not want to get their hands dirty and cannot see how intellectual pursuits, like the fields, need active cultivation. The nostalgic, *ancien régime* quality to Columella's vision of how Romanness has fallen away from a farming ideal is immediately recognizable but this is not just a rehash of Cato's 'things aren't what they used to be' lament, or of Varro's send-up of the clichés.

Nam prata et salicta, genistaeque et harundines, quamuis tenuem *nihilominus aliquam desiderant* industriam. Columella, *Rust. Praef.* 28

For meadows and osier-beds, clumps of broom and reeds, although they require *minimal effort*, still they require some.

The Preface clearly signals that how humans and the natural environment together generate landscape will be important; this is a significant reason for reading Columella paradigmatically here. The Preface's hints are followed up early in book 1, where Columella proposes a list of those who have taught cultivation to 'speak', and eventually 'sing', in Latin, so that tending the land can be conscripted to the project of cultivating Roman citizen identity.[93] With Latin instated as the ideal language of agricultural discourse, Columella then shows how politics and farming connect. We learn that, after the daily grind

[90] See also Columella, *Rust.* 2.1.1–4.
[91] E.g. Verg. *Aen* 6.793–4, 8.314, 322–9.
[92] Columella, *Rust. Praef.* 20. Cf. Cato, *Agr. Praef.* 2: when praising a good man, one calls him a 'good farmer' and 'good cultivator'.
[93] Columella, *Rust.* 1.1.12–14.

in the Forum, a suburban estate is where the right-thinking and public-spirited Roman concludes his day – although the practicalities of finding sufficiently accessible land for all these suburban estates are vague.[94] Nevertheless, the possibility of engaged citizens splitting the day between participation in the *res publica* and cultivation of the land is presented as a specifically Roman act. The development of this element of Columella's platform (being in the country is one complementary aspect of citizen life rather than part of a binary either/or, good/bad scenario) is his major innovation.

Clearly, Columella's primary interest is in the wealthy, politically active citizen. He wants to avoid encouraging the 'wrong' sort of landowner, someone who takes more land than he can manage, and ends by creating a wilderness of sorts, populated by feral cattle, roving wild beasts, and the worst kind of slaves. Later in book 1, he turns more explicitly to the problem of time and motion: how does the public-spirited landowner overcome the reality of physical distance from Rome in order to combine urban duty with country cultivation? At 1.3.3 we learn that the ideal estate needs good access: the road network will allow the landowner to come and go with ease and to transport supplies and produce efficiently. Yet however efficient this imagined infrastructure may be, we might still doubt the idealistic vision of all the right sort of well-behaved citizens daily returning from the hurly burly of the Forum or the courts to conveniently available estates. Roman roads may be famously smooth and straight, but there is only so much distance that a horse or carriage can cover in an afternoon, especially as winter evenings lengthen.

The goal of the fortunate would-be landowner is an estate where the climate is healthy and the soil fertile, with some gently inclined east- or south-facing slopes.[95] The estate should include cultivated land, woodland, and land in the rough, and the land immediately around the homestead should be flat. Despite acknowledging a practical requirement for level ground, hills and slopes feature vividly

---

[94] Ibid., 1.1.19. On what constitutes the *suburbium*, see Purcell 1987a; J. R. Patterson 2000; Witcher 2005. Cf. Columella, *Rust.* 1.3.12. J. W. Mayer 2005's major study sums up all the issues (in German).

[95] Columella, *Rust.* 1.2.3–5 (see also 1.3.1–2). Cf. Cato, *Agr.* 1.1–4. On healthfulness, see e.g. Cic. *Fam.* 16.18 (his Tusculan estate helps to cure Tiro). Cicero also imbues *salubritas* with metaphorical overtones; for example, he observes that in troubled times – July 44 BCE – what one wants is a remote, healthy, and delightful bolt hole (*Fam.* 7.18.2; cf. *Rep.* 1.1 and Cato's abandonment of healthy Tusculum). Cf. Cic. *Fam.* 12.2.1: Antony's drunken carousing at the Tiburtine villa he picked up in the confiscations exemplifies 'bad' land use.

in Columella's scenography. So we find that some hills will need to be treeless (for cultivating grain), and to have plateaux for particular crops; others, given over to olives and vines, will also have copses providing wood for vine supports and other structures. Untilled hills, useful for grazing, should ideally bubble with springs for irrigation and domestic use. Even stony hills can have their uses, providing raw materials for construction. What quickly becomes evident, as Columella observes wryly, is that his perfect villascape is unlikely to be found in the reality of Italy's *available* farmland – particularly, we might imagine, if it has to be in daily commuting reach of the city of Rome itself. It becomes increasingly clear that this version of ideal Roman practice is only going to be available to those with significant cash wealth, political clout, or inherited property; or to those for whom local and Italian concerns are of more interest than (urban) Roman politics. Later on, as we will see, Columella grapples with regionality in a way that suggests an awareness of a shifting focalization in the peninsula.

Siting the house, once the ideal estate is obtained, is the next dilemma with which the text confronts the eager novice landsman. The micro-climate is important: building the house on ground elevated on a hillside avoids the extremes of valley or mountain-top weather. Columella looks all the way to Rome's eastern provinces, to Athens' former Peloponnesian rivals Boeotian Thebes and Euboean Chalcis, for examples of intemperate places to be avoided; by contrast, the canny Roman *paterfamilias*, halfway up his hill, will be keeping his family safe from burning heat or fierce cold (and avoiding the dangers of 'rivalling' Roman authority). Moreover, sitting pretty on an elevated plateau keeps the house near the streams that typically babble down hillsides in spring and summer, but out of the path of winter torrents raging past. This description is crammed with sensory stimulation, a pattern that continues into Columella's next observation that the availability of water makes cultivation possible.[96] Naturally occurring spring water is best, we initially learn, but other options show how the reality of farmland is likely to depart from what nature offers.[97] It may be necessary to sink a well to access sufficient water; if the water drawn up is brackish, then build rainwater cisterns. But here Columella brings us up short: the naturally irrigated villa turns out to be *less good* than one where the farmer has to intervene in the water supply. Healthier

---

[96] Columella, *Rust.* 1.4.10–5.1.
[97] Purcell 1996b is an excellent starting point; Bannon 2009 looks in depth at water rights and use in Roman Italy.

water comes from artificial cisterns than from a year-round spring because rain water channelled by human ingenuity and technological skill through clay pipes is the superior product. Technocracy trumps nature. Nonetheless, a babbling brook has significant impact on the somatic experience of country life. Not only does it alleviate the worst of the summer heat, it also adds to the *amoenitas* (delightfulness) of a spot. Hence, if nature fails to provide one, then streams should be canalized to the villa, adding to the sensory charm and emphasizing the landowner's control of the landscape. Position relative to water remains a significant motif:

Sin summotus longius a collibus erit amnis et loci salubritas editorque situs ripae permittet superponere uillam praefluenti, cauendum tamen erit, ut a tergo potius quam prae se flumen habeat et ut aedificii frons auersa sit ab infestis eius regionis uentis et amicissimis aduersa; quoniam plerique amnes aestate uaporatis, hieme frigidis nebulis caligant, quae nisi ui maiore inspirantium uentorum summouentur, pecudibus hominibusque conferunt pestem… Eademque semper mare recte conspicit, cum pulsatur ac fluctu respergitur, numquam ex ripa, sed haud paulum summota a litore… Nec paludem quidem uicinam esse oportet aedificiis nec iunctam militarem uiam, *quod illa caloribus noxium uirus eructat et infestis aculeis armata gignit animalia, quae in nos densissimis examinibus inuolant, tum etiam nantium serpentiumque pestes hiberna destitutas uligine, caeno et fermentata colluuie uenenatas emittit, ex quibus saepe contrahuntur caeci morbi, quorum causas ne medici quidem perspicere queunt…* haec *autem praetereuntium uiatorum populationibus et adsiduis deuertentium hospitiis infestat rem familiarem.*   Columella, *Rust.* 1.5.4–7

But if the river is far removed from the hills, and if the healthfulness of the area and the elevated position of the banks permit the siting of the villa above flowing water, care must still be taken that it have the stream at the rear rather than in front of it, and that the front of the building face away from the region's harmful winds and towards the most friendly: most rivers in summer give off warm mists, and in winter dank fogs. These, unless they are dispersed by the greater force of the winds' breath upon them, bring devastation to livestock and mankind… Similarly, a villa that overlooks the sea is always well-aligned: reverberating from and showered by the waves, but never right on the water's edge; instead, some distance removed from the shore… And nor should there be any marsh-land in the vicinity of the buildings, and no *military road* adjoining; because the former spews out a pestilential emanation in hot weather and breeds insects armed with savage stings, which attack us in dense swarms. It is then too that it sends forth plagues of swimming and creeping things bereft of their winter swamp and infected with poison by the mud and decaying filth. From these are often contracted mysterious diseases whose causes not even doctors are able to ascertain… *the highway*, moreover, damages the estate because of the incursions of passing travellers and the ceaseless need to provide hospitality for those who turn in seeking lodging.

Urbana rursus in hibernacula et aestiua sic digeratur ut spectent hiemalis temporis cubicula brumalem orientem, cenationes aequinoctialem occidentem. Rursus aestiua cubicula spectent meridiem aequinoctialem, sed cenationes eiusdem temporis prospectent hibernum orientem… Ambulationes meridiano aequinoctiali subiectae sint, ut et hieme plurimum solis et aestate minimum recipiant.   Columella, *Rust.* 1.6.1–2

The manor house should thus be zoned into winter and summer apartments in such a way that the winter bedrooms may view the sunrise at the winter solstice, and the winter dining rooms look toward the sunset at the equinox. The summer bedrooms, on the other hand, should look toward the equinoctial midday sun, while the dining rooms of that season should face the winter sunrise… The promenades should be exposed to the equinoctial midday sun, so that they shall receive both the maximum of sun in winter and the minimum in summer.

Here we have a hugely complex set of parameters for how the estate as a whole, and the dwelling in particular, make the most of but also engage in a dialogue with their environment and the senses. Nature can inflict devastation, but the first of these extracts highlights a different sort of threat: that posed by uninvited people travelling through the estate's environs. The dilemma of hospitality is particularly interesting. Columella's tone suggests that, far from benefiting the landowner by displaying his property to wayfarers, the well-connected estate is all too vulnerable to the depredations of people in transit. Columella here specifies the perils of becoming a rest-stop on a military highway. What might we infer? The term '*militaris uia*' seems to suggest a road endlessly subject to the beat of legionary feet, but while that connotation lurks beneath Columella's choice of language, the 'military' aspect was probably a qualitative descriptor marking this as more than a back road or byway.

What he is actually saying is that having a major highway (a 'motorway' or 'interstate' in our sense) nearby diminishes the landowner's control over his estate and its boundaries.[98] These routes traversing the countryside deracinate the zoning of an estate as private and open it up to a wider landscape over which its owner has no control. If we think back to Columella's opening gambit (every good landowner is also engaging in public affairs in the city), we might even wonder whether the negative tone here has more complex implications. Not having a major highway adjoining one's estate means that either the property is close enough to Rome to make for a feasibly short

---

[98] Made clear at 1.5.7. For background and discussion of practicalities, see Laurence 1999: 103–8.

journey, or that a thriving local political centre is the focus of one's attention, or that one has completely cut oneself off from all levels of citizen activity. A major public highway populates the landscape with transitory and unknown quantities, it breaks the connection between ethnicity and locale, and it also imposes an external mark-up on how the individual estate is perceived, approached, and departed from. By contrast, the relationship between water (rivers make for another kind of communication network) and the villa is dialogic and positive, even though Columella is careful to warn of all the dangers that water can pose. We can see, therefore, that, whereas there can be friction between the estate and other wholly manmade interventions in the landscape, natural features are far more amenable to partnership, even if apparently more mysterious and threatening.

This rhetoric makes the estate's topography and situation into facets of a quirky and at times tetchy, but essentially benevolent, scenography. It undergoes a shift when Columella suggests that, to find out what kind of land one is entering into a relationship with, a more intimate approach is necessary.[99]

Saporem quoque sic dinoscemus: ex ea parte agri, quae maxime displicebit, effossae glaebae, et in fictili uase madefactae dulci aqua permisceantur, ac more faeculenti uini diligenter colatae gustu explorentur; nam qualem traditum ab eis rettulerit umor saporem, talem esse dicemus eius soli. Sed et citra hoc experimentum multa sunt, quae et dulcem terram et frumentis habilem significent, ut iuncus, ut calamus, ut gramen, ut trifolium, ebulum, rubi, pruni siluestres, et alia complura, quae etiam indagatoribus aquarum nota, non nisi dulcibus et uenis educantur.

Columella, *Rust.* 2.2.20.

We shall also make distinctions of taste as follows: from that part of the field that displeases us most, clods of earth dug up and steeped in an earthen vessel should be mixed thoroughly with sweet water. Then, after being carefully strained as one does with dreggy wine, the decoction should be tested by tasting. For the liquid will carry whatever taste is transmitted from the clods, and such we shall declare to be the taste of that soil. But apart from this experiment there are many signs that show that ground is sweet and suitable for grain: take note of the rush, the reed, grass, clover, the dwarf elder, brambles, wild plums, and a host of other things that, well known too to trackers of water, are not fostered except by sweet streams.

This symbiosis requires detective work and forensic testing, right down to actually swallowing an earthy potion. But the landscape intrinsically and extrinsically continues to signal its willingness to cooperate. Far

[99] Cf. Verg. *G.* 2.238–47.

more straightforward is another aspect of man in the Roman landscape, the meadow, which Columella attacks via speculative etymology:

et ideo necessarius ei cultus est etiam prati, cui ueteres Romani primas in agricolatione tribuerunt. Nomen quoque indiderunt ab eo, quod protinus esset paratum nec magnum laborem desideraret. Marcus quidem Porcius et illa commemorauit, quod nec tempestatibus adfligeretur ut aliae partes ruris minimeque sumptus egens per omnis annos praeberet reditum neque eum simplicem, cum etiam in pabulo non minus redderet quam in faeno... Cultus autem pratorum magis curae quam laboris est.   Columella, *Rust.* 2.16.1–2, 2.17.1[100]

[To the meadow] the ancient Romans attributed the primacy in agriculture. They also attached the name [*pratum*] for the reason that it was ready made [*paratum*] from the start and did not require much effort. Marcus Porcius [Cato], indeed, also recorded the following: that it is not destroyed by storms like the other parts of the farm, and, though needing very little expenditure, year after year it keeps performing; and this is not a single return, since it yields no less in pasture than in hay... The *cultivation* of meadows is, in fact, more about *care* than *labour*.

Columella then details the sometimes violent measures for grooming and maintaining these ready-made landscapes of production: vigorous, shrubby, and thorny growth has to be eradicated; pigs' snouts need to be kept from rooting, and grazing animals, with their destructive hooves, must be excluded. Fertilizer needs to be spread and stones removed, before finally the meadow is left to hay. The meadow, if guarded and tended, and rescued from neglect if necessary, is luxuriantly productive. Given the right sort of landowner, equipped with the appropriate skills, knowledge, and ability, a beneficial partnership between man and land is, in Italy, inevitable.[101]

The above passage sharpens our focus on a familiar pattern. Columella's interest is in developing a philosophy of labour and exploring agricultural epistemology rather than guiding a complete novice through the minutiae of farm-lore and the pragmatics of back-breaking toil. We see this again when, discussing viticulture, he observes that, although the landowner should endeavour to plant vines by species in separate plots – each bounded by paths and perimeters – he himself knows no one who has managed to achieve this because all young vines look alike. His rationale for urging his audience to attempt the impossible is (drawing on Plato) to tell us that striving to achieve beauty by way of the organizationally perfect vine-laden slope

---

[100] Cf. Varro, *Ling.* 5.40.
[101] Columella, *Rust.* 2.17.1–7, 3.8.5. Cf. Varro (see above). On the natural environment as nurturing 'mother', see e.g. Columella, *Rust.* 3.8.1, 3.10.10–11.

– a layout that would grace a formal garden – represents a worthy goal in itself.[102] He warms to the task as he explains why one should persevere:

et ut a leuioribus incipiam, primum, quod in omni ratione uitae non solum agricolationis, sed cuiusque disciplinae prudentem delectant impensius ea, quae propriis generibus distinguuntur, quam quae passim uelut abiecta et quodam aceruo confusa sunt. Deinde quod uel alienissimus rusticae uitae, si in agrum tempestiue <consitum> ueniat, summa cum uoluptate naturae benignitatem miretur… Sed haec quamuis plurimum delectent, utilitas tamen uincit uoluptatem. Nam et pater familias libentius ad spectandum rei suae, quanto est ea luculentior, descendit; et, quod de sacro numine poeta dicit: 'et quocumque deus circum caput egit honestum', uerum quocumque domini praesentis oculi frequenter accessere, in ea parte maiorem in modum fructus exuberat.　　　　　　　　　　　　　　　　　　　　　　　Columella, *Rust.* 3.21.2–4

And so to begin with the least weighty argument: in the first place, in every way of life (not just in farming), those things that are separated into their proper kinds are a more extensive source of delight to the sensible practitioner of each discipline than are those that are thrown hither and thither, so to speak, and jumbled together into an indiscriminate heap. Secondly, because even the greatest stranger to rustic life, if he should enter a<n arable> field at the right moment, would admire with great pleasure the benevolence of nature… But though all these give the greatest delight, still utility prevails over pleasure. For while it is the case that the head of the household comes down the more gladly to the spectacle of his property inasmuch as it is a magnificent sight, it is also true that, as when the poet says of the sacred deity: 'wheresoever the god has turned his goodly head', truly, wherever the person and eyes of the master frequently come to call, that's where the fruit flourishes in richer measure.

This is also all about hermeneutics. Columella constantly alludes to his role in transmitting knowledge from the works of previous big names in the genre, using core philosophical material where necessary. His landscapes' hyper-productivity depends on understanding and information (one has to know the climate, the appropriate methods of cultivation, the most suitable crops, the most destructive pests, and their habits), and also on the (poetically) almost-godlike owner's educated gaze, which in itself stimulates and is stimulated by agricultural productivity. An absentee landlord will get the landscape he deserves.

Columella left his readers agog for Virgilian flights of fancy by ending book 9 with bees. Book 10, notionally a verse coda to his

---

[102] Ibid., 3.20.4–5.

revitalization of farming as a priority for interesting and well-rounded citizens, is also clearly a capstone for Virgil's 'unfinished' *Georgics*:[103]

Superest ergo cultus hortorum segnis ac neglectus quondam ueteribus agricolis, nunc uel celeberrimus.   Columella, *Rust.* 10 *Praef.* 1

So what now remains outstanding is the *cultivation of gardens* [horticulture]: a sluggish and neglected chore for ancient farmers way back when, but now the height of fashion.

What we realize pretty quickly, as has been pointed out by Henderson's luxuriant reading, is that this is not just '*Georgics* 5'.[104] It also dips into the aesthetics of the *Eclogues*' pastoral world *and* shows cumulatively how the garden as microcosm of the city-state converses with the nature of Rome itself. Just as we saw with Varro and Cicero, landscape has a political quality.

As in Varro, Columella presents us with a speaking-named character: Siluinus, his addressee. 'Woodsman', or perhaps 'Forester', has had the benefit of Columella's nine prose books outlining the site of the productive estate, agricultural land and its qualities, arboriculture, viticulture, and then the familiar faces of large and small livestock, before winding up with what Varro also put closest to home in the *leporarium*: fowl, fish, game, and bees.[105] As readers of Varro and Virgil – and perhaps of Xenophon and Plato too – we know how bees can transform even prosaically utilitarian farms into political laboratories. What transpires here is that we move further into the analogy, strolling from bee-friendly flower meadows to the explicitly tamed and domesticated garden.

This horticultural spot is simultaneously part of and also separated physically and epistemologically from the wider landscape, so the aspiring gardener needs to think carefully about how to manage the design process.[106] One way or another, the landscape itself, if suitably chosen, will cultivate (y)our garden as it nourishes itself; the verb *educo* shows how the land gives plants a good 'education'.[107] The

---

[103] Columella, *Rust.* 10 *Praef.* 3; 10.2–3. Virgil's Corycian gardener in *Georgics* 4 has in turn been read as an allusion to the (now fragmentary) *Georgics* of Nicander; on this, see Harrison 2004. Kronenburg 2009: 132–84 connects up Varro and Virgil persuasively. See also Johnson 2004 on the Epicurean background. J. S. Clay 1981 or Perkell 1981 are good introductions to Virgil's gardener.

[104] Henderson 2004a: 13.

[105] As one of this *Survey*'s anonymous readers pointed out, *Siluinus* also suggests 'woody' in the sense of 'unfinished' or 'raw material'; an ideal addressee for a didactic poem.

[106] E.g. Columella, *Rust.* 10.6–16.

[107] Ibid., 10.13, 23–6.

small scale of 'gardening' (as contrasted to arable or pastoral farming) refines the relationship between 'city' and country further – the garden emblematizes the regionality of Italy and its autonomous landscapes. It is not long, however, before Columella unravels the developing harmonious diversity that garden space seemed about to offer. Suddenly, the relationship between man and soil becomes intrinsically violent, with a kind of inward-looking and violent incestuousness that may leave us queasy.

> *Nescia plebs generis matri ne parcite falsae.*
> *Ista Prometheae genetrix fuit altera cretae:*
> *altera nos enixa parens, quo tempore saeuus*
> *tellurem ponto mersit Neptunus, et imum*
> *concutiens barathrum lethaeas terruit undas.*
> ...
> *Nos fecunda manus uiduo mortalibus orbe*
> *progenerat, nos abruptae tum montibus altis*
> *Deucalioneae cautes peperere...*
> *... et curui uomere dentis*
> *iam uirides lacerate comas, iam scindite amictus.*
> *Tu grauibus rastris cunctantia perfode terga,*
> *tu penitus latis eradere viscera marris*
> *ne dubita, et summon feruentia caespite mixta*
> *ponere...*   Columella, *Rust.* 10.58–62; 65–7; 70–4

> Common folk, ignorant about your origin, lest you spare your 'mother'
>   know she's fake.
> *She* was the mother of the Promethean stock;
> another parent bore *us.* Way back when tempestuous
> Neptune submerged the earth with his waves and, as quaking
> shook the abyss, terrorized Lethe's waves.
> ...
> *Us* it was that a fertile hand, in a world devoid of humankind,
> created. To *us,* who on that day were torn out from mountains high,
> Deucalion's jagged rocks gave birth...
> ... using now the ploughshare's curved tooth
> tear her greenery tresses, now rip apart her mantle.
> With weighty rakes slash strips in her reluctant back;
> with wide mattocks scrape her vital organs.
> Don't hesitate: once mixed with the top layer of turf and while still warm,
> set them down so that they lie spread out...

Virgil is one obvious allusion, but Columella's inclusive use of '*plebs*' ('common folk' or, in a political context, old Roman families who are not patrician, or 'founding fathers') hints at a version of citizenship in which continuity is vested in a visceral relationship with the environment and landscape, rather than in political structures or authority.[108] Our *labor*, then, is to show how even 'we' wild ones, made from the rocks and mountains where humankind now rarely ventures, can participate fruitfully in a family relationship with the earth. That it is a warped, vicious relationship, in its beginnings, is gradually mitigated by Columella's description of how the gardener (*olitor*) sates the starving, frozen earth come spring.[109] In a Stockholm Syndrome-style scenario, captive earth, fed and then with 'hair' combed and newly spick and span in clean garb, then falls for her abuser.[110] The destruction of 'Promethean' humankind (born of earth) and the triumph of Deucalion's stony descendants hints at the need to purge a decadent and morally bankrupt humanity, a topos repeated annually and symbolically when the land stops producing food to sustain us (winter), leading to violence (ploughing) and renewed fertility.

The renewed landscape produced by this union is first of all a riot of flowers: white, gold, purple, and blue hues jostle for starring roles before giving way to a scene less straightforwardly aesthetic.[111] The flowers encourage a **scopophiliac** sensuality that is all about the Gaze; next, sexual activity is explicitly in the spotlight, and thence other senses are targeted. Dramatic shifts in scene and perspective transform the text's production of isovist space, shifting from the confined, jewelled garden into a panorama of empire: seeds and bulbs from Greece, from north Africa, from Assyria take root pell mell with 'cabbage', the crop that describes an itinerary of Italy while making Italy a synecdoche for the whole world.[112]

To follow Columella's lead, see Figure 1 (and consult Bradley, Isayev, and Riva's recent volume on Italian regionalities[113]).

> *Tum quoque conseritur, toto quae plurima terrae*
> *orbe uirens partier plebi regique superbo*
> *frigoribus caules, et ueri <u>cymata</u> mittit:*
> *quae pariunt ueteres caesposo litore <u>Cumae</u>,*

---

[108] Verg. *G.* 1.62–3. Gowers 2000 deals in detail with allusions to Virgil in Columella. See also Henderson 2002a; Doody 2007; and (in brief) Cowan 2009.

[109] Columella, *Rust.* 10.80–85; he feeds his victim with manure and sewage.

[110] Ibid., 10.94–5. Stockholm Syndrome occurs when a hostage becomes emotionally attached and even loyal or sympathetic to her or his captor. It is named for the hostages taken in a bank raid in Sweden, in August 1973.

[111] Columella, *Rust.* 10.96–104.

[112] On the different regions of Italy in brief, see J. R. Patterson 2006: 60–9; in more detail, the invaluable Farney 2007.

[113] Bradley, Isayev, and Riva 2007.

quae Marrucini, quae Signia monte Lepino,
pinguis item Capua, et Caudinis faucibus horti,
fontibus et Stabiae celebres, et Vesuia rura,
doctaque Parthenope Sebethide roscida lympha,
quae dulcis Pompeia palus uicina salinis
Herculeis, uitreoque Siler qui defluit amni,
quae duri praebent cymosa stirpe Sabelli,
et Turnis lacus, et pomosi Tyburis arua,
Bruttia quae tellus, et mater Aricia porri.   Columella, *Rust.* 10.127–39.

This moment is when it comes together: in all the soils of
the globe it thrives, for common folk and arrogant king alike,
its stalks in winter and in spring its *shoots* it presents.
This is the one that historic *Cumae* produces on its grassy shore,
produce of Marrucine territory too, and of Signia on Mount Lepinus,
and ditto for luxuriant Capua, and gardens at the Caudine Forks,
the famous Stabian springs too, and the Vesuvian countryside,
even cultured Parthenope, dewy with Sebethos' stream;
it has grown too where the sweet Pompeian marsh is neighbour to
Herculean salt pits, and where Siler pours out his crystalline waters,
where the tough Sabellians promote a *multi-sprouting stock*,
and at Turnus' lake too, and the fields of orchard-town Tibur,
in Bruttian earth, and in mother (of leeks) Aricia.

In reworking Cato (on cabbages), the Spanish-born Columella is simultaneously rewriting a seminal document of culture and showing how the relationship between Rome and Italy continues to generate column inches.[114] These lines riff on Virgil's 'praises of Italy', and nod to Varro's opening conceit: Tellus' painted Italy.[115] Columella's shtick is to home in on Italy's lower leg, taking us on an associative tour from Rome's environs to the south. En route we are whisked past a series of what Soja terms 'iconic emplacements', sites that reflect paradigmatically on the exopolis.[116] Here, the virile Greek cabbage is the MacGuffin, hooking readers for a retrospective exposé of cultural hybridism in Italy's most historically saturated and patriotically significant landscapes – ideal examples of 'realandimagined' space. Highlights are what this whistle-stop itinerary is about, and directional terminology is almost entirely absent (no examples of 'from here

---

[114] Cato, *Agr.* 156–8. The vitality of this theme in Latin texts continues to shape interpretations of archaeological data, an issue addressed by Attema 1996 and 2005.

[115] Verg. *G.* 2.136–76, composed in Naples (4.564); Varro, *Rust.* 1, discussed above.

[116] Soja 1996: 249.

you…', 'turn right at…', or 'south of…'), with the exception of the vague 'neighbour' and 'pours out'.[117]

The first stop, Cumae, site of Aeneas' katabasis, evokes the prophesied nature of Rome's destiny. Drawing on the Greek term κῦμα – the swell of the sea, pregnant with possibility (the verb κύω) – brings Greek offshoots to Italy; Κύμη, one landfall, becomes historically Italian and then Roman Cumae just as new ways of understanding what Rome represents, how its origins might most productively be defined, and how its relations with its neighbours could be explained all help to redefine the peninsula and gloss the landscapes of Magna Graecia. *Cyma* will take us full circle: the cabbage, a Greek delicacy too, reinvents Rome's most Greek sites as part of a conversation about how ethnic and political, not to mention topographical, boundaries occupy a Trojan–Latin–Roman interface.[118] Cumae represents extreme liminality: on the coast (land/sea), it was also a mythical point of contact between old and new worlds, between past, present, and future, and between gods and mortals (recall Lorrain's vision, this *Survey*'s cover).

Reading on, keeping an eye on the map, Columella pushes us towards a complex and detailed analysis. This historically resonant landscape is textualized using complex associative patterns, and framed in terms of consumption, sensory experience, and emblematic sites. It therefore repays analysis as 'thirdspace': a combination of geographic, representational, social, political, historical, imaginary, and perceptual elements and signs.[119] We might start with some history and practicalities: in the late fourth century BCE, Appius Claudius Caecus undertook two projects that radically transformed perceptions of spatial relations on the peninsula and redefined the dialogue between Rome and Italy: the Via Appia – shooting out south-east from Rome, through the Pontine Marshes, then eventually cutting cross-country to zip through Capua and past the Caudine Forks, before speeding via Tarentum to Brundisium – and Rome's first aqueduct, the Aqua Appia.[120] These conduits connected Rome to Campania and the cities of Magna Graecia, drawing together the peoples who had fought Rome in the Samnite Wars but also marking up the countryside as a

---

[117] Columella, *Rust.* 10.135, 136.
[118] *OLD*: *Cymaeus* sense 2 gives 'of Cumae in Campania'.
[119] Soja 1996: 2–3, and *passim*.
[120] Livy 9.29.5–7; Frontin. *Aq.* 5.1.3. The Aqua Appia's route, much of which was underground, is partly conjectural and not marked on Figure 1. It entered Rome from the south-east.

landscape configured by Roman power and vision.[121] The Via Appia, I suggest, helps structure our understanding of the tour.

Counterintuitively, we reach Signia (line 131), one of Rome's earliest colonies, via a detouring reference to the Marrucini. One of those Italian peoples who spent centuries switching between conflict and alliance with Rome, the Marrucini perhaps feature here to emphasize how the points of reference for topographic mark-up change when not focalized through Rome.[122] Columella juxtaposes Signia directly with Mount Lepinus, and Lepinus' ridge line makes the alert reader think about what lies on either side: the two main roads south that mirror its vector. Lepinus' ridge directly bisects the angle between the Viae Appia and Latina.[123] These two superhighways were almost contemporary (the Latina possibly a little earlier), and left Rome together before separating at today's Piazza Numa Pompilio.[124] The Latina linked Rome to the settlements north of the Alban hills, mirroring the Appia's progress through the marshes to the hills' south. Mount Lepinus formed an early natural boundary to Latium (setting one limit to Rome) and also held the sources of the rivers contributing to the Pontine Marshes – another 'boundary' feature – but readers are more likely to recall this as wine country (the south-west slopes produced the famous Setinian) than cabbage heaven.

Once part of Volscian territory, the Pontine Marshes were originally held in check in order to exploit the wealth of the agricultural plain, but this zone's proximity and productivity made it a natural target for Roman southerly expansion.[125] By the early third century BCE, Romanization of formerly Volscian territory was well under way. The Via Appia's trajectory cut through the heart of what soon became the Pontine badlands, plugged Rome directly into Magna Graecia's sphere

---

[121] On the Via Appia in brief, see Laurence 1999: 11–21, 56; Purcell 2007: 189–90. On the road's life and times, see della Portella 2004.

[122] Who would care about the Marrucini? The Marrucine family name Asinius came to Rome when citizenship was extended after the Social Wars. It gained prominence via the scholar, art collector, and politician Asinius Pollio (Consul in 40 BCE), but was already famously associated with Herius Asinius, the Marrucine commander killed in 90 BCE, and subsequently the Asinius tagged 'Marrucinus' by Catullus (12). The family continued to produce consuls in the Imperial era.

[123] Signia was believed (Dion. Hal. *Ant. Rom.* 4.63.1; Livy 1.56.3) to have been one of Tarquinius Superbus' colonies, plugging Columella's cabbagey itinerary into Rome's historical progress. Its commanding position over the Trerus valley (and Via Latina) at Mount Lepinus' north end made it strategically important.

[124] Haselberger, Romano, and Dumser 2002: 261.

[125] See e.g. Sallares 2002: 178.

of influence, and opened up access to the eastern Mediterranean.[126] Roman authority, exemplified dramatically and physically in the Via Appia, may also have been partly responsible for this landscape's transformation from lush agricultural zone to unworkable swamp.[127] Gradually, the space around this section of the Appian Way became a place where agriculture was impossible, zoned a health risk by malarial mosquitoes.[128] By Columella's day, the Pontine Marshes were a byword for nature's power to defeat Roman ingenuity; authors, thinkers, and educators such as Cicero and Quintilian played with the idea of the by then impossible feat – the draining of the water and reclamation of the 'wasteland' for Rome.[129]

Columella's next 'iconic emplacements' are the 'rich soil' of Capua and horticulture at the Caudine Forks. Capua, capital of Samnite Campania, evokes Cato and Virgil.[130] For Cato, Capua is simply part of the natural storehouse that Italy provides for canny farmers, yet Columella's juxtaposition of Capua and the Caudine Forks hints at a different perspective. Capua, a major political centre in its Samnite heyday, had defected to Hannibal after his triumph at Cannae (216 BCE) and gained fame as the place where he lingered instead of marching against Rome. In the Roman literary imagination at least, the treacherous fleshpots of Campania had diverted Hannibal from Rome, and therefore from victory.[131] First-century-CE experience offers a further mark-up: contemporary Capua, a major *entrepôt*, luxuriated in its high-profile position on the Via Appia as the conduit channelling the wealth of the eastern empire towards Rome itself. Making Capua '*pinguis*' connotes this well-fed prosperity, but also hints at the laziness or lack of mental acuity that too much of a good thing can bring

---

[126] According to Livy (6.5, 21), once Rome controlled the Pontine Marshes the land was soon parcelled up by wealthy aristocrats keen to exploit its agricultural potential, but the era of conflict had probably already seen some deterioration in the containment and drainage processes. See Sallares 2002: 179.

[127] Diod. Sic. 20.36.2 describes the physical mass of the Via Appia and its earthworks. A comparable issue is raised by Cicero (*Att.* 4.15.5) on flooding resulting from a Roman aqueduct connecting with the river Nar.

[128] See Plin. *HN* 3.59 (on the twenty-four towns that once exploited the fertile wetlands); 3.5.70 (on the loss of fifty-three peoples from Latium, in the wake of Roman control); 26.19 (this is 'lost' land). Tac. *Ann.* 15.42 describes a failed solution from Nero. Compare the insalubrity in e.g. Cic. *De or.* 2.290; Hor. *Sat.* 1.5.1, 7–8, 14–15; and (later) Sil. *Pun.* 8.379–82.

[129] Quint. *Inst.* 3.8.16. On Caesar's attempts, see Cic. *Phil.* 5.7; Suet. *Iul.* 44.3; Plut. *Vit. Caes.* 5.8.9. Contemporary archaeological survey continues to elucidate this zone, e.g. Attema 2005; see also Webography: de Haas.

[130] Cato, *Agr.* 135.2; Verg. *G.* 2.224.

[131] E.g. Livy 23.2, 10, 18.

(as Hannibal could testify).[132] Juxtaposed with Capua, the Caudine
Forks are next on our itinerary, site of Rome's momentous defeat
during the Second Samnite War.[133] Re-zoning this battleground and
symbol of poor Roman judgement for market gardening emphasizes
the greyscale that characterizes Roman perceptions of landscape. It
also recalls Bakhtin's useful terminology of the chronotope: a rich
historical nexus where time works thematically (two 'battlegrounds'/
two fertile landscapes/then and now).

Taking the Via Appia as a structural device makes some sense of
the journey from Virgilian territory (Latium) and Rome's destiny,
uniting Greek and Italian heritages (Campania, Cumae), through
a series of landscapes representing internal and external threats to
Rome, and concisely documenting early Roman expansion.[134] Moving
on, however, we are diverted off the main road and into southern
Campania.

Calling Neapolis (Naples) 'Parthenope' encapsulates the rich interface between Italy and Greece, and opens a literary gateway to Magna
Graecia. This name nods to the Siren called Parthenope, supposedly
buried there. It also alludes to Virgil's description of the *Parthenopean*
idyll of *otium* that he enjoyed there.[135] *Docta* ('Learned') *Parthenope* –
home to resting intellectuals and seductive Siren – yet again primes
readers for thinking hard.[136] *Parthen*ius, a Greek grammarian and poet
who famously arrived in Italy as spoils of war in the late 70s or early
60s BCE, ended up as rather more than a household slave to Catullus'
friend Helvius Cinna. He went on to act as unofficial mentor to a
generation of protégés (in particular the poets known as neoterics,
Cornelius Gallus, and of course Virgil) and spent his later years at
*Parthen*ope. Famously a centre for Epicurean philosophy, the Bay of
Naples was also where the first-century-BCE poet and philosopher

---

[132] *OLD s.v. pinguis*: 7, 8.

[133] 327–304 BCE. On the Samnite wars and Rome's early history, see Forsythe 2005 (n.b.
310–11). Livy (9.1–16) recounts the disaster and its aftermath: in 321 BCE the victorious
Samnites forced two defeated legions into a display of submission (passing under the enemy
yoke). For Livy, the Caudine Forks changed the outcome of the war (9.12.1–4).

[134] Purcell 1998 elucidates how significant the conceptualization of the Laurentine coast
as a zone of 'lost' peoples and cultures, given new meaning by Rome (heir to King Latinus'
Laurentum), was. See now C. Smith 2007.

[135] Verg. *G*. 4.563–4. '*Parthenos*' (παρθένος) also means 'virgin', cueing up a play on
'*Virgilius*'/'*uirginius*'.

[136] For usage, see Ov. *Met.* 15.712; Plin. *HN* 3.62; Stat. *Silv.* 3.5.79. Consult Servius on
Verg. *G*. 4.564.

Philodemus spent much of his time (at his patron Piso's villa).[137] Philodemus, like Parthenius, had a circle of protégés at the forefront of Latin literary culture. *Docta* invokes all this – Neapolis under an (even) Greek(er) name is the Hellenistic boot camp of 'Italian' poetics, which went on to make what we now term Latin literature.

This sampling of Columella's hyperlinks makes for laborious reading and slow travel, despite the brevity of the written lines. It also encourages readers to look behind dominant or conventional explanations, and this is born out when we get to Columella's water meadows and salt pits. While these are emblems of a landscape where humans and nature operate harmoniously, archaeological traces of centuriation on the territory between Vesuvius and Stabiae tell a different story of radical human intervention and of ethnic tension. As we move farther south, we meet a landscape where Rome's great enemies of the third century (Pyrrhus of Epirus, and Hannibal) found support, and it proved a fertile ground for conflict with Rome in the Social War of the early first century BCE. Columella's Sabellians are emblematic of different waves of territorial expansion – Greek, Italic, and Roman.[138] That Sabellian 'cabbage' is '*cymosa*' sketches in these patterns of cultural and political efflorescence, but it also recalls our first cabbagey halt: Cumae. This is surely no accident, since this is where the trip south ends: without warning, Columella whisks us back up the peninsula to Turnus' Lake. History comes into play here too. 'Turnus' might seem first and foremost (especially in this context) to evoke Virgil's antihero. The lake was indeed close to Alba Longa, and therefore fits satisfyingly into the *Aeneid*'s focus on the mythic landscapes of pre-Roman Latium but, oddly enough, it does not commemorate Virgil's Turnus.

Instead, we need to look to the later days of Rome's monarchy, and Tarquinius Superbus. Livy tells us how the king summoned the elite from the Latin states to meet him at the grove of Ferentina (near Aricia), but was himself a whole day late.[139] Arician Turnus took a stand against this insult, but misjudged how Tarquinius would respond: with calculated cunning he persuaded the assembled Latins, ready to

---

[137] Known now as Villa dei Papiri, Herculaneum (reconstructed in California as the Getty Villa, Malibu).

[138] Dench 1995: 179–83 discusses ancient perception; 186–212 presents and analyses traditional interpretations. Later on, the Bruttii, Oscan speakers like the Sabelli by the fifth century BCE, and defectors to Hannibal after the Battle of Cannae, send us tumbling back briefly to the toe of Italy.

[139] Livy 1.50. Cf. Dion. Hal. *Ant. Rom.* 4.45.

believe the worst, that Turnus himself was the one with designs on absolute monarchy.[140] The jittery Latins were so incensed that they devised a special form of execution: Turnus was drowned in the source of the Ferentine Water, and immortalized in the resulting Lake Turnus. Tense relations between Rome and Italy in the landscapes of mythic history underline how landscape speaks differently to different constituencies at different times. The two men called Turnus, both of whom flicker behind the toponym, nod to Rome's cultural and ethnographic overwriting of Italian identities while also alluding to the seepage still happening from subaltern voices in different contexts.

The final cabbagey halt is Turnus' hometown, Aricia.[141] Close to Lake Turnus and a major way-station on the Via Appia, Aricia recalls another story from this phase in Rome's early history.[142] Once Rome had made peace with the Etruscans, Latin Aricia became the Etruscan king's next target. Helpless Aricia was saved only by reinforcements from Sproutsville (Cumae). In Livy's version, the disconsolate and defeated Etruscans trudge back to their new ally, Rome, where they get a warm welcome and a neighbourhood in the making: Rome's Vicus Tuscus. We have swung right back up the coast and returned to the Via Appia, marching north. Our ultimate goal, if like Livy's defeated Etruscans we keep going, is Rome.[143]

V.4 Statius, landscape, and autarky: between authenticity and delight

In the late first century CE, Statius' hexameter *Siluae* (*Woodlands*) impressionistically mapped out a literary grove of estates and pleasure parks, and a milieu of wealthy patronage. The collection's title builds in a three-dimensional quality (physically, the book scroll is the 'wood') and configures it as a frame for the villas and landscapes it evokes. This collection of poems for patrons is inspired by and in dialogue with the kind of *otium* that elides the nitty-gritty of the economics of a country

---

[140] Livy 1.51.

[141] Plin. *HN* 119.10, 40–1 speaks of Aricia's fame for cabbages and leeks. Mart. 13.19 (in a collection of mostly foodie epigrams) notes that Aricia is celebrated for its Grove (of Diana) and its leeks.

[142] Livy 2.14.5–9; Dion. Hal. *Ant. Rom.* 7.5–6.

[143] Well worth looking at, as a modern take on Columella's project (albeit not with that aim in mind) is Tilly 1947.

estate.[144] Its 'woody' frame generates the landscapes and learned leisure that the individual poems so ostentatiously describe, while at the same time hinting at an *ur*-topography that predates artificial taxonomies and aestheticized views: what could be more authentic than woodland? Here, looking at two of Statius' 'villa' poems, we join him as he shuttles between the luxury estates of his wealthy patrons, dotted around the Bay of Naples and in fashionable Tibur.[145] We are plugging into a highly learned and allusive landscape, as we saw in Columella, while also participating in elite activity – leisure travel. Statius' verse villas – elaborately enriching the villas of his patrons with added philosophical nuance and mannered allusion to their cultural and intellectual achievements – are what happens next.[146]

The first of Statius' villa poems (*Silv.* 1.3) prioritizes perception and speech when drawing us into its Tiburtine landscape:

> *Cernere facundi* Tibur<s> *glaciale Vopisci*
> *si quis...potuit*   Stat. *Silv.* 1.3.1–2

whoever manages *to examine* [/perceive] the chill 'Tibur' of *eloquent* Vopiscus...[147]

Very quickly (just eleven lines later) Statius connects these terms to joy, pleasure, memory (and *mimesis*), and artifice. It is in the process of framing memory in words, and relating it directly to specific sites and symbols (**mnemotechnics**), that joy and beauty are brought into being and mapped out as alternative objects of cultivation. Ostensibly, this landscape is fashioned collaboratively by Vopiscus and nature, yet its overall architect is of course Statius, with his audience(s) as clients. Joining Statius in this space immerses readers in the sensory immediacy of the described villa and the complex and luxurious language of the physical text itself.[148] This is a site where chronological time ceases to operate straightforwardly (the chronotope struggles with the sensory overload) and narrative logic (the tour) is hard to follow. For the savvy reader, pleasure resides ultimately in the mnemotechnic process of

---

[144] Here we find no grumbling references to troublesome tenants or poor harvests (e.g. Plin. *Ep.* 9.37).

[145] Mattusch 2008 provides a vividly illustrated guide to villa culture around the Bay of Naples.

[146] Bek 1980: 196 examines the Villa Arianna (Castellammare) with reference to Stat. *Silv.* 2.2.

[147] Newlands 2002: 119–53 provides a detailed overview.

[148] Zeiner 2005: 77–97 details the luxury and materials that Statius' villas display.

recognizing and imaginatively redeploying the sights and sensations
on offer to create their own fantasy retreats.[149]

> *O longum memoranda dies! quae mente reporto*
> *gaudia, quam lassos per tot miracula uisus!*
> *ingenium quam mite solo, quae forma beatis*
> *ante manus artemque locis! non largius usquam*
> *indulsit Natura sibi.*   Stat. *Silv.* 1.3.13–17

> O long-to-be-remembered day! When it is recalled to mind, what
> joys, what weariness of vision amidst so many marvels!
> What a kindly quality the land has, what a fine appearance in this favoured
>   spot
> before ever *art's* handiwork! There is nowhere that, more lavishly,
> Nature has *indulged* herself.

Turning a space into a landscape means, as we have seen, defining
a frame and imposing points of view (whether physical or cognitive).
Just as much in Statius as in our other case studies, the frame for the
villa – what makes it and its landscape recognizable as zones of luxury
and spaces for thinking – is, precisely, the city; or at least the urbane
textualizing and intellectualizing qualities that it (and therefore 'our'
visit) generates, combined with the delightful prospect of 'recalling'
the villa's delicious cool from the stuffy summer heat of the city. In
this scene, Nature steps forward as a self-indulgent (*indulgeo*) Roman
aristocrat, engineering a grandiose villa project designed to please
and influence the discriminating spectator equipped with the right
epistemological toolkit (compare the visions conjured up in Figures 6
and 7). At the beginning of the poem Statius used epic, mythologically
saturated images to transport us into a parallel world where cupids
hover around the cool villa, and shifting combinations of familiar
stereotypes of elite villa culture are the bones of the scenography:

> *...Nemora alta citatis*
> *incubuere uadis...*   Stat. *Silv.* 1.3.17–18

> ...A lofty grove over swift
> waters hung...

---

[149] Taisne 1978 discusses Statius' villas as 'painted' scenes. See also Wallace-Hadrill 1983
(suggesting wariness in identifying literary–artistic cross-overs), and contrast Leach 1988, *passim.*

Figure 6 Jakob Philipp Hackert, *Villa of Maecenas and the Waterfalls at Tivoli*, 1783. Oil on canvas. 121.5 × 169 cm. Inv. no. GE-7156. The State Hermitage Museum, St Petersburg. Here (and in Figure 7) the relationship between human features and landscape is what unifies the scene. Hackert re-imagines the site using a dialogue between water, natural topography, and architecture, familiar from ancient literary texts discussing villas. The foaming water of the Aniene effectively separates the main group of (contemporary, rustic) figures (lower right) from the 'villa' (and from the 'Classical' past). Their lack of interest seems to echo the uncertain status of the supposed villa's relationship with nature – it is envisaged here as a ruin in the making, overtaken by foliage (the site is now identified as the temple complex of Hercules Victor).

> *Scilicet hic illi meditantur pondera mores;*
> *his premitur fecunda quies, uirtusque serena*
> *fronte grauis sanusque nitor luxuque carentes*
> *deliciae, quas ipse suis digressus Athenis*
> *mallet deserto senior Gargettius horto.*   Stat. *Silv.* 1.3.90–4

> Here, without doubt, your custom is to ponder weighty matters;
> in this spot is to be found productive calm and virtue, smooth-browed
> and serious, together with healthy brilliance and delights lacking
> in luxury; of such a kind that the Gargettian old man [Epicurus] himself,
>   would have preferred
> and departing from his own Athens, forsaken the garden.

Figure 7 Charles-Louis Clérisseau, *Waterfall in Tivoli,* 1750/5. Pen and Indian ink and brown wash, brush and brown and grey wash, and white. 35.2 × 28.5 cm. Inv. no. OR-11516. The State Hermitage Museum, St Petersburg. The buildings on the heights (top right) draw the eye, but also represent both end and starting point for the two main directional signs in the image (the waterfall, pouring down, and the blind-arcaded 'embankment' that directs the gaze from mid-left to upper right, and echoes the shadow across the rocks, lower left to upper right). Where the two central streams of water converge, we find the (expected) group of (again, contemporary, rustic) figures. Clérisseau's friends and admirers included some enormously influential figures (the English neo-classical architect Robert Adam, the art historian Johann Joachim Winckelmann, and the artist Giovanni Battista Piranesi).

Epicurean *ataraxia* (freedom from disturbance) involves structured withdrawal. The Epicurean Garden, evoked in better-than-life form for Roman aristocrats, represents philosophical cultivation, evokes a lost reality, and further enriches the experience of elite landscaped space.[150] Continuing the theme of recognition, Epicurus (via Cicero) advocates shifting one's attention to the past (using memory) in order to get a sense of perspective on the here and now (*auocatio* calls one away from present 'evils'; *reuocatio* brings past pleasures into present experience).[151] Moreover, through hope (*spes*) and anticipation, future pleasures become 'present' reality.[152] Knowing one's Epicureanism makes it easier to see how and why different ways of experiencing and understanding time, including the cultivation of memory, are important features of the villa experience.

Set this against *Siluae* 2.2 (Pollius Felix's seaside villa near Surrentum), and again the allusive and architectural processes of recall are to the fore:[153]

> ...*Placido lunata recessu*
> *hinc atque hinc curuae perrumpunt aequora rupes.*
> *dat Natura locum montique interuenit udum*
> *litus et in terras scopulis pendentibus exit.*   Stat. *Silv.* 2.2.13–16

> ...Within a limpid recess it is the crescent
> waters – here and there – that the curved cliffs pierce.
> Nature proffers the space; the watery shore interrupts the mountain
> and departs inland between overhanging crags.

> ...*uix ordine longo*
> *suffecere oculi, uix dum per singula ducor,*
> *suffecere gradus. Quae rerum turba! Locine*
> *ingenium an domini mirer prius?*   Stat. *Silv.* 2.2.42–5

> ...Scarcely through the long procession
> did my eyes hold out, scarcely, whilst through the items I was led,
> did my steps hold out. What a multitude of things! Is it at the place's
> innate qualities or its master's that I should marvel first?

---

[150] See Cancik 1968 (on *Silv.* 2.2); M. L. Clarke 1973; Lee 1978.

[151] Cic. *Tusc.* 3.33, 3.76, 5.74; *Fin.* 1.18.60. Cf. the approach outlined in Niebisch 2008.

[152] See Schroeder 2004.

[153] Older but still useful commentaries are Argenio 1970; D'Arms 1970: 117–59; Nisbet 1978. Now, see Nauta 2002: 222–3 (in brief); Newlands 2002: 154–98; Zeiner 2005: 178–90. This villa gained a new lease of fictional life in Caroline Lawrence's 'Roman Mysteries' series (vol. 3, *The Pirates of Pompeii*; vol. 11, *The Sirens of Surrentum*), see Webography: Lawrence (a); Lawrence (c) blogs her visit; see also Lawrence (b).

Statius flags up the sympathetic interconnections between Pollius and place. The 'genius' of this place is that it makes redundant the need to act the docent: here, no one (our Guide tells us, implying no one with the right education) needs the services of a parade of marble and bronze, famous and admirable historical worthies (exemplary figures whose busts structured a garden's avenues and paths), or artificially controlled and tritely perfect views and vistas. Instead, the primary focus rests on the autochthonic and untameable qualities of the landscape as a living entity and guide. This is exemplified at lines 98–111, a lushly epic farmscape where vine-shoots offer handkerchiefs to Naiads, salt spray showers the vines, and satyrs disport in the shallows with lusty Pans.

> *Inde per obliquas erepit porticus arces,*
> *urbis opus, longoque domat saxa aspera dorso.*
> *Qua prius obscuro permixti puluere soles*
> *et feritas inamoena uiae, nunc ire uoluptas.*   Stat. *Silv.* 2.2.30–3

> Thence through the zigzag heights creeps a colonnade,
> on the scale of a city, and with lengthy spine it conquers the jagged rocks.
> Where formerly with foggy dust the sun was mixed
> and there was an unlovely savagery in the path, now to journey is a
>   pleasure.

Statius may seem to deny the need for a scripted tour, but Pollius' estate turns out to be defined by controlled and controlling vistas (one famous example: a feature designated as the maritime arch forms an access route and viewing platform; get the picture by cooling off in a likely contender for the pool, now called 'Bagni della regina Giovanna') and literary mark-up (far from being an unmediated immersion in a natural landscape, the baroque scenography borrows from the tradition of literary villascapes and the conventions of Hellenistic epic). This deception – what seems most uncomplicatedly natural is in fact the result of human ingenuity, literary hermeneutics, and landscape architecture – is, it transpires, key to the experience.[154]

> *...quid mille reuoluam*
> *culmina uisendique uices? Sua cuique uoluptas*

---

[154] See also e.g. Stat. *Silv.* 2.2.52–62 (in some places nature has given way to the one who tends, worships, and gentles 'her' – Arion, Amphion, and Orpheus here acknowledge the supremacy of this landscape's occupier); 2.2.90–91 (marble mimics grass). On the paradoxical qualities of Statius' landscapes, see Myers 2000.

atque omni proprium thalamo mare, transque iacentem
Nerea diuersis seruit sua terra fenestris.   Stat. *Silv.* 2.2.72–5

Why should I rehearse the thousand
rooftops and the turn-and-turn-about views? To each is its own pleasure,
to every room an individual sea, and across the expanse
of Nereus its own landscape serves [/protects/observes] each different
       window.

Reading these lines highlights the empathic qualities inscribed in the
landscape. On personification in *Siluae* 2.2, Newlands observes:

the villa's appropriation of the various views marks the wealth and social prestige of the
owner and the Roman impulse for control of land. A fine view was an essential feature
of the Roman villa, and houses were designed with rooms on individual axes to frame
artfully the most attractive landscapes... Distinction here between the outside world
and the inner one is blurred... Transformed into decorative pictures, the landscape
appears calm and unthreatening. The villa's role as controller of nature is thus yet again
represented as benevolent. Essentially the villa assumes the role of artist, selecting
and ordering the raw material of nature into attractive form so that the distinction
between actual and painted landscape is pleasingly blurred. ...this ordering of nature
into pleasant views is [also] metaphorically related to the ordering of the passions. The
active role of the villa here as the controller of nature emphasises the strong metonymical
connection between house and owner... In particular, the pleasure (*voluptas*, 73) of the
view is incontrovertibly linked with the Epicurean concept of pleasure as freedom from
anxious desire.[155]

Newlands makes Statius' prioritization of technocracy his key development of Horace's landscape aesthetics.[156] What she does not discuss is
whether the implicit, practical grind of gardening and villa life will
inevitably erupt into every such textual scene. By personifying these
estates and giving them an aestheticized and introspective life of their
own, Statius seems to be tampering with a key part of Roman identity
– the citizen's role as farmer and inheritor of traditional agricultural
values dating back to the founding fathers. Readers can fight back by
knowing their Cato, Virgil, Varro, or Columella, but nature's artificial
and non-agricultural qualities seem here to sever the expected nexus
of autarky, fertility, and good government. Wherever you look in this
voluptuary landscape, pleasure and Venus focus solely on aesthetic
and intellectual production.[157] One might argue that, in the context of

---

[155] Newlands 2002: 172–3 (citing Vitr. *De arch.* 6.4). See also Bergmann 1991.
[156] Newlands 2002: 139–41, on *Silv.* 1.3 (cf. Newmyer 1984).
[157] Cf. e.g. *Silv.* 1.3.81–4.

Domitian's Rome, keeping away from the city and prioritizing cultural rivalry and philosophical excellence was a good tactic for a wary senator, but Domitian's interest in art, literature, and religion, gives bite to these excursions into philosophically theorized and aesthetically complex landscapes.[158]

A century and a half or so earlier, desire for luxury was excluded from Lucretius' Epicurean scenography,[159] and in their austere, stripped-down simplicity Lucretius' landscapes offered the chance to learn how to recognize and benefit from landscape's ethical effect. Statius' connection of pleasure to luxury and an Epicurean lifestyle suggests instead what Newlands has termed 'the assimilation of Epicurean philosophy to a life of wealth and privilege'.[160] Myers identifies how Statius works up Vopiscus' life of '*docta otia*' (highbrow leisure): we see a complex artifice of delightfulness; we suspect that enormous wealth, unconnected to such a villa's commercial viability, generated and still invigorates it and its *mores*.[161] The endgame is not a descent into the kind of luxurious total abandon that corrupts society as a whole, nor does the ideological self-display in *Siluae* 2.2 propel Pollius into the dangerous political limelight, or even public service.[162] Statius' lavish verse itineraries around his patron's country villas never suggest that these are other than isolated, inward-looking spaces; they exhibit little in the way of local or contextual ties nor accessibility or networking within the wider landscape (for example, Vopiscus' writing is a solitary activity; only Pollius and his wife occupy their villa). These villascapes have none of the civic engagement (willing or otherwise) of those of Cicero or Pliny, nor even the extravagantly horrified allure that tinges descriptions of Lucullus' properties or Nero's Domus Aurea. Nevertheless, Statius' poems make these villas visible even in Rome, advertising the 'invisible possession of philosophic capital as a cultural and social value'.[163] In a world where 'villa creation and development is as close to a military campaign' as a cautious Senator gets, contemplating Statius' dehumanized estates, drained of the cut and thrust of dialectic and civic duty, offers Romans an opportunity

---

[158] Cf. *Silv.* 5.3.227–9; on Domitian and the cultural politics of literature, see Coleman 1986.

[159] E.g. Lucr. 2.20–33. See Giesecke 1999: 3.

[160] Newlands 2002: 137.

[161] Myers 2005; Stat. *Silv.* 1.3.105–6, 108–9.

[162] Stat. *Silv.* 1.3.105–10; 2.2.121–42. On trading public life under Domitian for autonomy out at the villa, see Myers 2000, Spencer 2008. See Schroeder 2004: 145–6 for the philosophy in brief.

[163] Zeiner 2005: 190.

to re-energize and question the politics of leisure and its ethical consequences for the empire.[164]

The Domitianic Zeitgeist fostered religious piety and cultural production, and Statius' villa poems here show how a landscape might package qualities of character, interests, and good taste, making them safe to boast about, at a distance at least. The quiet silence of the apparently isolated estate, generated by technology and funded by wealth, marries Aristotelian emphasis on the importance of cognition in pleasure to Epicurean stress on the need to experience the landscape in its simplest building blocks. Statius' vivid sensory descriptions encourage both approaches. The polished and high-concept landscapes in both *Siluae* 1.3 and 2.2 depend implicitly upon traditional knowledge to cultivate them (landscaping techniques; architectural memory; past seasons), on recognition of good (or appropriate) and wrong growth (to ensure appropriate fertility), and on hopeful anticipation (fruitfulness despite fallow seasons; the leap of faith when seeds are planted at the dead time of year; a progression from ignorance to understanding). At the same time they prioritize pleasure (remembering and recognizing the practical and intellectual *epistemes* upon which they depend) and exclude the sweat of physical *labor*. Pleasure in these landscapes is overwhelmingly subject to reading in terms of time and space, suggesting that these villas offer another example of landscapes that need 'thirdspace' readings.

V.5 Ekphrasis: Pliny's artful landscapes

Pliny's villas are one prime context for his first nine volumes of collected letters, and recent work by Myers in particular shows how important it is to consider these landscapes alongside Statius' villa poems, even though they seem at first glance very different.[165] Reaching Pliny sets us a little after Statius, and about a century and a half later than our earliest landscape texts. Nevertheless, his villascapes strongly recall us to a world familiar from Cicero's use of landscape as a place to think.[166] Issues that we encountered with Varro and Columella also

---

[164] Von Stackelberg 2009: 80; cf. Zeiner 2005: 189, where the villas are the contemplative reward for the man who has reached the Epicurean ideal.

[165] Myers 2005.

[166] That said, writing to Q. Lepta in February 45 BCE, Cicero comments (perhaps with some irony) that his town house was at that time the match for any of his villas or even the wilds ('*desertissima regio*') in offering productive *otium* (*Fam.* 6.18.5).

feature. Here, we visit Pliny's Tuscan (mountain) and Laurentine (maritime) villas, and those at Lake Larius (Como), properties where he lets us peek into the villa's dual role as aesthetic backdrop for both intellectual self-fashioning (recalling not just Cicero but also Statius) and pragmatic business – the guarantor of revenue that keeps Romans securely within their social ranks (see Figure 2 for villa locations).

Pliny's descriptions of villa life suggest the Technicolor world of nostalgia, where everything is a little more like itself than reality admits. As du Prey has commented, these 'too good to be true' villas are above all sites of inspiration, and become 'the ideal embodiment of what life in the country can mean'.[167] Much has been written on how we might or might not use the letters to 'reconstruct' the villas themselves, and also how these letters tell more broadly on life in Rome during and in the wake of Domitian's unpopular rule.[168] Despite, or because of, the hyperreal quality of the detail on offer, the relationship between reality and productive fiction in Pliny's scenography remains open to debate. Key to understanding these villascapes is an awareness that the tours Pliny offers are all about the interface between representation (what he says and how he says it), perception (how readers understand and experience the scenes), and authority (Pliny's).

Starting near Rome, we can visit Pliny's villa at Laurentum (see Figure 8[169]). The long letter addressed to Gallus in which he first outlines the delights of this area talks 'us' briefly along the highways from Rome (Ostiensis and Laurentina).[170] These *Viae* provide access to his estate from either direction, but the trajectory in either case is from Rome, leaving the city to join Pliny at the seaside. We think immediately here of Columella's gloomy warnings about estates located too near to major roads, yet for Pliny this infrastructure collapses space and distance positively, letting landscape be put to good use for honing and performing citizen identity.[171] The part

[167] Du Prey 1994: xxi–xxii, who is explicitly interested in the relationship between buildings and nature.

[168] For a start, Bergmann 1995b and du Prey 1994 offer excellent introductions and surveys of what such villas might have been like, but see also Tanzer 1924; Pinon and Culot 1982; de Neeve 1992; Förtsch 1993; McEwen 1995; and, briefly, the architectural studies by Sundermann (1984, 1987a and b) and Porphyrios (1983); Leach 2003 and Myers 2005 tackle Pliny's representation of villa culture accessibly.

[169] On the vividly dramatic qualities of this model, complete with miniature figures, see du Prey 1994: 185–7; 293–4.

[170] Plin. *Ep.* 2.17. Cf. Webography: Lawrence (d).

[171] Cf. Cic. *Q Fr.* 3.1.4: how a man keeps up the *local* infrastructure tells a lot about his character.

Figure 8 Pliny's Laurentine villa: imaginative reconstruction created by Clifford F. Pember (see Pember 1947, where he says he aimed to make it like a movie set). Pember (1881–1955) initially trained as an architect, before turning successfully to set design (at Ealing Studios; for Hitchcock at Gainsborough Studios; in Hollywood, including with D. W. Griffith; and also on Broadway and in the West End). The model (and this view in particular) speculatively showcases Pliny's private suite. It emphasizes a dynamic relationship between the main house (right-hand side) and the *zotheca*, and the 'pavilion' (lower left). Pember's lavish (and colourful) vision prioritizes architectural zoning and encourages the idea that Pliny's persona is given not only focus but also authority by the access routes, plantings, and rocky shore, all leading towards the 'panopticon'. Note the formally planted garden, with built features drawing the gaze; the combination of colonnades and porticoes (forms with roots in the Greek world) with more ostentatiously utilitarian architectural forms; the layout, whereby Pliny's 'retreat' is both the focus of the rest of the villa in terms of spatial dynamics and also the most inaccessible feature ('nature' secludes and protects it on both sides – it juts out on a peninsula, and is flanked by the garden and the gently 'terraced' rocks leading to the sea; the *cryptoporticus* makes access control along the formally authorized route easy).

of the virtual journey following the major arteries is over in a few words/seconds, compressing the perception of distance separating city and country but also encouraging the reader to focus on the final, local road networks. Hence it is only when the reader-visitor reaches the turn-offs from these speedy (in every sense) highways that the description elongates – that is, we shift from thin to fat space. As we read on, we move more slowly through the text, and with heightened aesthetic triggers traverse Pliny's more detailed vision of the landscape around his estate, until finally we reach it.[172]

The local track is sandy and best ridden rather than travelled in a carriage.[173] But if one follows Pliny's advice, the vistas are full of aesthetic and practical interest as the road widens and narrows.[174] This letter presents a villa designed around the interplay between external and internal space (later, when we visit his Tuscan property in the Apennine hills, he encourages scrutiny of the interface between core designed garden space and peripheral or enclosing naturescapes). Arriving at Pliny's inextravagant (his description) seaside estate, one particular situational feature is emphasized throughout: the relationship between house and sea (perhaps we recall Columella's advice on siting the villa near the shore? We certainly remember Pollius' villa, as described by Statius).[175] The tour proceeds. The ground-floor dining room projects towards the open sea, which washes it with spray when the wind drives the waves inland (Figure 8 helps us to imagine this). The sea recurs as a visual feature in the small dining room (lit by light reflected from the water) and the swimming pool, too, affords a view of the sea; stepping upstairs one finds that the upper dining room commands a panorama of the whole coast, picturesquely dotted with houses ('*uillae amoenissimae*'); another dining room (primarily looking towards the garden and driveway) is secluded from maritime storms yet still within earshot of the gentle murmur of the waves; the view from yet another garden-facing dining room is specified as not encompassing the sea, but being no less lovely than a maritime vista.

Whereas Columella focused on the technical specifications for orienting rooms in tune with seasons, and the measurement and experience of time in his year-round model villa, Pliny prioritizes a sensory scheme, organized around his typical usage of the villa in winter and spring. The covered walkway, or arcade ('*cryptoporticus*', a portmanteau term that Pliny coins from Greek) that leads away from the orchard-garden provides vistas to both sides, but favours the maritime views with more windows. This walkway leads eventually to

[172] See Ricotti 1984 (a recent attempt to locate this villa).
[173] Plin. *Ep.* 2.17.2. If you are driving, paradoxically, this road takes longer to traverse. '*Grauius et longius*' is how Pliny terms the driving experience; *grauius* ('heavy-going'), also connotes boredom and wearisomeness – it is more fun to travel light.
[174] Ibid., 2.17.2–3.
[175] Ibid., 2.17.5, 10–13, 15–16, 20.

Pliny's real love: a suite of rooms he designed himself. A solar faces the terrace that flanks the walkway on one side and, inevitably, gives onto the sea view on the other; a bedroom has folding doors opening onto the walkway, and a window *'prospicit mare'* ('gazes out to sea'). A third facet of Pliny's delightful suite of rooms is the alcove suitable for a couch and a couple of chairs. This nook is cardinal, since it encapsulates the estate's attractions for Pliny:

a pedibus mare, a tergo uillae, a capite siluae: tot facies locorum totidem fenestris et distinguit et miscet.   Plin. *Ep.* 2.17.21

at its feet, the sea, at its back, villas, at its head, the woods: so many are the views and sites that one gazes upon separately or even all at once through each and every window.

This alcove or bay (esoterically titled *'zotheca'*) offers a segregated space suitable for one or two people at most. A kind of toposcope, it dips its toes in the sea, commands the screening woodland, and returns the gaze of the neighbouring villas (note how Clifford Pember's reconstruction emphasizes this feature as a whole, Figure 8). It performs seclusion with ostentatious excess, while at the same time putting 'Pliny' and Pliny's political and financial ability to afford such a retreat on display.[176] Encapsulated in this suite, then, are all the key aspects for the ideal elite rural landscape: we see nature tamed to the extent that it engages in a visual dialogue with the villa-dweller and presents a series of emblematic framed views that in turn encourage Pliny (and his reader) to operate his aesthetic sensibility on them. What looks best on a sunny day? Perhaps forest and sea need to be gathered into a cooling, refreshing, visual package. Does a wild storm prompt Pliny to look towards his neighbours? Or to retreat to the more secluded adjoining bedroom, where even storms are imperceptible? A version of untamed nature is important for the experience, but equally important is the knowledge that Roman (and, here, explicitly Plinian) ingenuity is capable of stereotyping and segregating, and then domesticating, natural phenomena. This luxurious niche fits Pliny like a second skin – with feet, back, and head symbolizing the ideal landowner at ease, manipulating his quintessential villa vistas.

Returning to the villa's seascapes, we learn that the amenity value of the sea is complemented by the estate's water sources – sweet springs.[177]

---

[176] Translucent screen doors (*speculares*) mark this out as a room on which money has been spent.

[177] Plin. *Ep.* 2.17.25.

Structurally, elaborating on the sea ticks off one of the *zotheca*'s three cardinal views. The others quickly follow: the woods that Pliny framed in his *zotheca* are not just aesthetically pleasing but also, prosaically, provide wood for the villa. Ostia (and Vicus Augustanus, a coastal village just past the estate next to Pliny's) provide additional bathhouses and supply all the other necessary provisions: so here is the third element in the *zotheca*'s outlook – the neighbouring villas. Pliny's villa itself provides the fourth visual field. Pliny is, it turns out, much more interested in describing the designed aspects of the landscape than he has been in rhapsodizing on the authentically natural features of the estate. The shoreline (for example) is enhanced by the pleasing variety of style in the groupings of nearby houses and detached properties. Adopting a reverse perspective and looking inland from the sea, Pliny suggests that the numerous villas are sufficiently individuated to give the appearance of little cities thronging the coast.[178] This perspective shifts ninety degrees when we learn that another way of experiencing the relationship between land and sea is to stroll the boundary – the shore; usually, the sand is firm enough, thanks to the waves, to make an excellent natural promenade. Hence, the shoreline is at its most successful when it is like a manmade environment.

Like a panopticon, Pliny's pavilion puts him at the centre of the paradigmatic landscapes of his estate. The estate turns around him and, in particular, around his private writing-suite, as if captured using a 360° lens in order to provide the ideal panoramic backdrop against which he can perform. Pliny expresses emotional attachment to this estate when he closes – it is the retreat where he loves to spend time.[179] We can cross-reference this imaginative and emotional response to the villascape at Laurentum if we scroll back to *Epistle* 1.9. Famously, this letter tells Minicius Fundanus how unproductive the urban round of *negotium* is when compared to the profitable *otium* of life at the Laurentine villa.

---

[178] Ibid., 2.17.26. As we see from Cicero, the scenic coasts were always popular (e.g. *Att.* 14.16.1). Interestingly, Pliny is sniffy about the usefulness of the sea (a wholly 'natural' zone) for providing anything more than basic sustenance (*Ep.* 2.17.28). Self-sufficiency in terms of inland produce is emphasized, and the villa manages the two key requirements to ensure this: water and shade (and these in turn generate the poetic *locus amoenus*). On the villas of this coastline, see Claridge 1997–8.

[179] Plin. *Ep.* 2.17.29.

O rectam sinceramque uitam! O dulce otium honestumque ac paene omni negotio pulchrius!
O mare, o litus, uerum secretumque μουσεῖον, *quam multa inuenitis, quam multa dictatis!*

Plin. Ep. 1.9.6

What a genuinely well-lived life! What sweet and appropriate leisure – practically speaking, more splendid than any 'business'! What a sea, what a shore, truly a private *Musery*: a place where research and composition flow fluently!

Again, writing to Julius Naso, Pliny emphasizes the paradoxical qualities of his Laurentine landscape: a maritime site, so perhaps not the most obviously 'productive', still it is the landscape that keeps giving:

Nihil quidem ibi possideo praeter tectum et hortum statimque harenas, solum tamen mihi in reditu. Ibi enim plurimum scribo, nec agrum quem non habeo sed ipsum me studiis excolo; ac iam possum tibi ut aliis in locis horreum plenum, sic ibi scrinium ostendere. Igitur tu quoque, si certa et fructuosa praedia concupiscis, aliquid in hoc litore para. Vale. Plin. *Ep.* 4.6.2–3

I possess nothing there except a roof over my head, a garden, and the sands hard by, yet alone of my properties it is bringing in a return. For that's where I do the majority of my writing, and rather than the agricultural land, which I lack, instead I tend to myself through study. Hence in place of full granaries I am now able to show off to you a full case of scrolls. So if you too long for a reliable, high-yielding estate, get one on this coast. Best wishes.

We can see this theme on display well over a century earlier, in Horace.[180] *Epistle* 1.16 is couched as a pre-emptive strike, warding off inquisition from 'Quinctius' (represented as a prominent man about Rome) as to what kind of produce his estate delivers. Quinctius appears to stand in for those who visualize the countryside as a zone for profit and productivity. The generic quality of the opening lines is underlined by Horace's enumeration (and dismissal) of potential produce as descriptors for his farm: arable crops, olives, fruit, pasture or vine-wrapped elms.[181] Horace turns the tables on Quinctius briskly – instead, the letter will loquaciously ('*loquaciter*', 1.16.4) describe the topography and terrain of his estate. *Loquaciter* draws in the chatter of birds, gossip, and verbal extravagance, making for a poem that is intrinsically and structurally out of sync with the notion of efficient

---

[180] R. F. Thomas 1982: 8–20 is especially useful here.

[181] The presence of vines twining around elms is, here, another possible tweak to the alert reader. This topos should be familiar to Horace's ideal audience from e.g. Catull. 62.49–58; Varro, *Rust.* 1.8.6; Verg. *G.* 1.2 (cf. Hor. *Carm.* 4.5.30; Quint. *Inst.* 8.3.8). For detailed discussion of the motif, see Demetz 1958. On the practicalities, see Fuentes-Utrilla, López-Rodríguez, and Gil 2004.

labor in a traditional sense. Horace's plot of land 'produces' instead a flood of language.

Returning to Pliny we see him develop a clear, but inverse, relationship between cultural production and large-scale agricultural landholding. The waywardness of nature (and perhaps of 'life' in general) makes it impossible to guarantee the production figures for his large, agriculturally fertile Tuscan property.[182] At Laurentum, where the holding is relatively small, close to Rome, and affected by proximity to the sea, other criteria operate. The activity there is overwhelmingly humane – Pliny cultivates himself rather than his crops.[183] The Laurentine villa operates, as recent scholarship observes, with one particular aspect of Pliny's persona as its focus: his Roman self.[184] If we turn our gaze now to Pliny's other homeland – the landscapes among which he grew up before taking root in Rome – we find echoes of the tension in defining citizen identity topographically that we met earlier in Cicero.[185] Pliny was born at Comum (Como) in northern Italy, in 23 CE; his continuing landholdings there make few appearances in the collected letters, but three instances are noteworthy. In book 2, Pliny's eulogy of the recently deceased Verginius Rufus is given a personal quality by a family tie embedded in local land use: Pliny's loss is greater than anyone's because of the love that was between them.[186] Why? They came from the same region, from neighbouring towns, and had adjoining fields and property. Verginius (who lacked an heir) became Pliny's guardian, and was like a father to him. Comum, then, is marked up as a region where collections of landholders form settlements with direct topographic and sociological links to their landholdings and the landscape as a whole. The division of the land itself has hugely personal implications – as depicted here, the shared boundaries lead to a grafting of one family onto another.[187]

---

[182] Cf. Plin. *Ep.* 9.16. Here Pliny bewails the appalling grape harvest: it forces him to transform his only harvest (poemlets) into young wine ('*nouum mustum*'), which he 'ferments' before serving. On Pliny and agriculture, see de Neeve 1992.

[183] See e.g. *Ep.* 1.3. Myers 2005: 114–15 tackles the absence of agricultural 'produce' in the two long villa letters. Riikonen 1976 surveys a range of literary angles on intellectual labour in the countryside.

[184] Compare Leach 1990 (who makes it more about a kind of self-cultivation) with Riggsby 1998 and Henderson 2003 (who emphasize the public/private interface).

[185] See Chapters III and V.1. As Dench 2005: 122–251 shows, issues flagged up by Farney 2007 as hot topics for identity-fashioning in the Republic persisted in elite culture through the first century CE.

[186] Plin. *Ep.* 2.1.7–8.

[187] Writing to Julius Valerianus (*Ep.* 2.15), Pliny comments that his mother's landholdings 'are delightful because they are maternal': the land stands in affectively for Pliny's mother.

Comum itself features early in Pliny's collection. Writing to Caninius Rufus, he opens by exclaiming:

Quid agit Comum, tuae meae <u>deliciae</u>? Quid suburbanum <u>amoenissimum</u>, quid illa <u>porticus</u> uerna semper, quid <u>platanon opacissimus</u>, quid <u>euripus</u> uiridis et gemmeus, quid subiectus et seruiens lacus, quid illa <u>mollis</u> et tamen solida gestatio...   Plin. *Ep.* 1.3.1

How are things at Comum, the *darling* of us both? What's happening at your *truly delightful* out of town villa, with its eternally springtime *portico*, its *deeply shady plane* trees? And what about your '*canal*', green and sparkling as it feeds the lake below, and your *smooth* and yet firm driveway...

The qualities and spaces that Pliny ascribes to his friend's villa are at once charmingly personal and at the same time stereotypical of the *locus amoenus* and the ideal villascape (what might it have looked like? The Getty Villa gives a hint, Figure 9). Comum becomes the friends' shared plaything (note the Catullan terms '*deliciae*', '*mollis*'), a landscape to be read in detail. This opening hints at an artifice continued when Pliny comments on the villa's ability to defy the seasons, to echo the Academy (with its plane tree), and to poke gentle fun (perhaps) at the pastoral tradition's topographical vocabulary of the 'charming spot'. Here, the watercourse recalls the landscape-garden features alluded to by 'Atticus' when praising Cicero's Arpinate estate, discussed in Chapter V.1. This dislocated *euripus* (from the Greek, εὔριπος) similarly alludes geographically to the strait between Boeotia and Euboea in Greece, but, closer to home and in Latin, it is the term for an artificial canal (one crossed Rome's Campus Martius) and also for the watercourse in Rome's Circus Maximus.[188] There is, therefore, a double artifice: this fake 'stream' with a Latinized Greek name recalls the Hellenic roots of pastoral (Euboea) and landscape as a setting for intellectual activity. When kept away from these vistas and sites, Pliny compares himself to a sick man uselessly filled with desire for stimulation, refreshment, and inspiration. In this he is solidly in tune with earlier thinking, linking verdant and well-designed vistas to good health; Vitruvius, for example, particularly endorses strolling

---

Cf. *Ep.* 7.9.5: Pliny's Larian estates inherited from his mother and father are priceless and irreplaceable, but he is happy to sell other less familially significant land that he has inherited in the area to his (and his mother's) friend Corellia.

[188] Cic. *Leg.* 2.2. See e.g. Strabo 9.2.2; 10.1.2. The Euripus in the Circus was originally a channel separating the audience from the track, but some time in the later first century CE this was filled in, and instead the central *spina* was transformed into a similar waterway. The Euripus on the Campus probably connected Agrippa's bathing complex to the Tiber.

Figure 9 The Outer Peristyle at the re-imagined Getty Villa in Malibu, CA. Note the peristyle's *trompe-l'oeil* frescoes, and the 'naturalistic' scale and positioning of the water sculptures. Although not fully evident here, the Getty Villa also takes advantage of its canyon location to create dramatic views of the sea and to manage the vistas available to the arriving/departing visitor.

along well-laid-out avenues and through landscaped gardens as a healthful activity.[189]

These themes recur in different form when Pliny describes for Licinius Sura a topographic curiosity closely associated with his birthplace.[190] The oddity is part natural and part manmade: a spring rises in a mountain overlooking Lake Larius, runs down over the rocks, and is detained briefly in a little artificial picnic chamber (*cenatiuncula*) before flowing on down into the lake. Three times a day this spring alternates between gushing forth and drying up. This phenomenon draws people up into the mountains to observe and to enjoy – reclining by the spring, Pliny sketches the scene as picnickers refresh themselves from the water that is also the object of their touristic attention. This offers a rare glimpse of people actively seeking out picturesque and (relatively speaking) *natural* beauty spots, but the underlying impetus for this in Pliny's view is still epistemological. The

---

[189] Plin. *Ep.* 2.8.2. Vitr. *De arch.* e.g. 5.9.5, 5.11.4.
[190] Plin. *Ep.* 4.30.

site, modelled as a kind of outdoor or grotto *triclinium*, is enjoyed specifically because of the puzzle set by its tricksy and complex water 'feature'; it is rather more like a piece of garden hydraulics than a work of nature, or, arguably, it makes nature compete against humankind, to create the most complex 'artifice' and alluring scene.[191]

One further letter (*Ep.* 9.7) adds colour to Pliny's dialogue with the landscapes of his childhood. Writing to Voconius Romanus, Pliny describes how, out of all his many villas, two of his properties on the Larian shore are equally the most pleasing and also the most hard work. For our purposes, they are intriguing because of the way in which he represents them as integrated into the natural shoreline of Lake Larius, but still not wholly or straightforwardly native to the site:

Altera imposita saxis more Baiano lacum prospicit, altera aeque more Baiano lacum tangit. Itaque illam tragoediam, hanc adpellare comoediam soleo, illam quod cothurnis, hanc quod quasi socculis sustinetur. Sua utrique amoenitas, et utraque possidenti ipsa diuersitate iucundior.   Plin. *Ep.* 9.7.3

One, built on the rocks *as at Baiae,* looks out over the lake; the other, again very much *as at Baiae,* sidles up to the lake. Hence my habit is to call one Tragedy and the other Comedy, since one is held up on tragedy's platform soles and the other seems to be in comic slippers. Each is charming in its own way, and in its difference from the other is the more attractive to the occupant.

Pliny's repeated simile reinvents Comum and Lake Larius as a faux Baiae. Personifying the villas as actors presents the landscape as a stage set for Plinian command performances, and a backdrop against which he can script significant aspects of the origins of his public persona. Drawing on cognitive linguistic theory we might explain Pliny's project thus:

...we build mental spaces from our originating 'reality' or 'origin' space, projecting elements from one space into another by means of such principles as identification (access), counterparts (projection), conflict constraint (optimization), inheritance (floating), and structure transfer (matching), drawing always on background or contextual knowledge.[192]

---

[191] Pliny's Uncle Pliny includes this spring in his section on portentous and otherwise mysterious water sources (*HN* 2.232). Tellingly, perhaps, the section's key contemporary allusion is to Nero: when all is not well (here, towards the end of Nero's principate), rivers do strange things such as flow backwards.

[192] Fludernik, Freeman, and Freeman 1999: 391, drawing in particular on Fauconnier (e.g. 1994). See also Herman 1999.

Using Baiae as a mark-up for Lake Larius makes a strong statement, linking Pliny's homeland directly to Rome's summer playground and also to the mythical Campanian landscape that first greeted Aeneas when he made landfall. Reading this letter makes it hard not to find Pliny in both sites at once – one the location of Rome's origins, the other, of Pliny's. Using counterparts and comparison, Pliny ensures that being in Baiae will always (after reading the letter) recall his northern homeland and vice versa. The two landscapes become points of reference for each other.[193] By naming his littoral villas Tragedy and Comedy, he ensures that every time his readers subsequently visit any lakeside villa, his cultured performance will be in the back of their minds. The literary and intellectual drama of these villas follows on the heels of his derogatory comments (in the collection's previous letter) about days wasted by the mob at the Circus; taken together, these two letters suggest that Pliny takes landscape very seriously as a way of presenting who he is and how to view him.[194]

Tragedy provides a (universalizing) panorama of the whole lake from its ridgeline position, whereas Comedy (finding interest in more humanly scaled detail) commands just one bay, but provides sinuous changing vistas from along its waterside terrace.[195] Landscape and literary expectations are in harmony. Tragedy, despite making such a visual statement, and with its straight (*rectus*) driveway – nothing natural about this – extending above the shore, encourages no reciprocity: the water never touches it; it sees and makes its point by being seen. Comedy instead lets landscape (ordinary, everyday life) guide its structure, and even enters into the spirit of things by physically breaking the lake surface (a kind of frame). Where Tragedy offers **hegemonic** oversight of the fishermen below, Comedy is so closely in sync with the requirements of life by the lake that its bona fides as a villa comes into question: it becomes like a boat, from which its reclining occupant can fish.

Pliny closes by saying that the two villas in themselves are still incomplete. They are certainly incompletely described, should a reader try to reconstruct them. They represent, we can infer, a long-term and ongoing project, and, like Pliny himself, they require ongoing cultivation. The more thought that he puts into how and what they

---

[193] Contrast Cicero's comments (10 May 51 BCE): his Cumaean villa has become a mini-Rome (*Att.* 5.2.2).

[194] Plin. *Ep.* 9.6.1, 3–4.

[195] Ibid., 9.7.4.

mean, the more he refines and enhances the kinds of statement they make about Plinian ethnoscapes.

Leaving Pliny's first homeland, our final visit is to his Tuscan property. This is the scenography that features most frequently and notably in his collected letters – in its scope, complexity, and sensory and intellectual charm it also provides an ideal backdrop for the visit to Hadrian's Tiburtine villa with which this *Survey* closes. The first extended description is addressed to Domitius Apollinaris.[196] Like Pliny's other villascapes, there is a strong literary element to the description. At Laurentum, the landscape helped him to hone his citizen networking through writing and thinking. Comum's villas, wholly unsatisfactory as indicators of believable architectural space, showed how allusive and vaguely delineated landscape could still perform autobiographically when enriched with the right sort of cultural tags. In Tuscany, Pliny's domestic arrangements (the house, its rooms, and spatial verisimilitude) are rather like dark matter: we know they are there, but their significance for understanding the scene as a whole is hard to determine. The focus here is on how the garden and wider landscape produce qualities significant for Pliny's purposes (compare the combination of artifice and nature at Powerscourt, Figure 10), and we meet the landscape setting as a vividly expressed, natural, 360° *pinacotheca*:

Magnam capies uoluptatem, si hunc regionis situm ex monte prospexeris. Neque enim terras tibi sed formam aliquam ad eximiam pulchritudinem pictam uideberis cernere: ea uarietate, ea descriptione, quocumque inciderint oculi, reficientur.   Plin. *Ep.* 5.6.13[197]

You will get great pleasure if you gaze down upon this landscape from the mountain height, for you will seem to see beneath you not real land but a kind of painted image of extraordinary beauty: in variety and layout it will refresh the eyes wherever they fall.

This letter delights in describing the climate, the environs, and the charms (*amoenitas*) of the estate and its setting.[198] Pliny's south-facing property is on the Tiber, and nestled in the Apennines: far from the insalubrious Tuscan shore.[199] Here, his health is at its peak, and he loves it because he has designed it himself.[200] There is an impossibly

---

[196] Plin. *Ep.* 5.6. Contrast the approaches of Myers 2005 and von Stackelberg 2009: 125–34.

[197] Cf. Cicero's negativity on 'artistic' scenery (*Att.* 15.14); and Columella, *Rust.* 3.21.2–4.

[198] Plin. *Ep.* 5.6.3.

[199] Ibid., 5.6.11–12, 14–15, 2. Du Prey 1994 is a mine of information on the search for this villa's location.

[200] Ibid., 5.6.46, 41.

Figure 10 Powerscourt Gardens, Co. Wicklow, Ireland, view from the main terrace towards the lake with Triton fountain. Key features here are the two gilded rearing winged horses ('Pegasus'), the terracing and plantings (which echo the 'real' landscape beyond the estate, where the Sugarloaf rises in the background to complete the sense of enclosure and harmony), and the amphitheatrical quality of the isovist (note also the topiary mimicking the hills and the terrace decorated with 'pebble' mosaics).

sempiternal quality to the scenes that he lays out for us: everything is always fresh, moist, green, and parti-coloured, free from excessive heat or toil. Other letters tell us that this estate was primarily (from a business point of view) about viticulture, but cash crops make little impact on how this letter conceptualizes landscape.[201] Interaction with Rome, far from being a daily affair or pressing concern, was seasonally modulated and related to produce rather than politics and ambition. This is also a historically saturated environment, populated with exceptionally elderly men – living links to ancestral custom. These greybeards represent local communicative (or collective) memory at work. Calendrical time also features: the Tiber operates infrastructurally, but only in autumn and spring, and even though the Tiber's presence provides a mainline to Rome, Rome has no control

---

[201] For the commercial aspects of this estate, see e.g. ibid., 8.2, 9.6, 37. Vineyards are often mentioned in this letter (e.g. 5.6.9, 27, 28, 29, 30, 39), as aesthetic features of the landscape.

over its flow.[202] Moreover, the Tiber goes one way, from here to Rome – unless one fights the current; by implication the city has little to offer in return for what this countryside naturally produces.

The hermeneutics of this landscape are developed and reiterated by the stories of the old men;[203] the old timers' oral histories, 'paragons of old-fashioned Italic rusticity and virtue', symbolize how time and history flow differently in the Apennine countryside, and make performance of the past a part of daily life.[204] This is underlined by the stagy sequel:

Regionis forma pulcherrima. Imaginare amphitheatrum aliquod immensum, et quale sola rerum natura possit effingere. Lata et diffusa planities montibus cingitur, montes summa sui parte procera nemora et antiqua habent... Prata florida et gemmea trifolium aliasque herbas teneras semper et molles et quasi nouas alunt. Cuncta enim perennibus riuis nutriuntur...

Plin. *Ep.* 5.6.7, 11

The region is exceptionally beautiful. Imagine an amphitheatre on such a vast scale that nature alone could fashion it [cf. the effect in Figure 10]. A broad and spreading plain is encircled by mountains, and the mountain heights have lofty, ancient groves... The meadows are bejewelled with flowers, and support clover and all sorts of other delicate little plants, always tender and fresh. For everything is fed by year-round streams...

The detail that Pliny lavishes on the built environment (the villa house and its amenities) matches that of *Ep.* 9.40 (Laurentum), but here he focuses our attention less on the villa's built structure and more on its intense relationship with a carefully depicted and highly cultivated landscape setting. Indeed, identifying and following a logical movement pattern through the estate, and understanding how each space relates to each new vista or where art ends and nature begins, is almost impossible, despite the profusion of information.[205]

Pliny later comments that there is a direct correlation between the acts of representing, reading about, and perceiving the villa phenomenologically; he uses the verb *uideo* ('see') to describe this complex experience, emphasizing the relationship between presence and sight.[206] Soja's study of space as a product of perception (vision and understanding), presentation (design, description), and practice

[202] Ibid., 5.6.12.

[203] '*Audias fabulas ueteres sermonesque maiorum, cumque ueneris illo putes alio te saeculo natum*' ('you'd hear ancient stories and old-timers' conversations: in effect, when you made a visit you'd think that you had been reborn in another era.' Ibid., 5.6.6).

[204] Farney 2007: 245.

[205] See du Prey 1994: 80–1 on the problems of pinning down where this estate was.

[206] Plin. *Ep.* 5.6.41. On Pliny's descriptions in this *Epistle*, see Chinn 2007.

(how it is used and experienced) is again helpful.[207] Seeing as a creative act is important from the start, since intrinsic beauty is not part of Pliny's programme of landscape scenography. 'Imagine an amphitheatre': the *form* of the area is beautiful once qualified by a defined visual frame of reference and described using an architectural overlay. The amphitheatrical model defines the banked seating (the hillsides) as zones for pleasurable rustic spectacle.[208] Pliny programs us to recognize nature's beauty via comparison with an artificial structure – specifically, one designed to encourage spectatorship.[209] Later vocabulary provides another option: the art gallery. When Pliny shifts to the metaphor of painting, the explicit agent shifts from *natura* to his human addressees (second person plural), and from the recommended lofty viewpoint readers can re-imagine natural scenery as works of art.

When we cross over from this external, framing landscape, we move into another spectacular world, introduced by a portico (an architectural feature that was often, though not here, an art gallery) and an open-air terrace.

Ante porticum xystus in plurimas species distinctus concisusque buxo; demissus inde pronusque puluinus, cui bestiarum effigies inuicem aduersas buxus inscripsit; acanthus in plano, mollis et paene dixerim liquidus… Pratum inde non minus natura quam superiora illa arte uisendum…   Plin. *Ep.* 5.6.16, 18

In front of the portico is a terrace laid out and divided up by box trees trimmed into many shapes; from there, a bank falls away on a slope, on which box trees delineate figures of animals facing from either side; on the plain is what I would almost call a pool, so liquid seems the acanthus that grows there… From there stretches a meadow no less of a must-see on account of its natural quality than the previously laid out garden…

'*Xystus*', a transliteration from Greek, hints at behind the scenes code-switching but even in its Latin spelling it is more ostentatiously Greek than '*porticus*' (a Greek structure, but a Latin word), and it highlights

---

[207] Soja 1996, developing Lefebvre 1991 as introduced in Chapter I. See also this *Survey*'s opening quote (Alcock 2002: 30). Von Stackelberg 2009: 126 tests this approach successfully on Pliny.

[208] Plin. *Ep.* 5.6.7–9: hunting, receiving the bounty of nature (farming is almost effortless on these fertile slopes). Down in the 'arena' the hard graft (5.6.9) is made visually appealing (to the notional audience?) by naturally ornamental flowers beside eye-refreshing streams (5.6.11).

[209] The 'shows' performed in the amphitheatre are paradigmatic mock-ups alluding to 'real' events and cultural archetypes, e.g. the wild-beast hunt; the battle. Viewing a staged micro-event is most meaningful if a shared cultural memory of its inspiration is in play.

cultural and linguistic interference. Pliny's guiding hand sends us out into his garden via these two Hellenizing features rather than through his rooms, in the first instance, emphasizing the probable complexity of the space we are invited to enter. Narrative and three-dimensional structure are implied by a set of supposedly ideal routes, scripted by a complex array of plantings. Their visual charm depends on heavy-duty gardening (which Pliny only hints at) and intellectual activity (which his description requires and encourages) to cement the symbiosis between 'man', villa, and landscape.[210]

Topiaried box features strongly (evergreen, slow-growing), and even actively participates in the project by configuring itself into animal shapes. With box as one unexpected sleight-of-hand artist (who would have expected topiary to design and maintain itself?[211]), it is unsurprising that what follows is also a piece of deception: below the portico, its garden terrace, and the slope populated by box-animals, lies a swathe of acanthus. Acanthus, equally famous as a sculptural relief motif, tricks the eye into believing that one gazes on a limpid pool.[212] The topiaried environs of this 'pool' are framed by a tiered box hedge, beyond which lies a quasi-natural feature: a meadow. Meadows, as outlined by Columella, are far from 'natural', but Pliny chooses here to emphasize their natural qualities – juxtaposing *natura* with *ars* and making the two subject to the force of the apt gerundive '*uisendum*' (a 'must-see').

Natural and artificial landscapes are, in this scheme, equally integral to the aesthetics of the experience as a whole. Beyond, fields, meadows, and woods stretch out indefinitely into a (descriptively) hazy background. Here Pliny's unspecific directional verbals and vague relational comments emphasize the difference between this villa's seclusion from Rome and the well-connected and more ostensibly believable qualities of the Laurentine villa's site. The effect is to make it as hard as possible for readers to imagine where Villa Pliny stops and real life begins.

Shifting back to the house itself (returning initially to the *porticus*) is achieved textually without recourse to words denoting real-time movement in time and space. The transportation is sudden, but eased by the fact that 'nature' is also a significant contributor to the comfort

---

[210] See McEwen 1995: 20–4.

[211] Plin. *Ep.* 3.19; *topiarii* (landscape gardeners, topiarists) are a *sine qua non* for a well-kept estate.

[212] See e.g. Vitr. *De arch.* 2.7.4.

and visual delights on offer indoors. Pliny briefly guides us first to a dining room.[213] Next he takes us to a central suite of rooms with delightful views, which seems to represent one of the villa's private retreats.[214] The suite surrounds a courtyard shaded by four planes and centred on a splashy fountain.

Est et aliud cubiculum a proxima platano uiride et umbrosum, marmore excultum podio tenus, nec cedit gratiae marmoris ramos insidentesque ramis aues imitata pictura.

                                                           Plin. *Ep.* 5.6.20–3

There is also another room, *green* and *shady* from the *nearby plane tree*; it is *embellished* with *marble* as far as the dado, and also (in no way ceding the prize to the *marble*) an *eye-deceiving fresco* of *branches* and *birds* perching on *branches*.

We have seen that the dense shade of the plane tree evokes Greek philosophizing, so Pliny's description of the suite's second room suggests a thoughtful space where sensory and intellectual pleasures blend and encourage scrutiny of the interplay between art and nature, reality and imagination (compare Figures 16 and 17). This room is enthusiastically artificial in its transportation of a profusion of nature indoors and onto the walls. In a manner reminiscent of garden rooms and small, enclosed, highly decorated courtyard gardens (often termed *uiridiaria*), such as those found at the villa thought to have been Poppaea's at Oplontis, the compact description captures and contains the mind's eye resolutely, depicting a fantastically expansive internal mural landscape that provides the natural vistas otherwise missing from the experience. We return to *uiridiaria* later (and in Chapter VI). The lack of specificity as to what trees or which species of birds are painted, or what the colour scheme of the marble is, gives free rein to the reader's imagination (far more vividly personal than what Pliny could hope to specify) but within constraints. Marble and paint combine to create an artful woodland (complete with ornamental birds), but one corralled into the architecturally appropriate zone on the wall.

Pliny then continues the tour of the house before turning us back outdoors.[215] There we enter what he calls the part of the property with the best design and the most charm (*amoenitas*): the hippodrome

---

[213] Plin. *Ep.* 5.6.19.
[214] Ibid., 5.6.20–3.
[215] Ibid., 5.6.23–32.

garden. The viewer, Pliny says, sees its main area all at once – that is, he represents it as one isovist.

Medius patescit statimque intrantium oculis totus offertur, platanis circumitur; illae hedera uestiuntur utque summae suis ita imae alienis frondibus uirent. Hedera truncum et ramos pererrat uicinasque platanos transitu suo copulat... Alibi pratulum, alibi ipsa buxus interuenit in formas mille descripta, litteras interdum, quae modo nomen domini dicunt modo artificis: alternis metulae surgunt, alternis inserta sunt poma, et in opera urbanissimo subita uelut inlati ruris imitatio. Medium spatium breuioribus utrimque platanis adornatur. Post has acanthus hinc inde lubricus et flexuosus, deinde plures figurae pluraque nomina.

Plin. *Ep.* 5.6.32, 35–6[216]

The centre is fully open so that, immediately on entering, the whole space, encircled by plane trees, is available to the gaze; these are clothed in ivy so that the tops are naturally leafy whilst the lower parts are leafy with borrowed foliage. The ivy winds around trunk and branches and links each plane tree with its neighbour as it spreads... Here and there box divides up the lawn, clipped into thousands of shapes; some even form letters that spell out the name of the master or the gardener. Others rise up in the form of mini-obelisks, which alternate with fruit trees. Suddenly, in the midst of this urbane work of art, a mock rural scene unfolds. The open middle ground is enhanced by low plane trees on either side. In the background, acanthus spreads out, glossy and sinuous; then more figures and more 'names'.

Plane trees (evoking a calm, static, and controlled landscape) denote the central space. They in turn are redefined and compromised by freely twining ivy that has turned individual trees into a garland of sorts, no longer semiotically intact nor sterile. The riot run by the ivy over all but the tops of the planes suggests the lurking potential for uncontrollable fertility and danger immanent in natural landscaping, but nevertheless the overall image is of artful order: Bacchus at play in a pastoral scene. The design may pick up on a weak joke once made by Cicero to his brother: his gardener had smothered one of his villas – house and colonnade – in ivy, making his Greek sculptures look like topiarists caught in the act, touting their wares.[217] If this is a nod to Cicero, the connections between ivy, poetry, and Bacchus heighten the textuality. Embedded in the plural form of 'ivy' (*hederae*) is an allusion to the ivy-icon denoting word division on inscriptions.[218]

These samples give a flavour of the complexity of the hippodrome garden as a motif (Hadrian had one too – see Figure 19 – and one

[216] Martial's 'garden' epigrams offer a useful comparison; see Kuttner 1999a: 370–1.
[217] Cic. *Q Fr.* 3.1.5.
[218] Saenger 1990: 55 n. 27 puts the first use of ivy as orthographic icon in the first to second century CE.

featured in the imperial residence on the Palatine Hill). The inner
edge of the frame (planes, transformed into a garland of Bacchic ivy)
is studded with box trees (between the planes) and then encircled
by (poetic, Apolline) laurel. Ivy links the planes to one another and,
as a motif for writing, epigraphic 'ivies' transform the space into
one monumental inscription marking Pliny out as an intellectual: a
devotee of wine, literature, landscape-gardening, and aesthetics, and
a man who can see beyond the superficial forms of things. This is his
monument, rather than the more expected array of marbles (we should
note in passing that statuary is surprisingly absent). Such a reading
is encouraged as one reaches the curved end of the 'hippodrome',
where here and there names are clipped out from box trees (spelling
'P.L.I.N.Y.' and his now nameless 'gardener'). The omnipresence of
Pliny (narrator, guide, part of the landscape) makes it hard to see the
sights from any other perspective. Here, somewhere near the garden's
far end, trees morph into obelisks (just right for a racetrack), living
monuments sit side by side with fruit trees, before the whole highly
artificial (*urbanissimus*) scene reforms as a rural pastiche, and topiary
and acanthus gradually blend into the middle distance.[219]

From here we return in our final extract to the top of the racetrack,
to a room (just off a marble outdoor dining space, or *stibadium*) where
Pliny sets his Graeco-Roman hybrid *zothecula*. The room (*cubiculum*)
comes with a solid locational tag (it faces the marble dining pavilion
at the top of the hippodrome), but with little else to relate it to the
specific topography of the estate or dwelling. Externally, it tells a
story of designed simplicity where art and nature work harmoniously:
gleaming (but otherwise plain) marble walls are smothered in a vine.
Folding doors tell us that this room is an in- and outdoor space but,
looking out from inside, the implied and specified views are restrictive
(we assume the enveloping vine blocks vistas) and the *uiridia*, or
'greeneries' make for no distinction between species or plantings.
Linguistically, *uiridia* suggests *uiridiaria* – small, enclosed gardens that
made greenery the star turn and were often decorated with *trompe-
l'oeil* frescoes (depicting gardens), which blended the walls with the
real plantings (compare the effect on display in Figures 16 and 17).
So this small room simultaneously suggests a view out into immersive
greenery and hints at vistas into an architectural and artistic Greenery.

---

[219] Plin. *Ep.* 5.6.35–6.

Mox zothecula refugit quasi in cubiculum idem atque aliud. Lectus hic et undique fenestrae, et tamen lumen obscurum umbra premente. Nam laetissima uitis per omne tectum in culmen nititur et ascendit. Non secus ibi quam in nemore iaceas, imbrem tantum tamquam in nemore non sentias. Plin. *Ep.* 5.6.38–9

Next an alcove withdraws: both in the room and separate from it. Here there is a bed, and despite windows on each side the light is still dim on account of the surrounding shade, caused by a flourishing vine that climbs over the whole building, pushing right up to the roof top. *You* cannot *lie* there in any other way than as if in a *grove*, but you would not risk feeling rain in the way you would if you were in a *grove*.

Vanishing into an alcove, the room forces its occupant to imagine himself out in a fantasy, wild-woods setting (an even more enclosing 'greenery'). This quirky playfulness exemplifies the letter's scenography. Here, Pliny shows art bettering reality by making introspection the key to perceiving nature most effectively, and he structures his account to encourage consideration of how exactly art betters nature. The combination of *nemus* and *iaceo* in the first clause of the last sentence enforces the notion of pastoral verse, quiescence, and the world of *otium*; the sentence's opening negative (*'non'*) reminds us that readers/ visitors are in Pliny's (and the alcove's) power. The relaxation that this room enforces is better than any real-life Arcadia. The shade is like but, as the comparative ablative emphasizes, definitely not woodland shade, and this artifice is echoed in the little room's outlook onto designed greeneries and the *vine*-shaded and gleaming white marble dining area (complete with its semicircular couch: *stibadium*, from the Greek στιβάδιον), where complex plumbing (Roman hydraulic know-how) sends streams of water into a basin whose surface forms a floating table.[220] 'Light' food floats on the water in containers shaped like little ships or birds. The birds evoke woodland, but the ships (perhaps emblematic of decline from Golden Age grace) might remind us further of the artifice: everything here has been transported; the illusion only passes muster if one carefully obeys the visual cues.

Reading *Epistle* 5.6, Pliny says, is just like physically visiting the villa.[221] This should mean the reverse is also true – the 'realandimagined' villa visit is a textual experience and tells a story. Pliny's letter gives us plane trees, which link to the Academy (Pliny the philosopher); plane trees' shade, plus acanthus, draw in pastoral verse (laurel seals the

---

[220] Plin. *Ep.* 5.6.36–7. On water in outdoor triclinia, see Ricotti 1987; Kuttner 2003.
[221] Plin. *Ep.* 5.6.41, 44. Henderson 2002b, 2003 (villas generate writing); cf. von Stackelberg 2009: 133.

image of Pliny the author and connoisseur); ivy and vines evoke
Bacchus (Pliny the bon viveur); ivy-icons and topiary box-letters
connote monumental inscriptions, the biggest contrast one can get
to the notionally 'private' epistle (Pliny's public status). In *Epistle* 5.6,
looking outside (and looking beyond the estate or letter, in search
of orientation or context) always involves turning the gaze inwards
again. When combined with the letter's mash-up scenography of art
and nature, this makes an ideal introduction to the painted landscapes
and sites of real villas to which we turn next.

VI SPACES AND PLACES

si hortum in bibliotheca habes, deerit nihil. Tusculum late May/June 46 BCE, Cic. *Fam.* 9.4[1]

If you have a garden in your library, there will be nothing lacking.

...any purposeful arrangement of natural objects...with exposure to the sky or open air, in which the form is not fully accounted for by purely practical considerations.[2]

Pictures and spaces, like literary texts, tell a story. This chapter, together with the *Survey*'s envoi, tackles a range of these stories. At our first two sites we focus on painted landscapes in suburban villas (the Villa 'Farnesina', and the Villa of Livia at Prima Porta, near Rome). The next two, the famous but now mostly lost Horti Sallustiani and Porticus of Pompey, open a window onto the political and civic role of peri-urban Roman landscape gardens. Rounding off the survey, a stroll around the parkland of the emperor Hadrian's villa near Tibur (modern Tivoli) uses the contemporary site to reflect on villa visits then and now.

How can we get a sense of the visual and physical qualities of Roman landscape? Ancient agriculture and planting schemes leave few ostensible traces, and although there are literary texts and landmark studies of plants and crops to which we can refer, this chapter turns first for help to painted vistas.[3] Without these frescoed instances of visual trickery and wishful thinking from the walls of Roman houses and villas, re-imagining the archaeological remains of designed landscapes and their conversation with the built environment and lived experience in their heyday would be very difficult.[4] We have already seen how Latin authors enthusiastically textualized and mediated the natural world; their vision prefigures sixteenth- and seventeenth-century

---

[1] Addressed to Varro, with whom he was planning to meet up.

[2] Working definition of a garden: Cooper 2006: 12–14 (citing M. Miller 1993: 15).

[3] Kuttner 1999c: 8 for caveats. Jashemski 2002 gives chapter and verse on plantings, using Pompeii as a focus. Barker and Lloyd 1991 present useful examples of fieldwork in landscape archaeology; Villedieu 2001 showcases the Palatine Hill. On horticulture, von Stackelberg 2009: 35–47 sums up; for the detail, see Jashemski's massive two-volume study of Pompeian gardens (1979/93) and Jashemski and Meyer 2002 (a comprehensive work on Pompeii's natural history).

[4] In a series of key studies, Purcell (1987b, 1995, 1996a) and Wallace-Hadrill 1998b make clear what is most important. Jashemski 2007 sums up.

artistic reinvention of 'landscape' but was also in close dialogue with a wide range of practical and utilitarian agendas. Fragmentary echoes of how utility and aesthetics combined in ancient designed landscapes can still be tracked down in surviving Renaissance and later landscape gardens; visiting these estates shows how agriculture could frame ornamental parks, which in turn worked as performance venues displaying the power and taste of their owners in support of their political ambitions.[5] Exploring one or more of these sites, tripping out to Hadrian's Villa at Tibur, and factoring in the texts we sampled in Chapter V, will all help to make more sense of what landscape could mean in ancient Rome.

VI.1 Landscape as background and foreground

Returning to terminology, the problem identified in Chapter I remains: how do we tease out what constitutes a specifically *ancient* 'interest' in landscape as an artistic subject or object, or as experiential space, and relate it to contemporary reception? Chapter I suggested some further reading and introduced the roots of modern Western landscape discourse in sixteenth-century art. Chapter II's investigation of aesthetics pointed out how Romanticism's Sublime delighted in reinventing the natural environment as an alien and disturbing landscape, with some features recognizable from Bacchic nature (although hard to reconcile with the ethos of most ancient representations). The Western, post-Renaissance and in particular post-Romantic use of the term 'landscape' prioritizes the aesthetic qualities of nature, and often muscles out (or idyllizes) functional utilitarian features and voices. Combined with an emphasis on nature as wild(er)ness, this could lead to the assumption that there was little significant equivalence between classical and modern

[5] Consult Andrews 1999: 67–75 for a succinct summary. More expansively, useful approaches are presented in Hunt 1991, 1996; Ehrlich 2002; Helmreich 2002; Christian 2008. The great landscape gardens typically have well-illustrated websites, but see also Webography: *Garden Visit* and Catena Digital Archive of Historic Gardens and Landscapes. If you are planning a trip, visit (e.g.) in the UK: Mount Stewart (Co. Down), Rousham (Oxfordshire), Stourhead (Wiltshire), Stowe (Buckinghamshire), Wrest Park (Bedfordshire); in Ireland: Powerscourt Gardens (Co. Wicklow – see Figure 10); in France: Parc des Buttes-Chaumont and Parc Monceau (Paris), Désert de Retz (Marly), Versailles; in Germany: Sans Souci (Potsdam), Dessau-Wörlitz (Wörlitz); in Italy: Villa Aldobrandini (Lazio), Bomarzo (Lazio), Villa d'Este (Lazio), Villa Lante (Lazio), Sacro Bosco (Lazio), Villa Borghese (Rome), Villa Doria Pamphili (Rome), Villa Medici (Rome); in Russia: Peterhof (St Petersburg), Tsarskoe Selo (near St Petersburg); in the USA: Monticello (Charlottesville, VA), Hearst Castle (San Simeon, CA), Vizcaya (Miami, FL).

landscape discourse and interest in the farmed countryside, but we have already seen how much this oversimplifies the position.

We can restart here by focusing on ancient landscape frescoes. Like those that often decorated churches, stately homes, and aristocratic villas, they present architecturally fixed vistas, tied for the most part permanently to one building, relating spatially to a defined physical and economic environment, and connected directly to one aristocratic commissioner and (typically) his household.[6] Like ancient landscape frescoes, when mural landscapes once again began to open up imaginary windows within Europe's grand buildings they did not need to include human figures in order to speak intimately about and to the families and socio-cultural milieux who gazed at them, who inhabited the rooms their vistas extended, and who typically depended on extensive landholdings for their prosperity. As we will see, the architectural spaces from which mural landscapes are viewed condition and specify their perspectives, authorizing three-dimensional reading strategies very different from those encouraged by portable art works or objects, even when similar scenes were on display.

Landscape art had become a sign of prosperity and power that a time-travelling Roman might have recognized. With its roots in the development of a newly humanistic and environmental rather than religious iconography, 'natural' scenery was taking centre stage by the seventeenth century. Its popularity in the wealthy and powerful Italian courts, and at Rome, helped to secure the place of 'landscape' in the new neo-classical style. As Nicholas Poussin (1594–1665)'s influential (beautiful, occasionally threatening, but never agricultural) visions make clear, this was an emblematic vision of landscape as a combination of pagan Golden Age idyll and Christian moral and social order, a development that increasingly became linked to the exploration and discovery of 'new' worlds and European imperialism.[7]

---

[6] See Andrews 1999: 53–75. Bek 1980: 164–203 outlines how villa art and architecture connect.

[7] Cosgrove 1998: 140–2 sets out the general argument. Giorgione (1477/8–1510)'s famous *The Tempest* prefigures a fascination with symbolic post-classical landscapes in which figures, nature, and built structures play complementary roles. Cf. landscapes by Agostino Tassi (1578–1644), and (as on this *Survey*'s cover) Claude Lorrain (Gellée) (1604–1682) (like Poussin, both spent time working in Rome). Two recent major exhibitions emphasize continuing interest in landscape: 'Poussin and Nature' (The Metropolitan Museum of Art, New York, 2008), and 'Agostino Tassi (1578–1644): un paesaggista tra immaginario e realtà' (Palazzo di Venezia, Rome, 2008). Cosgrove 2007 discusses how changing geographical knowledge affects vision and understanding – see the exhibition 'Magnificent Maps: Power, Propaganda and Art' (British Library, London, 2010). Vautier 2007 examines how 'Rome' in all sorts of ways remained a key feature of artistic development right up to the nineteenth century.

This was the era of increasingly elaborate landscape gardens across Europe, designed to establish the political and cultural authority of their owners, but in time the so-called Picturesque movement of the eighteenth and nineteenth centuries eventually redefined both this kind of 'landscape' and the more ostensibly natural countryside as a touristic or dilettante pop-culture spectacle (see Figures 6 and 7).[8] 'Untouched' nature joined the landscape gardens and parks of great estates (see Figure 10) as stops on a day-tripper's itinerary. This kind of increasingly commercialized experience allowed visitors to take a tour without engaging directly with the politics of an uninhabited (or depopulated) countryside, an invisible workforce, or the original agenda of landowner or designer.[9] Marxist cultural critics argue that the term 'landscape' *always* veils the reality of rural labour and social inequality, transforming the countryside into escapist scenery rather than a place of work (or a place from which authentic 'workers' have been cleared).[10] This may seem far removed from ancient experience, but land rights were a burning issue in the late Republic and, as we noted earlier (for example, in Chapter III), rural to urban migration and perceptions of changing patterns of land use were of huge concern for ambitious politicians.

Away from the frescoed palazzi and the patronage of wealthy churchmen, landscape art was developing and gaining early popularity in northern Europe in particular in a slightly different way: as a portable souvenir or household chattel, and this adds another flavour to the mix. The *bulk* market for most landscape art (and therefore its main form of exposure to the widest range of people) was concentrated in painted scenes on canvas, in mass-produced prints, and in landscapes on porcelain or pottery. These landscape scenes made the countryside a commodity at a time when cities, commerce, and trade were flourishing. The currency of landscape in this context was mostly about a different kind of progress to that of neo-classicism: mobility and change (and, eventually, a kind of nostalgia). By the mid-seventeenth century the Netherlands, for example, was a major European trading economy, whose wealthy merchant class operated as a powerful oligarchy. A popular import was Chinese porcelain, which encouraged the development of the famous Delftware; this in turn was frequently decorated with rustic views. Mass-produced 'landscapes'

---

[8] Ackerman 1990 is the landmark study.
[9] Chard 1999: 209–48 traces this pattern in touristic responses.
[10] See e.g. Daniels 1989.

on homeware spoke most vividly to those living and working in a flourishing, urban, and highly mobile cash economy.

Summing up, to get the most out of the term 'landscape' when studying ancient perceptions and modern developments means using it to explore how 'certain classes of people have signified themselves and their world through their imagined relationship with nature, and through which they have underlined and communicated their own social role and that of others with respect to external nature'; these 'insiders' cannot 'walk away from the scene as we can walk away from a framed picture or a touristic viewpoint'.[11] Even when such scenes apparently lack human figures, they are still populated landscapes, closely connected to the real 'figures' for whom they provide a backdrop. The decline in fresco-painting and the early decoupling of landscape art from architectural form and its social hierarchies, and from a direct relationship with the land, is one major reason why we might now struggle to think ourselves into a Roman worldview.[12] However, although the fixed contexts for defining space as landscape have shifted (and continue to shift), by tagging space as 'landscape' we still specify landscape as a valuable commodity, high in cultural as well as real capital. Roman 'interest' in landscape, defined in this way, represents a nexus of intellectual, aesthetic, and practical reward, where landscape works as 'a medium of exchange between the human and the natural, the self and the other. As such, it is like money: good for nothing in itself, but expressive of a potentially limitless reserve of value.'[13]

VI.2 Landscape and scale: gardens

The garden is the smallest parcel of the world and then it is the totality of the world.[14]

---

[11] Cosgrove 1998: 15, 19.

[12] Andrews 1999: 166–75 sums up how changing relationships between natural order and social hierarchies affected 'landscape'. Other developments (e.g. impressionism and the invention of photography) are also summarized clearly by Andrews 1999: 177–223.

[13] Mitchell 1994a: 5.

[14] Foucault 1986: 26 (in the context that the earliest kind of 'other' space, or heterotopia – a place embodying contradictory or culturally troubling sites, and providing space for exploring them safely – is the garden). Cf. Cyril Connolly's melancholy, metaphoric usage: 'It is closing time in the gardens of the West and from now on an artist will be judged only by the resonance of his solitude or the quality of his despair' – 'Comment', in *Horizon* December 1949–January 1950.

Over the course of the first century BCE one specific kind of landscape, the 'garden', changed – horticulture came to symbolize the harmony between human (art) and nature that was so lacking in the contemporary world. Garden space is particularly important in this chapter, although Latin terminology has foxed those eager to specify exactly what was meant by *hortus* (typically, garden singular) and *horti* (plural, often a large estate or pleasure garden).[15] This urge to pin down the semantics overlooks the sophisticated way in which the term 'garden' still operates, drawing together a multifarious range of garden art, landscape elements, and uses – some of these, although fewer than one would hope, are highlighted in the reopened ancient Roman 'garden' display at Rome's Musei Capitolini; what we mostly see there (and what mostly survives) is just a tiny sample of the art and decor, offering little insight into ancient gardens' utilitarian roots.[16]

For one modern example of what we are dealing with, consider London's Kensington Gardens in the light of Cooper's detailed study of what gardens mean.[17] This space is now simultaneously a public park, a royal estate (*horti* as collective plural), a collection of diversely planted and structured individual gardens (*horti* as individuating plural), and a green oasis in a teeming metropolis.[18] 'Gardens' in the plural still suggests an expansive and multi-use landscape, populated with decorative, utilitarian, and ideological aspects and sites; plural usage also tends to imply narrative or metaphorical complexity. The singular 'garden' suggests smaller-scale space, though perhaps every bit as complex in structure, planting, and symbolism. In space-syntax terms, 'garden' allows comprehension as one isovist (all points are theoretically at least visible or intelligible from all other points), whereas 'Gardens' more typically comprise convex space (multiple isovists, where not all meanings, vistas, or itineraries are notionally available simultaneously).

Ancient gardens operate within the broader remit of landscape, but also bring the wider landscape into the domestic setting – as we have seen in Pliny.[19] Previous chapters also emphasized the importance

---

[15] For a sketchy summary, see Beard 1998. Von Stackleberg 2009 looks briefly but thoughtfully at what gardens mean in a Roman context.

[16] Review: E. Fentress 2007. See Cima and Talamo 2008.

[17] Cooper 2006.

[18] Different but comparable examples include New York's Central Park; Paris' Jardin des Tuileries and Bois de Boulogne; Dublin's Phoenix Park and St Stephen's Green; and London's Hyde Park. Kingsbury and Richardson 2005 present an accessible and thoughtful array of discussions.

[19] See Wallace-Hadrill 1994: 44–5.

of reading Roman landscapes as part of an established Graeco-Mediterranean conversation about how humankind relates to the natural environment.[20] Persian 'Paradises' (Greek παράδεισος; Latin, *paradisus*) – Royal parkland – became a primer for environmental design in the Hellenistic courts, providing one additional point of reference for the development of landscape semiotics in the late Republic.[21] Despite nuances of foreign, regal luxury, landscape gardens rapidly became emblematic of Rome's new imperial status as cultural arbiter and collector. The increasing prominence of large-scale, aesthetically complex gardens in the highly charged political climate at Rome in the first century BCE encourages an ideological reading, particularly with the unprecedented appearance of public gardens around the city. In this era, vistas and landscapes previously restricted to elite *otium* in the *suburbium* and Campania increasingly formed part of the peri-urban experience.[22] They showcased Roman power – or the power of individual Romans – to combine different elements of designed landscape (market gardening, farming, recreation and relaxation, authority) in a coherent and even ideologically challenging package, a trend underscored in the propagandist display of rival generalissimos such as Pompey and Caesar, both of whom provided Rome with public gardens not far outside the city walls.[23]

For most Romans, daily life made food the keystone of gardening. The majority of gardens were in some way 'kitchen' gardens, whether on a grand scale, with 'warrens' and oceanic fish ponds, or more like modern allotments, with mixed planting of vegetables, ornamental cultivars and flowers for cutting, or merely a trough of herbs and vegetables for the pot.[24] This, as we have seen, does not

[20] Follow up on wider context using e.g. Segal 1963 (literary focus); Ridgway 1981 (Greek sculpture as garden ornament); Osborne 1987, 1992 (the history behind the scenography); M. Carroll 1992, 2003 (accessible surveys cover lots of ground); Hughes 1994: 45–72, 130–48, 169–80 (environmental concerns); Farrar 2000: 1–11 (usefully descriptive); Alcock 2002 (combines archaeological and historical approaches); Cole 2004 (applies gender theory); Hutton 2005 (adds an ancient tourist's view to the mix); and Barnett 2007 (how religion affects landscape).

[21] For Persian Paradises (e.g. Cyrus' at Pasargadae), see Stronach 1989 and (more wide-rangingly) Conan 2007; in brief, see Farrar 2000: 9–10; Briant 2002: 442–4. Semiotically fluid, 'paradise' denoted enclosed space – royal parkland; formal, structural, and aesthetically complex gardens; gardens where plantings rather than pavilions were the focus – and both domestic and public functionality. Water featured frequently, as did shade.

[22] Adams 2006.

[23] See Grimal 1984: 65–89. On Pompey's gardens, see below. On Caesar's gardens, made public in his will: Coarelli 1996; D'Arms 1998; Haselberger, Romano, and Dumser 2002: 142–3. Discourses equating man-modelled landscapes with political power feed into the late Republican worldview via Xen. *Cyr.* 1.11, through Polyb. 31.29, and into e.g. Varro's tamed 'nature' (see Green 1997: 440).

[24] Von Stackelberg 2009: 10–13 sums up.

mean that they lacked design or visual interest. Even the humblest of plantings has the potential to be easy on the eye as well as practical, and aesthetics played a significant part in the conceptualization and discussion of utilitarian gardens.[25] Martial's humorously ironic comparative description of a tiny *hortus* shows how a modest plot can assume grandiose qualities.[26] His 'window-box' garden takes on the characteristics of a lavishly appointed hunting villa, with all the key features of a quintessential rustic landscape: woodland, farmland, livestock, and flowers. In this pint-sized property, woody rue makes for a Grove of Diana, a rose petal stands in for a garland, a mouse takes on the epic proportions of the Calydonian boar, while, caterpillars or no, the harvest barely fills a snail-shell. Thus, in a garden, size isn't everything; a small, complex space, particularly one in which mixed plantings change seasonally, is also likely to be extremely 'fat' space and a densely allusive text, tightly scripted in terms of seasonal and laborious time, topography, and aesthetics.

Martial's *hortus* encapsulates the simultaneously emblematic and representational qualities of the painted landscapes and *trompe-l'oeil* gardens that became a popular feature of interior decor in the late first century BCE, and persisted into the first century CE. These painted representations of nature are at once fantastic, imaginary, and hyperreal; they also offer us a vista into what (elite) Romans wanted or even expected to see through their windows, and how they understood the relationship between inside and outside space, and this is where we start.

VI.3 Imagined landscapes: the Villa 'Farnesina'

[In discussion with his son, Andrews realizes that for the boy] the countryside had a repertoire of several scenes visually auditioning to be landscapes. What, then, constitutes a 'scene'? ... Can we arrest the moving panorama at any point and be satisfied that the segment of land now in focus is a landscape?[27]

---

[25] For good starting points, see Conan 1986; Littlewood 1987: 9–10; Purcell 1995, 1996a; Beard 1998. Turner 2005 takes a long view; Wolschke-Bulmahn 1997 explores ideologies of garden design versus nature in the twentieth century.

[26] Mart. 11.18. Martial variously denotes the minute property as '*rus*' (country estate) and '*hortus*' (garden). See also Plin. *HN* 19.59. For discussion, see Linderski 2001.

[27] Andrews 1999: 5.

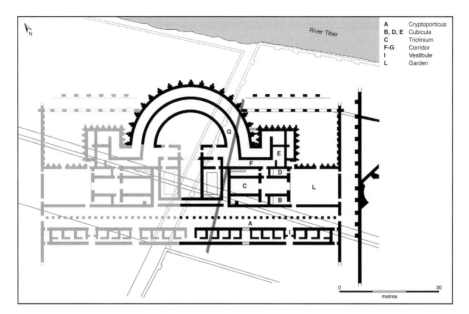

Figure 11 Villa 'Farnesina', based on G. Gatti's 1880 plan (*Notizie degli scavi di antichità*, April, Table IV, 2a).

Situated across the Tiber from Rome, the large, symmetrical Villa 'Farnesina', only partly excavated, is often associated with Augustus' aide Agrippa, husband of the Princeps' daughter Julia (follow the discussion using Figures 3 and 11).[28] It is a tempting identification (detailed in Beyen 1948), but the Tiber bank was prime real estate and some caution is justified.[29] Today, the Via della Lungara presents no ancient villa but, instead, a glorious Renaissance palazzo, decorated to order for the Chigi family in the early sixteenth century.[30] The excavated Augustan-era site was completely backfilled. To find evidence (at the time of writing), visit the Palazzo Massimo, one home of the

[28] On the excavations (written up in *NSc* April 1880, 127–42, Table IV), a result of embankment works regulating the Tiber in 1879, see in brief Bragantini and de Vos 1982: 17–24; Dolciotti 1998b.

[29] Agrippa may or may not have been the owner, but the eclectic mix of frescoed scenes recovered from the excavated rooms has much in common with the decor of other villas from this period. For brief coverage, see Bergmann 1995a: 104–5; Bragantini 1998b; Haselberger, Romano, and Dumser 2002: 272–3; Wyler 2006: 215–16. At greater length, see Leach 1988: 226, 240–1, 261–76 (comparing the Villa 'Farnesina' to the Palatine Casa di Livia) and *passim* (on landscape painting from villas around Vesuvius). More generally, see Leach 1985; J. R. Clarke 2005; Moormann 2007.

[30] The name 'Farnesina' stuck after the villa came into the hands of the Farnese family in the late sixteenth century.

Museo Nazionale. This museum displays a treasure trove of frescoes including those recovered from the Villa 'Farnesina', and from the Villa of Livia (*ad Gallinas Albas*) at Prima Porta.

A number of excellent analyses focus on the colourful landscape vignettes from a series of the Villa 'Farnesina's' small rooms. The jewel-like quality of the scenes in these *cubicula*, brilliant with vivid colours and set amid painting schemes that mimic richly inlaid marble, costly wood, and gems, shows the views off as if they were paintings adorning a gallery. Their subject matter is mostly small-scale, with images strongly evocative of an Alexandrian Greek background.[31] Bergmann comments that 'the empire was inherently collective' – make this 'eminently collectable' to understand how this villa's decor showcases the pick-and-mix eclecticism in landscape aesthetics and ornament.[32] The scenography is emblematic of the tutti-frutti qualities of later first-century iconography at Rome. It shifts between what are termed 'second' and 'third' styles,[33] showcasing and defining viewers against a complex array of landscape effects so that we and they exemplify the *voyant-visible*, presenting a sophisticated panorama of Rome and the Mediterranean in dialogue.

Our focus is the less ostentatiously spectacular landscape frieze that decorates the corridor F–G, connecting the south wing to the central hemicycle.[34] The corridor makes strolling feet map out this key architectural feature whose curved wall partly at least defined the villa's terraced riverside gardens and visually commanded the Tiber. Its position facing the new temple (Pantheon) and leisure complex sponsored by Agrippa on the Campus must have drawn the eyes of those strolling across the river in the parkland and traversing the still relatively undeveloped Campus plain.[35] The hemicycle may have been a landmark even in the further distance, potentially visible perhaps a kilometre and a half away at Augustus' Mausoleum, or farther still, from Sallust's estate or the luxury Pincian hillside villas north of the

---

[31] E.g. the rooms designated *cubicula* B, D, and E.

[32] Bergmann 1995a: 106. The *triclinium*, for example – a south-facing room, open to an enclosed garden with mock-portico decor – combines a delicately sketched landscape, complete with statuary, figures, and natural and artificial features (picked out on a black background), with a narrative frieze around the upper part of the walls (Egyptian-style judgement scenes: see Bragantini and de Vos 1982: 234–9). Wyler 2006: 217 explains that the artist created 'an emphatically new language'.

[33] On these 'styles', see J. R. Clarke 1991: 31–72; Strocka 2007. See also Kuttner 1998.

[34] See 'pull-out' page in di Mino 1998 (discussion in Bragantini 1998a).

[35] To get a sense of the topography, explore the *Digital Augustan Rome* online map (see Webography: Romano).

Figure 12 Rome, view south-west across the 'ancient' Campus from the Pincio (Villa Medici); the sightline includes the Mausoleum of Augustus (behind the central church) and stretches towards the Gianicolo (the green slopes give a hint of the verdant estates of the Janiculum in antiquity). The Villa 'Farnesina' site (Via della Lungara) is further along on this sightline.

city (such as that enjoyed by Lucullus – the Villa Medici occupies this part of the hill today and its terrace offers views giving a sense of the scope and interest of ancient vistas; see Figure 12). The hemicycle certainly engaged monumentally with Tiber traffic, and, with its curved façade, visually referenced the curved *cauea* (auditorium) of Pompey's theatre.[36]

It is unlikely that the curved portion of the corridor provided direct access into the hemicycle, but its arc emphasizes to viewers and amblers that this is a monumental luxury villa (not a townhouse), a 'theatrical' space, a place with surplus room, and one whose form and

[36] On the place of villas in the landscape (in general), see Mielsch 1987. On this villa's design, see Favro 1996: 166 – its innovative combination of existing forms with radical changes in scale makes the villa an interesting (domestic) companion piece for the public Baths of Agrippa across the river. See also Lugli 1938: 5–27; Yegül 1992: 181–3. On Augustan-era changes to the northern Campus, see Palmer 1990; Rehak 2006.

therefore the kinds of experience that it encouraged were part of a new wave in peri-urban villa design. Unlike the binary in/out dynamics of the *domus*-house, in this villa moving farther 'in' requires decisions about routes, and means moving (or even meandering) through garden courts from a north-west or south-east direction, approaching clusters of rooms leading to corridor F–G, or into the 'main' central public space (the 'auditorium'), before facing the same sorts of spatial and directional decisions when the routes reverse themselves in mirror image.[37]

For Vitruvius, corridors (*ambulationes*) were by design and tradition best suited to decoration with landscape frescoes, and wild or 'satyric' landscapes are typically associated with the stage sets for 'satyr' plays.[38] This overlap marks up landscape scenes as a world of gods, myth, performance, and unknowability, which in turn redefine the space they decorate.[39] Vitruvius also makes clear throughout book 6 that displaying the self via appropriate architectural features is closely aligned to a Roman's ability to persuade others to see him on his own terms.[40] Demonstrating his command of the shared symbolic values of self-display, rooted in domestic decorative use of theatrical imagery, substantiates the homeowner's right to take a major role in civic life and to compete politically to represent and guide the citizen body.[41] Vitruvius comments metaphorically that a shared semiotic system of values and references is necessary to decode trajectory and movement through a landscape-frescoed corridor, and chooses the word *doctrina* (implying a system of key skills) to indicate the kind of life-training that makes it possible to choose and follow an appropriate route

[37] The *cryptoporticus* (recall Pliny's enclosed walkway or arcade) provides an alternative direct axial route following the line of the roadside shops; on the *cryptoporticus* as a design feature, Zarmakoupi (forthcoming) looks set to prove definitive. On privacy in Roman domestic space, see Wallace-Hadrill 1994: 17–37; Nevett 1997; Riggsby 1997. On the relationship between access, routes, social identity and hierarchies, see Grahame 2000: 15–23. On applying space-syntax theory, see Grahame 2000: 24–36.

[38] Vitr. *De arch.* 7.5.1–2, 5.6.9. On painted landscapes, Leach 1988 is still a go-to study; other important recent work includes Bergmann 1991 (and on landscape and myth, 1999); J. R. Clarke 1996; Allison 1992; Tybout 2001; O'Sullivan 2007.

[39] E.g. the fountain, pergola, grotto, shrine, cliff-face, and faux-wilderness of *Cubiculum* M (north wall) at the Boscoreale (P. Fannius Synistor) villa, near Pompeii (now in the Metropolitan Museum of Art, New York); Ov. *Am.* 3.1.1–4; Sen. *Ep.* 41.3. See Lehmann 1953; M. L. Anderson 1987: 17–36. On the Roman Gaze, see Sharrock 2002.

[40] On Vitruvius, see McEwen 2003 (*passim*); Wallace-Hadrill 2008: 147–9, 193–6.

[41] Relevant additional discussions to factor in include Bergmann 1994; Wiseman 1994; Bodel 1997; Kuttner 1998; Wallace-Hadrill 1998b; Grahame 2000: 7–9, 15–22; and (ranging widely) Hales 2003.

(*iter*).[42] His list of typical iconic vignettes therefore prioritizes scenes *characteristic* of landscape, such as harbours, promontories, shores, rivers, springs, canals, shrines, groves, hills, cattle, and shepherds; and, where appropriate, statues of gods and legendary subjects.[43]

In antiquity, discrete art works, frequently booty documenting Rome's triumphal imperialism, were typically housed in porticoes – another kind of 'corridor'.[44] As Leach's wide-ranging discussion shows, Roman colonnaded gardens and *porticus* art galleries made reference to each other in terms of use, design, and decor.[45] The delicate, sketchy, and muted landscape vignettes lining corridor F–G seem, however, to recede rather than vying for attention as individuated works of art (or 'booty') – see Figures 13–15. Now, initially at least, they catch the glance rather less than their quirky 'frames': impossibly slender and structurally incredible architectonic features (wreathed and garland-carrying 'caryatids') which emphasize both the linear perspectival qualities of the space and also the artifice of the emphatically 'framed' and regularly ordered alternation of quasi-rustic landscape 'views' and 'still-life' groups, concealed and revealed by the curving space of the passage. The painted 'frames' help to point up the complexity of this space by alluding to the colonnaded wall of a *porticus* gallery and encouraging the passer-by to read the landscape vignettes in a slew of ways: as vistas into imagined, physically inaccessible space; as hyperreal commentaries on the real peri-urban sights and sites just outside; as a way of structuring the speed and pattern of movement through the corridor; and as tells on the core activities, concerns, and successes of the household.[46]

The scenes of produce, musical instruments, theatrical masks, and so on that alternate with the corridor's landscapes remind the passer-by of the socio-cultural status of owners and guests as common participants in a complex system of patronage and friendship.[47] Owners and guests alike might expect to bring and be presented with (token) gifts in kind to signify and solidify their relationship – and

---

[42] Vitr. *De arch.* 6, *Praef.* 1, 2. See O'Sullivan 2006 (key study on walking and landscape-painting); La Rocca 2008: 71. Laurence and Newsome (forthcoming) focus on movement, showing how much interest this theme is now generating.

[43] Vitr. *De arch.* 7.5.2.

[44] Favro 1994; C. Edwards 2003.

[45] Leach 2004: 123–55.

[46] On looking 'through', see Kuttner 1999c. Short 2008: 121 outlines a complementary argument: '"IDEAS ARE LOCATIONS" is not only a linguistic metaphor, but also (and above all) a conceptual metaphor that provides a kind of semiotic "schema" for behavior as well as speech'.

[47] See Wallace-Hadrill 1989 (edited collection on patronage); Brunt 1965a (*amicitia*).

Figure 13 Villa 'Farnesina', Corridor F–G, pastoral landscape fresco (Palazzo Massimo Museum, Rome. Inv. 1232 F1: S2). See main text for detailed discussion.

perhaps to contemplate the nature of this friendship as they strolled past the sequence of images. As one gazes along corridor F–G, the repeating pattern of landscapes and still-life groups floating on a pale background signals visual and conceptual unity, and regularly forces the passer-by's eye back from the 'outdoor' pseudo-vistas to the architectural reality of the internal space and its day-to-day usage. Every few steps the stroller passes from landscape to painted 'support', to another cluster of iconic objects and consumables that evoke and give shape to the life of the cultured homeowner, his family, and his guests.[48] The 'Farnesina' strip differs from, for example, the painted 'Odyssean' Esquiline landscape[49] in use of colour but also in the ambiguity of continuous/fragmented narrative progress from scene to scene, and architectural context ('Farnesina' F–G is not a space designed for static use, such as a *triclinium* [dining room]). The effect

---

[48] Similar in muted colour, and pictorial style, are the (probably contemporary) landscape vignette from the excavations beneath the American Embassy in Rome (*in situ*); the Sala del Monocromo (Casa di Livia, Palatine Hill, Rome); columbarium decor in the Villa Doria Pamphili, Rome; the red room of the villa at Boscotrecase (Museo Archaeologico Nazionale, Naples). For detail on the 'still-life' scenes, see de Vos 1982; masks and other quasi-Dionysiac or satyric imagery are a persistent theme (Sauron 1994: 573–7).

[49] O'Sullivan 2007 is excellent on this.

is what Lynch terms a 'melodic' time series, and studying the effect shows how space, too, exerts an authority.[50]

Sampling a few of these landscapes shows how this might work. Our first vignette is primarily rustic and sacral (Figure 13).[51] This scene is densely allusive of pastoral tropes familiar from Chapter II, and enthusiastically picked up in verse shortly before this villa's decoration by Virgil.[52] Key qualities common to Vitruvian diktats and pastoral verse are all present: a sense of leisured labour, and iconic features such as trees providing shade, a deity (Apollo), flowing water, verdant greenery, grazing animals, and shepherds in conversation. Also typical of the pastoral franchise is a dialogic and dramatic quality. Literary pastoral's delight in self-conscious meditation on the nature of artistry, the fragility of harmony between humans and nature, and the relationship between urbane discourse and rustic integrity adds complexity to a stroll past these landscapes.[53] These are spaces encoded for contemplating the self and the qualities of Roman identity peripatetically, and this is borne out by Rome's location of philosophical enquiry in the stoas and peristyles of the educated and Hellenophilic elite – where walking is key to intellectual development.[54]

Another shuffling of pastoral motifs adds bite to a vignette where identifiably urban morphology intrudes – the gate and faintly visible rotunda on the left-hand side (1233 F2: S8).[55] These landscapes are evidently doing more than simply re-scripting pastoral motifs or reflecting the reality of the Roman world.[56] Just along the wall (1233 F2: S2) this crystallizes. We see a two-storey, riverside villa, set by a harbour (Figure 14). A central bridge connects the villa to a faintly visible pedimented and colonnaded structure suggesting a large, urban edifice, possibly a temple, across the river.[57] The scene picks up some pastoral emblems (evidence of human intervention in the landscape, water, trees, hills, a god-haunted quality) and mixes them with a

---

[50] Lynch 1960: 107; on autobiographical hegemony expressed through space, see Arnold 2008.

[51] Inv. 1232 F1: S2 ('S'2 refers to the Section or 'vignette' within the specified panel, reading left-to-right; 'F' refers to position on F–G); in detail, see de Vos 1982: 337–8. Bergmann 1992 is particularly useful for getting to grips with painted pastoral (especially groves).

[52] Pl. *Phdr.* 230b2–c5; Theoc. e.g. *Id.* 1, 7; Verg. *Ecl.*

[53] Comparing literary and painted pastoral, see Segal 1963: 50–1.

[54] See e.g. Cic. *Fin.* 5.1.1–2; *Rep.* 1.14, 18. Montiglio 2000; Nightingale 2001; Zetzel 2003.

[55] Leach 1988: 270–1 reads this slightly differently. Different again is de Vos 1982: 338.

[56] Cf. Leach 1988: 271.

[57] The scene splits down the middle, pivoting on the possible 'villa' that engages with river, bridge (both to the left), and rustic, pastoral landscape (to the right). See de Vos 1982: 338 and Leach 1988: 269–70 for conflicting interpretations of what this scene represents.

Figure 14 Villa 'Farnesina', Corridor F–G, riverside landscape fresco (Palazzo Massimo Museum, Rome. Inv. 1233 F2: S2). See main text for detailed discussion.

prosaic harbour where four fishermen are strenuously hauling in nets under Poseidon's statuesque gaze but also subject to the painted villa's oversight.[58] From the real Tiber-side villa 'Farnesina' we gaze across to the imagined waterside villa, which in turn looks down towards its own rustic scene.[59]

This painted villa and its landscapes prime us to look thoughtfully *through* the wall to the real villa's environs. Just north-west of Agrippa's new bridge across the Tiber, the Villa 'Farnesina' was a little further on again from Rome's working port area and the naval arsenal downstream, and lay to the north-east of the Janiculum hill. The frescoes emblematically rework the 'real' landscape surrounding the villa as a series of synecdochic, stripped-down pastoral miniatures, rather than as a directly representational *trompe-l'oeil* panorama. Stopping in this corridor and considering how the allusive imagery connects to lived experience means thinking about how close this villa (and perhaps its owners) are to the city's constraints, and how and why this particular set of landscape scenes works for the householder.

[58] To his right, below, crouches a figure making an offering and a man who seems to be playing leaping fish on a line. Below him sits a fisherman with a pole. These figures share a common and close focus, keeping them anchored in the left foreground. Resting on his trident with a dolphin beneath his right foot, this Poseidon-'type' dates to a Lysippan model from the late fourth century BCE. Beneath his pedestal sit a rudder (or just possibly, as Leach 1988: 270 argues, an anchor) and a globe.

[59] The right rear-ground is occupied with increasingly faint greenery, and possibly a hill, and the landscape's 'rural' section has little of the pastoral *joie de vivre* of the last scene discussed. Linking the two narrative units, one figure associated with the 'villa' confronts the rigged ship manoeuvring towards the central bridge with sails furled.

Figure 15 Villa 'Farnesina', Corridor F–G, pastoral landscape with *quadriporticus*, fresco (Palazzo Massimo Museum, Rome. Inv. 1230 G3: S2). See main text for detailed discussion.

Pausing also makes this more like a relaxed stroll through a country-house *porticus*, and the accessible positioning of the scenes and their iconographic range encourage a contemplative rather than a utilitarian or purposeful pace.

One final example (1230 G3: S2) takes us fully into the hemicycle (Figure 15). Centre left sits a vast, square-colonnaded structure with a large entranceway;[60] a basic pastoral zone (centre foreground) then meshes the left zone (perhaps a sacred precinct[61]) with the scene to the right. Here, at the high point of the ground sloping up from the colonnaded building, stands a woman carrying a pitcher on her head;[62] she faces a *syzygia* – a short entablature supported by two pillars – containing a drapery-swirled female figure, usually identified as Isis-Fortuna and holding a cornucopia.[63] On the entablature crouch two terminal sphinxes, enhancing the Egypto-curious aspects of the scene. One branch of a bifurcated and gnarled tree passes right through the *syzygia*, stretching towards the pitcher-carrier. The other branch, twisting up behind the shrine, supports an awning whose right end is

---

[60] This structure appears to have an external *ambulatio* built into the façade (with side entrances) in addition to a *porticus* enclosing the open central space.

[61] A *schola*, surrounding a feature that looks like an attenuated dipylon gate.

[62] De Vos 1982: 340 suggests that the woman's hands are occupied by spinning; Leach 1988: 268 proposes that the slope leads down towards a stream running across the foreground at which the sheep are drinking (with the arched feature to the lower left as a rustic footbridge).

[63] De Vos 1982: 340 makes out a lotus on the statue's head.

fixed to a high outcrop crowned with a Priapus. Beneath the awning a group watches exotic, Egyptian dancers accompanied by an *aulos*.[64]

Here, the empire's culture of collecting comes sharply into focus.[65] Key compositional elements (the Isis-shrine, the water-carrier, the dancers) hint at the increasingly cosmopolitan nature of Rome as capital, while alluding to the need somehow to integrate them with the rustic-idyllic qualities of Rome's mythic pastoral origins – cued up in part by the ancient gnarled tree and Priapus: here, locations are ideas. Visually, perspective encourages a bird's-eye view down into the open square of the *porticus*. It floats on the pale ground at what seems a distorted angle, suggesting a lack of secure foundations in this landscape and pointing up the surreal qualities of the vista. Despite its familiar elements, this structure is completely unprecedented within a sacral-idyllic scene.[66] Leach proposes that it alludes to contemporary Augustan building projects across the river. Agrippa's Saepta Julia, another rectilinear colonnaded structure, was directly in the villa's sightlines (on the far side of the artificial lake associated with Agrippa's Baths); it was also close to the Temple of Isis on the Campus, perhaps also in play through the frescoed *syzygia*, and Agrippa's new Pantheon.[67] Standing near the beginning of the hemicycle phase of the corridor, we look through the fresco to the real-life Saepta and Pantheon: art evokes but also offers a new angle on reality.

Moving along the landscape-frescoed villa corridor in either direction highlights the controlled and controlling nature of corridor space. These are commissioned, painted, and imagined scenes marking up a wholly enclosed space – yet the dialogic quality linking them to each other, to the exterior world, and (relationally) to passers-by encourages an imaginative approach. The landscape scenes mimic 'real' landscape in stylized fashion; their sketchy qualities and the curve of the corridor urge us both to stop to puzzle out the detail (risking the chance that others using the corridor may bump into us and start a conversation) and also to keep moving, to find out what happens next rather than to pause for deliberation. The painted structural elements designate false

---

[64] On this iconography, see de Vos 1982: 341 n. 27.

[65] On connecting nostalgia/utopianism to Egyptian and 'oriental' motifs in this era, see Grimal 1984: 84–6; von Blanckenhagen and Alexander 1990: 41–9; de Vos 1991; Sauron 1994: *passim*. Orlin 2008 shows how a tactical deployment of Egyptiana could help to redefine Romanness.

[66] Leach 1988: 267–8.

[67] Ibid.: 269 argues vigorously that the fresco's stream with footbridge cites the footbridge across the Euripus (Campus Martius), and develops this topographic argument for panel 1231 G1 S2 (a 'naval battle' scene).

edges to the scenes that the compositions themselves fail to script; they appear to be excerpts from an ongoing comic strip in which the effects of empire and the day-to-day life of the countryside jostle, suggesting also the complex cultural functions of elite villas; yet this reading ignores their hyperreal qualities as a sequence.

Here, so very close to Rome, the owners' approved decor suggests a stroll through a still rural world – small towns, farms, and village life – in which the rustic villa forms one constituent part. The contrast with the real and increasingly built-up environs of Rome – and the wealth and power of the villa owners – just across the river or over the 'garden wall' must have been striking. These part-'satyric', part-pastoral vistas are at once boundary markers (for the corridor and villa), surreal in their iconographic juxtapositions, and scenographic in Vitruvius' theatrical terms. To return to Augé: moving means repetitively 'taking up a position' and thereby taking a series of positions on the sites around us. 'Landscape' deployed as corridor decor invites comment because the sequence of thematically connected miniature isovists conjures up different points of view on narratologically disconnected sites. These scenes could not really exist in sequence along a single vector and outside a single line of windows, or outside one real colonnade. Yet they encourage recognition of the different kinds of promenade that a villa might have, or views and experiences that it might offer, thus helping to animate and refine our understanding of how villa space operated. Their dependence on movement helps define the space both as a passageway and as an intellectual experience. Again, one walks in order to think, and the experience of walking stimulates 'new reflection'.[68]

For Roman citizens, concerned to articulate a new sense of shared identity, the process of walking down this or similar corridors might well have seemed to signal a new way of perceiving the world and Rome's place within it. Its simultaneously generic and contemporary qualities might also have suggested to the passer-through that no two views out the window captured the same scene: by pausing at some scenes and not others we can see a more or less rural, a more or less politicized, or a more or less artistic and literary landscape for this villa. The subtle range of scenes on offer, with their multicultural hints at imperial horizons, suggest that viewers might still be reflecting on the embedded cultural tensions on reaching either wing of the villa,

---

[68] Fontana-Giusti 2007: 259; Short 2008: 121.

Figure 16 Villa of Livia (*ad Gallinas Albas*), Prima Porta, detail of Garden Room fresco (east wall, to the right when facing the entrance). Here we see a spruce tree, a quince (left), and pomegranate (right). A thrush perches above the quince tree; a pigeon sits below the spruce. One can just make out two cypresses in the background. Dark-green box sets off small, low, blue and yellow flowers (lower left, behind the balustrade); the 'filler' plant looks like oleander (dark green leaves; all the following plant identifications draw on Gabriel 1955). In front of the balustrade we can just about make out (left to right) an ivy (with violets entwined with it), an iris, and (in the recess) a hart's tongue fern. A sense of the painted 'lighting' effect is visible on the spruce's branches and the quinces in particular (hinting at a central light source, emphasizing the focal tree, adding depth to the perspective). It is not wholly obvious here, but the scene lacks shadows (adding to the surreal effect).

at the moment when they are confronted with the more explicitly Egyptianizing decor in some of the surviving rooms.[69]

VI.4 Total immersion: Livia's garden room (Villa *ad Gallinas Albas*, Prima Porta)

Coming from the Villa 'Farnesina', we have now seen how landscape frescoes can have some of the flexibility more usually associated with portable art. We have also seen in detail how pastoral iconography gives visual reality to a paradox: 'one is both invited and detached while involved in a process that heightens awareness of one's station in the present world'.[70] Pastoral's self-reflexive quality also features in the rather different visual frame of reference, a lushly vivid and verdant painted garden (see Figure 16) that one experiences in a sunken room at the villa of Augustus' wife Livia at Prima Porta (north of Rome on the Via Flaminia). This surviving room's totally immersive qualities of unified design and space challenge the beholder to suspend disbelief and give way to its idyllic and hyperreal profusion.[71]

Taking a step back, context helps to decode the visual effect. Augustus took a keen interest in 'greening' Rome and embraced the complex propagandist possibilities of combining an extensive building programme (leading to his famously 'marble' city) with lush use of nature.[72] The contrast between sparkling new public buildings and vivid greenery, juxtaposed at new and older sites such as Pompey's portico gardens, Augustus' own Mausoleum, and Agrippa's bathing and exercise complex, must have been striking and, on a hot Roman day, delightful.[73] Not just a respite from the relentless heat or the dusty

---

[69] Versluys 2002 discusses the politics of Egyptian imagery.

[70] Bergmann 1992: 21; cf. the more historicizing view of Silberberg-Pierce 1980.

[71] To follow up, sample: Kellum 1994; Reeder 1997a, 1997b; Liljenstolpe and Klynne 1997–8; Kuttner 1999c; Klynne and Liljenstolpe 2000a, 2000b; Reeder 2001; Settis 2002; Carrara 2005; Klynne 2005; Zarmakoupi 2008.

[72] E.g. Strabo 5.3.8 on the Mausoleum's gardens; Suet. *Aug.* 92.1–2 (on the 'miraculous' Palatine palm tree); Plin. *HN* 14.11 (on Livia's vine) and 15.70, 139 (on Livia's new fig and laurel varieties). See also Gallini 1970: 157–87 (on Bacchic nature in this context); Brilliant 1975 (on Augustus' laurels); von Stackelberg 2009: 89–92 (on Augustus and nature); E. A. Pollard 2009: 320–4 (on the imperial qualities of botanic gardens). Favro 1996: 176–80 briefly sums up on gardens and Augustan Rome.

[73] Conan 1986 discusses the relationship between nature and art in these terms. Castriota 1995 shows how this filters into the iconography of the *Ara Pacis*. Kellum 1994 relates it directly to Livia's villa. Compare Lloyd 1982. On nature, landscape, and the urban gaze, see Duret and Néraudau 2001: 235–41 (and on Strabo's Campus Martius, 329–31).

hurly-burly of urban life, appropriate control over the environment
suggested a harmony between citizen(-emperor), *Natura*, and the
realms of myth and deity. Roman power was also glossed favourably
by the increasing success of imported specimen plants.[74] Thriving
public gardens in Augustus' city signified a flourishing *res publica* and
a concord between humans and gods; they stood in for more explicit
propagandist assertion that the era of civil war, unnatural bloodshed,
and political devastation was over.[75] The (civic) laurel was particularly
significant for Augustus' appropriation of Apollo as a patron deity,
emblematic of the new-style government and a renewal of moral
order; at Prima Porta, however, a much more multifarious profusion
of planting presents a complex experience.[76]

An additional frame of reference is contemporary interest in
plant encyclopaedias, a genre that first gained popularity in the first
century BCE as literary spoils from libraries and collections newly
under Roman control began to make their way back to Rome.
Kuttner suggests that Livia's innovative, seasonally ambiguous,
and multifarious painted garden is a visual equivalent to the newly
available botanical handbooks.[77] These plant companion-books must
also have made a significant impact on public and private planting
schemes in the new wave of parks clustering around the city itself –
Pliny the Elder was later to comment that, in the wake of Pompey's
dendrophily, trees became key 'captives' or booty in Roman military
triumphs.[78] In particular, we may speculate that they prompted a new
educated awareness of the scientific and epistemological connotations
of particular fashionable combinations of non-agricultural flora.[79] One
might trace this awareness in the relationship between painted gardens
here and at other sites: vividly beautiful examples include frescoes from
villas at Boscoreale, Boscotrecase, and Torre Annunziata (Poppaea's

---

[74] On appropriate versus inappropriate in landscaping, see von Stackelberg 2009: 93–100.
The pomegranate's popularity is an excellent example, but see also the lemon, lupine, peach,
walnut (for a catalogue of plant evidence from Pompeii, see Jashemski and Meyer 2002: 80–180).

[75] See Kellum 1990.

[76] Kellum 1994: 211 n. 7; Sauron 1994: 571–3; Liljenstolpe and Klynne 1997–8.

[77] Kuttner 1999c: 29. See also French 1994: 92–103 (on Theophrastus). On Dioscurides
and ancient botany in general, see Pease 1952; cf. Plin. *HN* 25.5–8. On Pliny the Elder and the
natural catalogues, see Beagon 1992: *passim*; E. A. Pollard 2009: 324–9.

[78] Plin. *HN* 12.111. Sen. *Controv.* 5.5 gives a flavour of the issues. See Meiggs 1982: 276–8.

[79] The ability to read and facility to consult plant handbooks was accessible only to a few,
but even elite crazes in plants can quickly become wider cultural phenomena, e.g. the so-called
tulip fever that spread rapidly from seventeenth-century Amsterdam.

Figure 17 Fresco detail (*Oecus* 15) from the Villa known as Poppaea's, at Oplontis (modern Torre Annunziata, near Pompeii). Note the combination of architectural (framing), culturally significant, and natural features (peacocks, greenery, deep blue sky; double-height arcaded *porticus*, theatrical masks, gateway, tripod). Sauron 1994 decodes the scene.

Villa at Oplontis, *oecus* 15; see Figure 17), and the 'Auditorium' in Maecenas' Esquiline Gardens.[80]

Today, visiting the site of Livia's extensive estate, whose ridgeline position dominated the Tiber valley's course towards Rome, makes for a confusing experience. Instead (or in advance), the visitor can get a sense of the whole site by exploring the recently developed 'virtual' villa, which reconstructs the different phases of building and decor.[81] One

[80] As of Summer 2009, the Oplontis frescoes can be visited in situ (see also M. L. Thomas and Clarke 2007, and Webography: *The Oplontis Project*). The 'Auditorium' of Maecenas (Rome) is usually closed to the public, but guided visits are sometimes available (on the site, see de Vos 1983; Kuttner 1999c: 24–6, and Webography: *Iconoclasm* blog). See also the Villa 'Farnesina' *uiridiarium* (Dolciotti 1998a; Kuttner 1999c: 26); the Casa del Bracciale d'Oro, Pompeii (vividly illustrated in the 1991 exhibition catalogue *Il giardino dipinto nella Casa del Bracciale d'Oro a Pompei e il suo restauro* – consult Stefani and Borgoncino 2006).

[81] Webography: *The Virtual Museum of the Ancient Via Flaminia*. Terminals with the full interactive Multi User Domain, explored using avatars, are on site at the Museo Nazionale

entered the so-called Garden Room by stepping underground – surely, as with the 'Auditorium' of Maecenas on Rome's Esquiline Hill, an indication that this was a summer space, providing a fantastical escape from the heat of the sun. One emerged into a 360° painted garden, whose fertility implied plentiful sun and rain but never inflicted them on its occupants.

Entering the Palazzo Massimo's reconstruction hints at the somatic impact: first, cool, dim, almost bewildering abundance; then the cumulative effect of the frescoed foreground's detailed intensity gradually blends into more impressionistic representation of fertile greenery as the painted space 'recedes' toward the implied distance.[82] Viewing the room in virtual reality emphasizes the potential for subtle lighting to enhance the artifice, and also reminds us that if a *triclinium*, then the angle of gaze would ideally be quite different from that available to the museum visitor. Initial impressions of riotous nature and a myriad shades of green are quickly modulated if one steps up to the 'fence' to get closer to the 'garden'. Orientation is initially provided by a low (perhaps calf height, if standing, but closer to eye level if reclining to eat) painted 'wicker' fence (set 'behind' a dark border, where the walls meet the floor) with a central opening to the north and south, and occasional small birds.[83] The next perspectival plane is a well-tended grass walkway, with a decorative stone parapet forming the second boundary. Here a distinctively patterned ornamental tracery offers a frame, focuses the gaze, and encourages the viewer to linger.

A repeating pattern of individual small flowering and foliage plants (iris, ferns, violets, ivy) follows the parapets on each side and discourages the eye from focusing exclusively on the central feature of the shorter parapets: directly opposite each break in the wicker fence the parapet 'withdraws' into an angular recess. One expects an urn or statue, but instead finds a tree – pine (north) and oak (south).[84] On the (long) east and west walls, two similar recesses per side embrace

Romano, at the Terme di Diocleziano; elements of the Virtual Villa are downloadable. Forte 2007 details the project's results.

[82] Grau 2003 traces such total-immersion (or virtual-reality) techniques from antiquity to the present.

[83] Linderski 1989 is particularly interesting on painted birds.

[84] For detailed descriptive analysis of individual features, see Gabriel 1955. Note the 'woodland' quality hinted at by the choice of trees, and the fact that laurel is not one of the 'display' trees, despite its significance for the Villa as a whole. Kuttner 1999c: 28 suggests that the trees are monumentalized and aestheticized by their cooption in this way. This makes for another connection between controlled and riotous nature in the different painted zones.

spruce trees. These trees (vertical compositional elements) form a visual link between the room proper, the manicured pathway, and the seemingly wild natural profusion beyond. Further connections between the zones include the freeze-frame fluttering birds and the untamed vegetation, on the point of invading the walkway from over the parapet. The contrast between the three main zones (room, walkway, and lush planting) suggests a progression from central social order, through environmental order, into a world where *Natura* apparently takes charge.[85] Another reading might prioritize the schematic face-off between natural profusion and Roman love of taxonomy – the two confront each other across the path.[86]

Unlike Varro's theatrical aviary, this is not an ostentatiously 'artificial world of colonnades and bird-netting'.[87] For a start, the cultivation scheme looks plausible, at least superficially, and presents instantly recognizable plants easily cross-referenced today, with a minimum of extravagant hard-landscaping.[88] If we look harder, reading for symbolic potential, the scene starts to look less natural. Individual elements recall the densely allusive properties of the literary landscapes we have examined, with an array of possible scenographic keys including a Bacchic scheme. Ivy and violets conjure up a grape-laden vine, and mark up the year – spring flowering leads to autumnal harvest; the vine is Dionysus' plant, whereas violets supposedly protected against hangovers.[89] Dionysus' ivy activates the triumphal imagery of other foliage on display: oak, palm, laurel, myrtle, ivy, pine. It is noteworthy that all the plantings in this 'garden' (as in comparable examples of this scheme elsewhere) are sempiternal: vigorous, flourishing young trees, shrubs, and flowers. The typically gnarled and aged trees popular in pastoral or sacro-idyllic landscapes do not feature, keeping viewers in the room at the heart of the best of all possible worlds.[90] Kellum details

---

[85] See Kellum 1994: 215.

[86] On the wider implications, see Castriota 1995; R. Evans 2003.

[87] Varro *Rust.* 3.5.9–17. Kellum 1994: 217 also draws important connections with Virgil's *Georgics*.

[88] Caneva and Bohuny 2003; more generally, Jashemski 1979. On Greek plants, see Baumann 1993.

[89] Kellum 1994: 218–21. This relates to Bacchic nature (Chapter 2), and hints too at the ivy and violet garlands worn by Alcibiades in Plato's *Symposium* (212d, e). On ivy and Dionysiac imagery, see Kuttner 1999c: 13–19. On sacred groves, see Scheid 1993; on painted groves, see Leach 1988: 197–260 *passim*; Bergmann 1992; Reeder 2001: 75–83 (summary discussion focusing on Livia's Villa).

[90] Cf. the Ara Pacis' multi-seasonal produce. Looking past Virgil, Johnson 1990 (on Tibullus; see also Leach 1980) and Leach 1975 (on Calp. *Ecl.*) connect pastoral directly to politics and *anomie*.

the semiotics of laurel in myth (Apollo, Daphne) and for Augustus, but for discussion of how these images function as tropes within a wider discourse of painted *trompe-l'oeil* gardens, we turn to Kuttner.[91]

For Kuttner, garden-room frescoes are framing devices: they typically encourage the viewer to see the room as a pavilion or grotto with a designed garden prospect. Her analysis proposes that this room's decor reconfigures its central space as a grotto from which we gaze out into the open air (even though anyone using the room would recognize the impossibility of the isovist), but, if one gets too close, the different painting styles giving detail to foreground and creating an eye-deceiving perspectival distance become clear.[92] The artifice of this scheme is also highlighted by its architectural impossibility: a cave must have a back wall – here instead *all* walls are 'open', no (painted) structural supports are on display, and no particular perspective or panorama is strongly prioritized. Moreover, the once vividly painted stuccoed vault evokes artificial landscape features rather than natural grottoes; again, looking up may have forced viewers to recall that 'outside' the simulation is underground.[93]

If this room was used as a *triclinium*, then recalling Pliny's elaborate water features (and comparing it with, for example, the dining cavern at the Villa at Sperlonga, the 'Canopus' and 'Serapeum' complex [Figure 20], and the 'Maritime Theatre' at Hadrian's Villa, or possibly the 'Auditorium' of Maecenas at Rome) we may be surprised that no evidence remains of a water feature to heighten the grotto experience.[94] Moreover, this 'garden' includes no definitive painted water features (compared to, for example, the Casa del Bracciale d'Oro at Pompeii), sculptures, or urns (as in the frescoed *uiridiaria* from Poppaea's Villa at Oplontis, or from the Villa 'Farnesina');[95] without clear evidence of water (to nourish the greenery), the sense of mysterious luxuriance

[91] Kellum 1994: 219–21, 222–3; Kuttner 1999c.

[92] Kuttner 1999c: 15, 27. Gabriel 1955: 7–8 prefers to read the irregular yellowish-brown feature linking the ceiling and the painted garden as the rough edge of a thatched roof; Reeder 2001: 35–44 (also interested in the idea of an underground room 'pretending' to be underground) adopts the grotto interpretation, and draws comparisons with the 'Auditorium' of Maecenas (2001: 53–9).

[93] As Gabriel 1955: 21–3 observes, the painted 'lighting' strategy also fails to cohere fully, making for a slightly surreal effect, which the reconstructions proposed in Forte 2007 tackle, using artificial lighting schemes.

[94] In detail, see Lavagne 1988. Also Stewart 1977; Mielsch 1987: 121–8; Ricotti 1987 (with discussion of Hadrian's Villa); Ehrlich 1989 (ditto); Ridgway 2000; Weis 2000; Beard and Henderson 2001: 74–82; Carey 2002 (with discussion of Hadrian's Villa); Kuttner 2003. Compare the stepped water feature identified in the 'Auditorium' of Maecenas.

[95] J. R. Clarke 1996 and Bergmann 2002 (on the villa at Oplontis) are useful here.

is heightened.[96] The lack of built-in natural sound effects suggests that any imposed soundtrack would be occasional and dependent on the event or context, would heighten the sense of artifice, and would perhaps isolate any voices in conversation. The silent walls would in this way become a 'natural' audience.

Next, shifting to real rather than painted scenery, we wander back towards Rome and two famous landscape parks.

VI.5 Landscapes encircling the city: the Horti Sallustiani and Porticus of Pompey

The political qualities of the designed parklands surrounding Rome, and the *otium* they supported, show how importantly these public and private landscapes featured as part of integrated image-making packages for their wealthy owners.[97] Different kinds of experience were available, from a getaway from the heat and dust, to a philosophical stroll, an afternoon outing, a chance for seclusion, or something more akin to an art gallery or theme-park visit (cf. Figure 9). Underpinning all these landscape experiences was the ever-present authority of the garden's sponsor – visually and explicitly in the statuary and art on display, implicitly in the availability and fertility of the garden itself, and conceptually in the kinds of stories told or evoked by combinations of a visitor's personal memory, the garden's imagery, and specific conditions and contexts of a given visit.[98]

Roman memory, we have noted, was spatially dynamic, and closely attuned to the artificial qualities of Roman culture. Landscape gardens give us an opportunity to see the 'art of memory' at work.[99] Roman mnemotechnics (that is, the systematization of memory) operates by visualizing a 'memory' three-dimensionally as a landscape to be moved through: the would-be memorizer starts from a mental picture of some regularly articulated, designed space (stoa, basilica, portico...) that contains discrete iconic images or objects (herm, bust of Sophocles...). She or he then uses the icons as pegs on which to hang the key elements in a structured discourse. Mentally revisiting

---

[96] Kuttner 1999c: 27 makes a case for a painted stream being represented by the dark 'border'; see also Ricotti 1987. See Bergmann 2008 on the mysterious quality of such spaces.

[97] La Rocca 1986: 18–33 is a keynote study. See also Lloyd 1982.

[98] Here, Bergmann (1991, 1994) is particularly useful. See also Bartman 1991; King 2000.

[99] Sauron 1994: 446–74 (on *oecus* 15, Oplontis).

the sequence of 'statues' in the 'place' (that is, imagining oneself to be walking from one to the next in a specific order) allows one to reconstitute the speech or whatever is the object of memory.[100] As the unknown author of the *ad Herennium* notes, the mnemonic landscape of these memory nodes (*loci*) was ideally rather like a villa.[101]

Thus a prospective garden designer in the late first century BCE could start with a fairly well-defined discourse about what makes a pleasurable and usable landscape (shade, water, paths), and an awareness of the dangers of the wrong kind of hubristic associations.[102] Required ingredients include icons (a bust of Socrates, a herm, a Priapus or a Venus, a startled deer, etc.): booty arrayed in an appropriately articulated sequence to tell a story you want your visitors to see.[103] Roman landscape gardens deployed these features strategically to emphasize the relationship between orderly, productive (of pleasure or power) recreation, Roman civic identity, and practical philosophy. To visit them is to experience a controlled narrative of the relationship between owner, visitor, state, gods, and the natural world.[104]

Unfortunately, like most Roman landscape gardens, the Gardens of Sallust and Porticus of Pompey are no longer visible in situ. Moreover, nineteenth-century urban development redesigning Rome as a capital for the newly unified Italy eradicated most of the lingering traces of the changes in level that were key to estates such as Sallust's. In their time, however, these were two of Rome's most famous landscape parks.[105] They are the source of iconic images such as the 'Dying Gaul' (appropriated by the Ludovisi family in the early seventeenth century

[100] This draws on the processes as outlined and discussed in Yates 1966; Blum 1969; and Small 1997. For a range of contemporary approaches to the structures of memory, see Neisser 1989; Burgin 1996; Casey 2000, 2001; Brockmeier 2002; Ricoeur 2004.

[101] *Rhet. Her.* 3.31–2. See Bergmann 1994; McEwen 1995: 14–17 (succinct; focusing on Pliny's villas); Baroin 1998. Cf. van Eck 2000.

[102] See Varro *Rust.* 1.2.10. Ideas of Persia feed into a developing colonial perspective over the eastern Mediterranean as a lush, luxurious, and even dissolute zone; an imaginary and threatening landscape of kings, courtiers, excess, and transgression. See La Rocca 1986: 8–17.

[103] See Cic. *Tusc.* 2.9 (his own 'Academy' and 'Lyceum' remember 'real' spaces, but through a literary and philosophical filter); *Q Fr.* 3.1.1–6. Hill 1981 looks specifically at domestic usage, but see also Littlewood 1987; Kuttner 1995, 1999a; Bilde 2005.

[104] Summed up in Hartswick 2003: 16–20. Charlesworth 2003 presents a useful analogue (Stourhead, UK), while Moore, Mitchell, and Turnbull 1993, and Hunt 2003 consider the broader issues.

[105] There are elements of the Horti Sallustiani still in place, e.g. the delicate landscape frescoes (comparable to those in F–G of the Villa 'Farnesina') discovered beneath the American Embassy; and a vaulted (Hadrianic) structure accessible via Piazza Sallustio and open by arrangement or during events (Webography: *Horti Sallustiani*; see also Carpano 2000). Pompey's Portico lies beneath the charming backstreets that connect Largo Argentina with Piazza Campo

during construction on the site of the Horti Sallustiani).[106] This and other instantly recognizable statues from a range of ancient luxury estates are a highlight of any tour through the remodelled Capitoline Museum (take them home, in a richly illustrated book on sale in the Museum shop).[107]

Hartswick details what we currently know and can deduce about the Horti Sallustiani, making the important point that plantings were by no means a minor feature in these luxury estates. We have seen at Prima Porta how planting schemes can tell a subtle and allusive story.[108] There is, unfortunately, little contemporary evidence for the role of Sallust, disaffected politician-turned-historian (mid-first century BCE), in the design and layout of this estate. Its boundaries are uncertain (see Figure 3), but it was neighbour to the Horti Lucullani and stretched across the Pincian and Quirinal hills north of the city, taking in the valley between the two (and the stream – known now as Acqua Sallustiana – that ran down through it, draining eventually into the Tiber).[109] Clearly, this estate nestling just outside the city walls had an ample and (recalling Columella) almost ideal water supply. Like Maecenas' Esquiline Gardens, this estate also had mortuary connections: it was close by the Campus Sceleratus (located just inside the Porta Collina) where Vestal Virgins who broke their vows were entombed alive.[110] Moving on a generation, Sallust's estate took centre-stage when inherited by his great-nephew, another Sallust, who was part of Augustus' inner circle.[111] The estate finally passed directly into imperial hands, probably by inheritance: Agrippina (Nero's mother) was eventually widowed by the second Sallust's adoptive heir (Sallustius Passienus), and went on to marry the emperor Claudius.

de' Fiori. La Rocca 1986 discusses the Esquiline *Horti*, including the Horti Lamiani (on which, see Cima 1996); Cima 1986 homes in on the archaeology.

[106] On the 'Gaul' statuary's evocation of the Hellenistic court of Pergamum, see Marvin 2002: 205–11, 214–15. More generally, see Hartswick 2004: 104–8. Other famous icons include the Ludovisi and Boston thrones, Silenus with Baby Dionysus, a wounded Niobid, and the Borghese Vase.

[107] Cima and Talamo 2008 – although at €50 (June 2008) it's not an impulse buy. E. Fentress 2007 reviews the Capitoline '*Horti*' display. Its temporary counterpart (in Florence) was the ambitious 2007 exhibition exploring gardens from Babylon to Rome (and reconstructing two full-scale Pompeian peristyle gardens), catalogued in di Pasquale and Paolucci 2007, and reviewed by Marzano 2008.

[108] See also Talamo 1998.

[109] Hartswick 2004: 1–8 sums up the changing topography and possible boundaries.

[110] On the Esquiline Gardens, see Häuber 1998.

[111] Name-checked in Hor. *Carm.* 2.2. See also Tac. *Ann.* 3.30.2; Syme 1964: 283 suggests that the gardens only became ostentatiously luxurious under the second Sallust's ownership.

As is abundantly clear in Hartswick's account, despite the range of finds from the Horti Sallustiani, recovering a clear sense of what a garden visit might have been like at any given time is impossible.[112] Nevertheless, based on our case studies and factoring in Vitruvius' comments on the close relationship between designs of town and country properties, we can conclude that colonnades, statuary and sculptures, water, axial views, shrines, formal plantings, and designated walkways were prominent features in this as in other peri-urban parks, combining the static quality of architectural structures and immobile marble and bronze figures with the shifting sensations of the seasons and times of day, the fluttering of birds and humming bees, the babble of fountains, and the potential for (guided) choice among the various itineraries and paths (see Figures 9, 10, and 17).[113]

Visual and semiotic allusions to the Greek world filter through architectural terminology (stoa, peristyle, gymnasium) and thus nestle also in the semiotics of the likely architectural structures themselves. Sites in this estate, as in those of Cicero and his correspondents, probably had tags such as *Lyceum*, or *Museum*, or even *Amaltheum* (recalling the goat-nymph who nannied Zeus on Mount Ida, and the mythical cornucopia flowing from her broken horn).[114] Softening the crisp masonry and angular architectural forms, ivy and vines were probably important elements of the park's soothing greenery, and also significant for their Dionysiac exuberance and hint of mystery and danger.[115] Such plantings would also have evoked the convivial quality of elite estates as venues for self-display and grand entertainment, while at the same time recalling the agricultural focus of many of the more suburban and rustic villas.[116]

---

[112] See Talamo 1998 and Haselberger, Romano, and Dumser 2002: 146. For recent archaeological finds, see Piranomonte 2007. Compare Villedieu 2001.

[113] Hartswick 2004: 12. Vitr. *De arch.* 6.6.5. Aural qualities filter through e.g. Varro's discussion of aviaries (see Chapter 5) and Cic. *Leg.* 1.7.21; recall Pliny's fountains (also Chapter 5). Plin. *HN* 12.13, 35.116 located the Roman beginnings of topiary and painted *trompe-l'oeil* topiary in the Augustan era.

[114] Cicero's Tusculan estate had a 'Lyceum' and an 'Academy' (*Div.* 1.8, *Tusc.* 2.9 – see Leen 1991); his friend Atticus had an 'Amaltheum', like Gelon's 'Horn of Amalthea' in Syracuse from the early fifth century BCE (*Att.* 1.13.1, 1.16.15–18; see F. G. Moore 1906; Grimal 1984: 78, 304–6); on Oplontis, see Sauron 2007. More generally, see Ridgeway 1981; Gleason 1994: 19–21; Wallace-Hadrill 1998a.

[115] Recall Pliny's ivy (Chapter V.5), and the use of these features at Prima Porta. Wiseman 1998: 16 discusses the vineyards in this zone.

[116] Hartswick 2004: 14, and recall Chapter V on Varro, Columella, and Pliny. It is unclear how widely accessible to or closed off from the peri-urban landscape these elite estates were (physically or visually). Hartswick 2004: 16–17 argues that major 'national treasures' (art as booty) would be on public display at least occasionally (citing Cic. *Tusc.* 5.102); cf. C. Edwards 2003.

A frisson of danger as well as cultured delight must have amused and even possibly unsettled the visitor meeting a rosy hippopotamus reflected in a pool (cf. the two Pegasus statues, Figure 10), or being spied on by a Silenus or Satyr amid the foliage or peering out from a grotto; the presence of warrior Amazons too suggest that violence and perverse sexuality lurked as one took the air and strolled along avenues and colonnades, or gazed down the hillside or across the valley.[117] More prosaically, imperialism, conflict, and death, noble or ignoble, may have featured if the famous 'dying' and 'suicidal' marble 'Gauls', with their Hellenistic and Pergamene connotations, and the (possibly Greek-import) Niobids (inventoried in the Ludovisi collection) all populated the estate.[118] A marble group comprising figures identified as Artemis, Iphigenia, and a hind draws together sex, death, power, and danger as key landscape components.[119] The relationship between idyllic landscapes and (sexual) violence simmered in our discussion of Melior's tree (Chapter IV). If this range of immobile statues was characteristic of the estate's marble inhabitants, then the exuberant but also implacable, perilous, and inhumane qualities of nature seem to have been important to the range of itineraries, particularly where disturbing faces or cloven hooves poked out from amid greenery – an experience still available in Rome's Villa Sciarra, a terraced public park populated with slightly larger than life-size tableaux of sexy violence (see Figure 18) and complete with a living 'stage', theatrically framing statues of the months of the year.[120]

[117] For statues that seem 'real', see Pygmalion's creation (Ov. *Met.* 10.247–69); cf. Apul. *Met.* 2.4. On reality versus art, see Philostr. *Imag.* 1.28.2 (Elsner 1995 is particularly useful). An exotic hippopotamus (from the Ludovisi inventory) is on display in the Ny Carlsberg Glyptotek (Copenhagen). The Villa Ludovisi took over the site of Sallust's estate in the seventeenth century and was a rich source of sculptural finds; these are summed up by Haskell and Penny 1981: 27–30 (on the 'dying Gaul': 224–7; on the 'suicidal Gaul': 282–4).

[118] Consult Hartswick 2004: 93–104. The 'dying' and 'suicidal' Gauls from the Ludovisi collection are currently on view in the Musei Capitolini and Palazzo Altemps (Rome); a related kneeling 'Gaul' is on display in the Louvre (Paris). Elements of a 'Niobid' group can be seen in the Palazzo Massimo (Rome); this was a popular theme for sculpture groups: there are other examples (possibly from the Horti Lamiani, on the Esquiline) in the Uffizi (Florence) and the Ny Carlsberg Glyptotek (Copenhagen). Cf. Hepple 2001 on the 'museum garden' in sixteenth- and seventeenth-century England. Hölscher 2004 is interesting on how Roman 'art' related to Greek models and examples (Pollitt 1978 sums up the kinds of 'booty' pouring in).

[119] Hartswick 2004: 83–142 discusses sculptural finds currently identified as likely to be from the estate. See also Moltesen 1998.

[120] Though Cic. *Q Fr.* 3.1.5 debunks the reality effect. On the numinous quality of landscape, see Ov. *Met.* 3.155–62. Leen 1991 discusses how particular sculptural forms or figures were associated with different spaces (see also Vermeule 1968). On deviant luxury, women, and gardens, see Boatwright 1998. See Webography: *Villa Sciarra* (including statue groups of Pan and Syrinx, and Apollo and Daphne).

Figure 18   Apollo and Daphne statue group, Villa Sciarra, Rome. This couple, and an array of other 'classical' groups also still *in situ* (e.g. Pan and Syrinx; Diana and Endymion), were originally part of Giovanni Ruggeri's (early eighteenth-century) design for the grounds of the Villa Visconti (Brignano, Italy). The Wurtses, the American owners of the Villa Sciarra (from 1902), bought the Ruggeri sculptures as part of their landscaping vision for this new project. On George Washington Wurts' death (1928), his widow, Henrietta, made plans to give the Villa Sciarra to the Roman people as a public park, which concluded with a formal presentation to Mussolini in March 1930.

As terraced parks such as Rome's Villa Sciarra make clear, the theatrical qualities of the landscape itself, and its power to conceal and reveal through changes in level or apparently natural barriers (water, rocks, crevasses), will have taken centre stage. These, combined

– as discussed by Beard (1998) – with the artificially frozen limbs, evocatively Hellenic herms, artistic license in modelling, and playful approach to scale will have challenged, charmed, and delighted guests and owners alike. Part of the pleasure must have been in the process of recognizing the high-concept landscape for the artifice that it was, in scrutinizing the boundaries between nature and art, static and transitory effects, and enjoying the interplay of 'natural' and artistic structuring features. The tactile quality that characterizes surviving marble inhabitants suggests that there was pleasure to be gained from testing the limits of art and myth to enrich the meaning of landscape: these immobile figures may have been designed to fool the willing viewer into participating in the performance until the moment when cold stone broke the illusion.

Our second Roman park takes us down from the hills onto the Campus plain, and right up to the city's traditional boundary. Where Sallust's estate benefited from its location straddling a valley, offering the potential at least for elaborate vistas, terracing, and straightforwardly gravity-fed water features, Pompey's site presented flat, if marshy, ground.[121] Gagliardo and Packer (2006) sum up recent archaeological (re)thinking on the park but, to get a sense of how the park maps onto the contemporary city, Gleason (1990) still provides the best overview.[122] This garden differs from Sallust's *horti* not just in terms of scale, scope (designed as a public space), and context (association with the theatre and Temple of Venus Victrix) but also through architectural form.

This was a *quadriporticus*, a space defined by the architectural feature that enclosed it, gave it shape, and defined its paths and vistas: the rectangular colonnade (cf. Figures 9, 15). Vitruvius, writing thirty-odd years after this entertainment and relaxation complex had become part of Rome's landscape, emphasizes that planted colonnade gardens are a key feature of the ideal theatre, and also integral to urban design.[123] Gleason argues that this park is *the* archetype for the formally designed Roman *porticus* garden; it certainly provides context for the landscaped

---

[121] The Villa 'Farnesina' used terracing to maximize its river frontage; Lucullus' Pincian villa also took advantage of topography to enhance the monumental and experiential range of views and perspectives that it provided. On the use of terracing for maximum impact and spatial innovation, see Tybout 2007.

[122] See also Denard 2002; Haselberger, Romano, and Dumser 2002: 207. On the politics of the complex, see Temelini 2006.

[123] Vitr. *De arch.* 5.9.1–9.

environments contextualizing the auditorium-shaped features in the Villa 'Farnesina' and the Gardens of Maecenas.[124]

Pompey's *porticus* garden had made available for the first time to a mass audience a glimpse of the evocatively Hellenic and visually dense world of elite suburban villas. It was intelligible to a cross-societal audience specifically because it drew on the architectural vocabulary of the familiar smaller-scale structure and plantings of a *domus* garden, scaled up dramatically and re-imagined as a public-access but topographically controlled space, relating directly to the public and civic buildings on the Campus. Pompey's *quadriporticus* provided a new permanent expression of the festal qualities of Rome's year (in the theatre) and offered a temporary home to the then peripatetic meetings of the Senate.[125] Shops, too, formed part of the complex, nodding to the typical mixed-use rhetoric of urban streetscapes. As the detailed reconstructions proposed by Gleason (1994) show, Pompey's *porticus* surrounded a grove designed to present an effect at once harmoniously natural and highly urban and artificial: sightlines and perspective served a coherent (self-)promotional agenda.[126] Strolling in this garden's shade soothed eyes and mind, delighted the ear with babbling water, and imprinted on visitors the powerful patron who stood behind Pompey – Venus herself.

The theatre and temple of Venus were complete by the late 50s BCE, and then 'restored' by Octavian (soon to be Augustus) in 32 BCE. The dimensions of the *porticus* garden were in the region of forty-five by thirty metres.[127] The fragmentary Severan Marble Plan (the early third-century-CE *Forma Urbis Romae*) depicts a strictly symmetrical design for the garden, analysed in detail by Gleason.[128] Enhancing the structured design and offering movement, greenery, and shade, two double 'colonnades' of trees echoed the marble columns of the *porticus* itself, and provided further perspectival authority for how and

---

[124] Gleason 1994: 13. We might, here, recall Pliny's 'hippodrome' feature (Chapter V.5).

[125] Gros 1987. The Campus was traditionally a political and military space: military gatherings (e.g. soldiers preparing for a Triumph) and consular (and magisterial) elections – the Saepta – were key defining activities. See also e.g. the Villa Publica (the dramatic *locus* for Varro *Rust.* 3). Caesar was, in this period, giving both Saepta and Villa Publica a makeover. See also Sauron 1987.

[126] Compare Bergmann 1994, Kuttner 1999c. See also Gros 1999; Haselberger, Romano, and Dumser 2002: 207. Throwaway literary references abound; see e.g. Catull. 55; Prop. 2.32; Ov. *Ars am.* 1.67, 3.387; Mart. 2.14.10, 11.47.3. Fittingly, Pompey's nemesis Caesar was eventually assassinated in the Senate's meeting hall in Pompey's complex (44 BCE).

[127] Using Gleason 1994: 16, fig. 3 (reconstruction based on the Severan Marble Plan). This scale makes the length and breadth relate proportionally in a ratio of 3 : 2.

[128] Gleason 1994. See also Webography: *Stanford Digital Forma Urbis Romae Project.*

at what stages in the visit particular elements of the garden were on display. As discussed above, the 'back wall' of the stone colonnades themselves made available the typical *porticus*-gallery experience of statue-filled niches alternating with Greek works of art – in effect, trophies, showcasing Pompey's power, generosity, wealth, and military success.[129]

The central axis between marble and arboreal 'columns' led from the Curia (east), through the theatre, and on to the Temple of Venus (west), putting these two structures in dialogue via the orderly grove (perhaps, as we noted earlier with Pliny the Elder, evoking the serried ranks of a Triumph) and the theatrical and performative space between them. Gleason suggests that other emblematic trees such as laurel (victory) and myrtle (Venus) were likely to have featured too; if so, the orderly planes set off by the laurels' and myrtles' dark glossy leaves will have strongly emphasized not just Pompey's eastern victories but also his continuing subscription to Roman values.[130] The fountains commented on by Propertius (2.32.11–12) provide the final sensory feature. Glimpsed through the orderly plantings, the bubbling of water makes for a charmingly unpredictable visual and aural element, encouraging movement (to experience a new vista) and conversation. Indeed, opening up comfortable, stimulating conversational avenues and spaces for Rome (that is to say, presenting Rome with its own version of Athens' Academy or Painted Stoa) was a key innovation for a city unaccustomed to recreational public space.

Coarelli and Sauron (with different names in mind) both argue strongly that the *porticus* gallery was curated as a unity, combining Roman imagery with the sophisticated luxury of the Hellenized East; the central space, if we take Propertius' word for it, is both emblematic *locus amoenus* and Roman *imperium sine fine* (boundless empire) in miniature.[131] Also subtly enhancing the central axis of planes were regular features variously interpreted as fountain-statues

---

[129] E.g. Plin. *HN* 35.59, 114, 126, 132 (paintings). Mart. 11.47 describes the northern 'hundred-column' portico (*hecatostylon*) as located by a grove of plane trees in which lurked statues of wild beasts. Kuttner 1999a: 360–4 is excellent on the (female) statuary.

[130] Gleason 1994: 19. See also Kuttner 1999a: 364–8 (detailed discussion of literary context for the planes).

[131] Prop. 2.32.7–16. On the curatorship, see Coarelli 1971–2: 105 (Atticus); Sauron 1987 (Varro). Key recent studies are Kuttner 1995: 170–4; and 1999a. Zanker's influential reading of Augustus' Forum fits well with a controlled scheme in this earlier complex (1988: 193–5, 210–15). At Pompey's *porticus*, gilt-brocade 'Attalid' drapes kept the sun from important paintings (Prop. 2.32.11–12; Ov. *Ars am.* 3.387). On the statues, see Sauron 1994: 249–314 (at 266–80, a stroll through the colonnade); more generally, see Vermeule 1968.

or posts to support trophies or triumphal icons.[132] This prioritization of Pompey and the East meshed with visual and structural allusion to the suburban landscape – Latium's hills were dotted with temples embraced by groves.[133] Thus Pompey's 'grove' might mediate between politics (Curia) and rustic landscape (the 'mountain' *cauea*) in a completely different way, evoking the nostalgic ideology of Rome's mytho-historical origins as a woodland space under the care of roaming nature deities.[134] This *rus in urbe* quality seems to underscore Kuttner's implication that Pompey's complex kick-started the *topopoesie* that features so strongly in the literature of this era.[135]

At the Villa 'Farnesina', regular (painted) structural features drew the eye along corridor F–G. Here, the combination of trees, columns, and colonnades similarly encouraged a linear reading, but the axial vista's provision, between stone and living columns, of glimpses of colour and moving water served a purpose not unlike that of the 'Farnesina' landscape vignettes into a hyperreal countryside. Snatched, sketchy, or partial views suggest a whole world of interest lurking off-centre, and add a sense of dimensionality and exploratory possibility to an otherwise linear 'access' model focused between civic duty and the 'mountain' glades leading visually towards Venus' temple on its 'outcrop'. Gleason's argument that, rather than having a full-height permanent stone *scaena* (stage building) blocking the visual link between temple and grove, the original Pompeian scheme made use of temporary *scaenae* erected to order for each production, allowing a unified experience that was overwritten when Augustus remodelled the complex with a permanent *scaena* and closed the Curia, is particularly attractive in this context.[136]

This chapter has explored a range of landscapes, from mythic pastoral vignettes, complete with shrines, shepherds, trees, and more

---

[132] Summed up in Haselberger, Romano, and Dumser 2002: 207.

[133] Gleason 1994: 21 and Kuttner 1999a: 347 propose that we see in particular a link with the site and topography of the Fortuna complex built into the hillside at Praeneste (possibly redeveloped after Sulla's sack in 82 BCE; see also Hill 1944; Wallace-Hadrill 2008: 111–16).

[134] Kuttner 1999a: 357–8 proposes that the 'Maro' statue in the *porticus* garden is sited with specific regard to the complex's Curia, so as to evoke the visual and spatial dynamic between the statue of Marsyas and the Curia in the Forum Romanum. In this way, Pompey's garden becomes an alternative Forum.

[135] Venus' centrality to Lucretius' environmental study of human evolution also flickers behind this nexus. Kuttner 1999a: 359–71 follows Pompey's Porticus through the *Greek Anthology* and Martial.

[136] Suet. *Aug.* 31. See Gleason 1994: 24.

urban forms, through to the fantasy power to make seasonal time perform on command in the garden room at Prima Porta and other sites. We have seen how extensive parkland with the space to evoke imaginary Arcadian landscapes could transform Rome's environs into a powerfully charged expression of empire and a space perhaps to let down one's guard and enjoy the alternation of pavilions, fountains, planting, and avenues as a balm against the cut and thrust of city life down the road. Finally, we have looked at a single example of a large-scale formal garden, where the setting and landscape design made no concessions to nature's authority and owed everything to the controlling vision of its originator. Our final stop, at Hadrian's Villa, takes something from each of these kinds of landscape. The painted nature that will have brought life and interest to this villa is gone, but frescoed plantings and landscape scenery will still have helped shape the original relationship between villa and countryside.

AN ENVOI
GETTING (AWAY FROM) IT ALL AT HADRIAN'S VILLA

Powerful Romans were hugely alert to the ways in which landscaped nature, appropriately presented, could enhance their prestige and present them in the most flattering light. Octavian's re-scripting of Pompey's *porticus* garden just before the Battle of Actium shows just how acutely the semiotics of control over nature fed into the public propaganda of the last years before the Augustan Principate. Privately, too, we have seen Roman imperialism and personal iconography filter through the scenography of the Villas 'Farnesina' and *ad Gallinas Albas*. Nero's Domus Aurea, in the mid-first century CE, shows just how politicized the landscaping of nature could become, and how disastrously it could go wrong as viewed through the eyes of disaffected elite commentators such as Pliny the Elder and Tacitus.[1] To conclude, however, we travel east from Rome along the Via Tiburtina to Hadrian's Villa (see Figure 19). This large and complex archaeological site has been extensively analysed: MacDonald and Pinto's vibrant 1995 study should be any visitor's first port of call, followed by Ricotti 2001, which includes study of the gardens and the network of subterranean roads.[2]

Arriving today at Hadrian's villa by (stopping) public bus from Rome gives a sense of the distance this estate offered from the noise and hassle of the city (twenty-eight kilometres – about half a day's ride – west). Recent exhibitions and events in London, California, and Rome, not to mention its appearance (juxtaposed with Mussolini's EUR) in Julie Taymor's film *Titus*, have showcased its contemporary and persistent significance – and popularity.[3] Nevertheless, and despite

---

[1] See Chapter I above; MacDonald 1982: 25–46 introduces the architecture of the Domus Aurea.

[2] Also, De Franceschini 1991 (detailed archaeological study) and 2006 (recent advances); Adembri 2000 (the basic guide, usually on sale on site).

[3] Exhibitions: 'Hadrian: Empire and Conflict', British Museum, London, 24 July–26 October 2008 (Webography: *Hadrian: Empire and Conflict*; print catalogue: Opper 2008; rave review: Boatwright 2009). Colloquium: 'Hadrian's Villa and the California Garden', Stanford University, CA, 5–6 March 2005 (Webography: *Hadrian's Villa and the California Garden*); 'Villa Adriana, paesaggio antico e ambiente moderno', Palazzo Massimo, Rome, 23–24 June 2000 (Reggiani 2002). For general comments on reception, see Watkin 1992: *passim*. On Julie Taymor (dir.), *Titus* (1999), Clear Blue Sky Productions, see Taymor 2000 for production notes (and pp. 58–9 for images), and Theodorakopoulos 2010. Luigi Magni's 1970 comedy *Scipione detto anche l'Africano* also puts the villa to dramatic use.

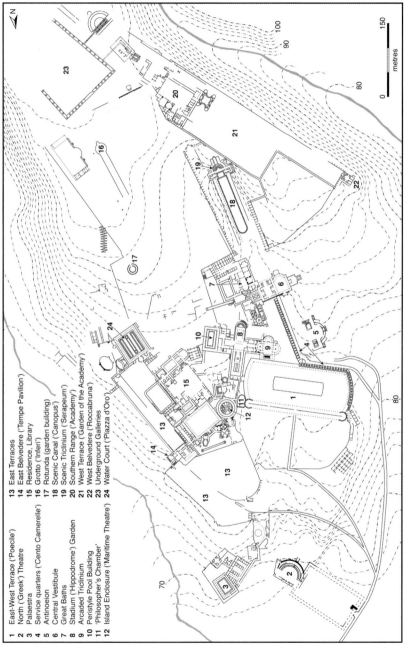

1 East-West Terrace ('Poecile')
2 North ('Greek') Theatre
3 Palaestra
4 Service quarters ('Cento Camerelle')
5 Antinoeion
6 Central Vestibule
7 Great Baths
8 Stadium ('Hippodrome') Garden
9 Arcaded Triclinium
10 Peristyle Pool Building
11 'Philosopher's Chamber'
12 Island Enclosure ('Maritime Theatre')
13 East Terraces
14 East Belvedere ('Tempe Pavilion')
15 Residence, Library
16 Grotto ('Inferi')
17 Rotunda (garden building)
18 Scenic Canal ('Canopus')
19 Scenic Triclinium ('Serapeum')
20 Southern Range ('Academy')
21 West Terrace (Garden of the Academy')
22 West Belvedere ('Roccabruna')
23 Underground Galleries
24 Water Court ('Piazza d'Oro')

Figure 19   Plan of Hadrian's Villa, Tivoli.

the extensive physical remains and its peaceful situation, the sheer
scale and fragmentary nature of the site makes it almost impossible to
understand its organization and to imagine its former appearance. It
is therefore particularly exciting that one spin-off from the Hadrian's
Villa Project is Chiappetta's imagining of different characters' routes
through the villa.[4] If one has not got Chiappetta in hand, or a copy
of Adembri (2000), a conjectural model of the estate in its heyday
(located near the modern entrance) helps.[5] Prefacing one's visit with
a trip to nearby Tivoli for a stroll through the Villas Gregoriana and
d'Este helps to flesh out the ancient villa's potential use of landscape,
and its likely sensory and intellectual qualities.

Forsyth (inspired by a visit to the Renaissance and later villas of
Tivoli, and by his hunt for Cicero's Tusculan villa, at Frascati) indicates
how seductive the relationship with a ruinous villascape such as this
can be:

Modern architecture and made ground are seldom picturesque either in the landscape,
or on canvass [sic]… In landscape we love ruined temples, a Gothic castle, a moss-grown
cell, more than the most elegant ['modern'] villa; because ancient Romans, a feudal
baron, and a hermit, being remote from our own times or manners, are more poetical
beings than a private gentleman or a modern prince. We know what the ['modern'] villa
and its inhabitants are; one glance gives us all, and exhausts the subject. But we must
fancy what a ruin has been; we trace and we lose its design, we rebuild and re-people
it, we call in history, we compose, we animate, we create; and man ever delights in his
own creation.[6]

Influential ancient literary references early on made the running for
this kind of imaginative mapping of Hadrian's estate, including the
description in the anonymous *Historia Augusta*'s life of Hadrian.[7] Here,
we get a seductive glimpse of what happens when an emperor reinvents
the (by the early second century CE) conventional theme-park model
of the luxury villascape. Not just Hellenized with a *Lyceum*, a *Poecile*,
and an *Academy*, we hear that this villa was conceived as a synecdoche
for empire. Like an early Disneyland or Las Vegas, its parts evoked
the provinces of Egypt (Canopus, Figure 20) and Greece (Valley

---

[4] Chiappetta 2008; see Webography: Frischer.

[5] For helpful discussion, site plans, and illustrations, see Webography: De Franceschini;
Ricotti. In print, see e.g. MacDonald and Pinto 1995: 2, fig. 1 (and extensive pull-out plan);
Adembri 2000: 6–7 (reconstruction), 98–9 (layout).

[6] Forsyth 1835: 261–2. See e.g. Christian 2008 for the beginnings of these ideas.

[7] *Hist. Aug.* 26.5 (fourth century CE); MacDonald and Pinto 1995: 6–8 provides a summary
of literary references. More generally, we need to keep the material covered in all previous
chapters in mind.

Figure 20 Hadrian's Villa, Tivoli, 'Canopus' and 'Serapeum' (Scenic Canal and Triclinium features). Note the reconstructed colonnade around the water feature, the Hellenic echoes in the statuary (e.g. Caryatid wannabes), and the scale of the vaulted 'Serapeum'.

of Tempe, Thessaly) on a far larger scale than ever before recorded in a garden feature. Grand official 'palace' buildings (the Central Vestibule, Circular Hall) complemented the more 'domestic' zones and structures, making this estate rival and reconfigure the power previously concentrated in the imperial palace on Rome's Palatine.[8] The hyperreal qualities of an empire available for an afternoon's stroll, and increasingly subject to personal responses and imaginative filling in of the gaps, make for a story that successive visitors have eagerly bought into.

Construction on the estate was in progress from 118–c.135 CE, and the original extent was in the region of 120 hectares (today, typically about 40 hectares are accessible); approximately 900 rooms and ambulatories have so far been counted, but much of the outlying

[8] Also mocked-up, we hear, were the Athenian council building (Prytaneum) and the Euripus (in Hadrian's *Poecile*).

estate has never been excavated and even major central structures lack complete excavation.[9]

Drawing on the *Historia Augusta*'s comment, we find that many sites have traditional identifications with redolent locales. The identifications for most are at best 'likely', with many dating to the time of the villa's rediscovery as a site of antiquarian interest in the sixteenth century.[10] Its named prospects and the densely evocative quality of many of its vistas are thus as much a product of the Renaissance imagination as of substantiated fact: for example, the underground tunnels and grotto identified as Styx, Hades (*Inferi*) or the Elysian Fields, and the Scenic Triclinium with its complex hydraulics (labelled 'Serapeum' to complement the identification of 'Canopus').[11] In addition, many of the standing columns that give such grandeur to the landscaped ruins today were re-erected by the Italian state when part of the site was first purchased in 1870. As further remains were excavated, weather and environmental damage (helped by bombing in 1944) continued to necessitate ongoing repairs. The site's extensive redevelopment to facilitate tourism has made it harder for the ordinary visit to recapture the designed relationships between structures, avenues, and so forth.[12]

The surviving rich decorative programme of art, statuary, colourful inlay, and marble has been extensively documented, but also dispersed to off-site museums, leaving the experience of the Villa today strangely monochrome. No consensus helps understand how coherently programmatic the original art collection and its display was. Indeed find-spots for much of the surviving statuary are insecurely documented. Some mosaics, marble pavements, and walls remain, many restored (an example is in the Arcaded Triclinium). The wealth of stucco decoration is almost entirely long gone (exceptions, for example, in the Great Baths). In addition, much sculpture probably vanished over the years – some taken for its artistic quality, interest (examples abound in the Vatican and Capitoline Museums), or use as material for lime-making. Some simply vanished, with much architectural decor, into the boggy area in the north-west quadrant

---

[9] Opper 2008: 132.

[10] The first identification of the site as Hadrian's Villa followed the visit of Pope Pius II and the humanist and historian Flavio Biondo (1461). Soon after, statue finds plus wider availability of the *Historia Augusta* led to growing interest in mapping the evocatively listed sites.

[11] Using MacDonald and Pinto 1995 for less evocative/speculative toponyms.

[12] On the UNESCO World Heritage List since 1999, the site continues to undergo changes as a result of conservation, facilitating public access, and archaeological work. The 'Doric' Temple, for example, is a work of restoration.

(just off the map, Figure 19). Decorative as well as structural marbles were robbed for reuse in later building programmes.[13] Even so, the chaotic profusion of remains, ongoing excavations, ruins, and greenery give a sense of how much more than just a lavish residence this estate was.[14]

It is initially tempting to find in this villa an analogue for the kind of 'villa-as-city' motif alluded to by Pliny when describing seaside villas, and a feature of invective against the Domus Aurea. After all, the size of the site and scale of its buildings dwarfs Pompeii, and representatively urban structures can be ticked off: baths, theatres, porticoes, avenues and colonnaded walkways, plantings, (possibly) a *palaestra*, fountains, temples, libraries, and public (reception) hall.[15] But in addition we find a grotto, pools, a hippodrome (stadium) garden, banqueting halls and lavish outdoor *triclinia*, extensive open (or unbuilt-up) space and belvederes, as well as a widespread network of underground tunnels, galleries, and service quarters, all recalling elements of the textual villas we visited in Chapter V; moreover, many typical urban features are (so far) missing.[16]

As MacDonald and Pinto comment, only a quarter of the sixty or so buildings are unambiguously identifiable, and the spatial relationship between them – together with the lack of a rectilinear street-grid pattern – makes it unlikely that the original scenography directly mimicked a new 'Roman' town.[17] It is more likely that the mass of buildings and surrounding parkland evoked the idea or symbolic value of Rome as imperial capital – the city whose political functions it partly usurped – and reflected to some extent Hadrian's ambiguous relationship with Rome, a place where he spent relatively little time. This estate allowed him to avoid the city centre by bringing the functions of the city out to Tibur, in the process providing an urban, political gloss to any visit

[13] See Raeder 1983 on the eclectic range of statuary. Piranesi's late eighteenth-century excavations record structures now lost (see his detailed and still hugely useful site plan: *Pianta delle fabbriche esistenti nella Villa Adriana*, 1781, in Pinto 1993, and online at Webography: Catena Digital Archive of Historic Gardens and Landscapes); also the 1751 revised edition of Contini's cartographic visualization of Ligorio's survey (*Pianta della villa tiburtina di Adriano Cesare*), in Ranaldi 2001.

[14] Gizzi 2002; Guarino and Bruno 2002.

[15] Newby 2002 locates the hypothetical *palaestra* behind the 'Greek' Theatre. For itineraries that emphasize this civic aspect, see Chiappetta 2008: 92–3, 126–7.

[16] E.g. no honorific arches, agoras, or shops, no basilicas, forum, senate house, or major official cult temples. See sample itineraries at Chiappetta 2008: 46–7, 70–1. Cf. the shops embedded in the peri-urban 'Farnesina'.

[17] MacDonald and Pinto 1995: 11.

to the estate.[18] Obvious comparisons can be made with the projects of two other philhellenic emperors: Nero's Domus Aurea and Domitian's Alban Villa;[19] but Trajan, too, enjoyed country estates (for example, Centum Cellae), a less awkward precedent.[20] Raeder's discussion of the continuity between villas of the late Republic, through these imperial estates, to Hadrian's Villa provides useful context to follow up.[21]

Topographically, the central area occupied a north–south sloping plateau with stream-filled valleys to north-east and south-west, feeding into the (still navigable) River Anio. All the strictures of situation for an ideal villa seem to be in place – good infrastructure (Via Tiburtina, Anio), a town nearby (Tibur), plentiful water (local streams and proximity to aqueducts en route to Rome from the Anio),[22] a physical situation that made hydraulics – and elaborate water features – relatively straightforward (the sloping plateau), and ample sunlight and cooling winds.[23] These physical features were then enhanced and subtly moulded. The height of the plateau became more dramatic through extensive terracing and the construction of deep substructures which, in conjunction with belvederes, authorized or prioritized particular vistas and caused the whole site to float upon a raised artificial horizon.[24] The villa made a dramatic statement of visual unity in its north-eastern and south-western terraced elevations (one catching the morning, the other the evening sun). These grand façades, particularly monolithic in form to the south-west, stood out as monumental enhancements of the villa's command of the landscape, also hinting that the natural environment supported and endorsed Hadrian's combined personal and public *auctoritas*.

It is difficult to envisage the impact of the range of East Terraces from Tibur's villa-rich heights; visually, planting would have affected how the estate imposed on the view from Tibur and the main access

---

[18] We cannot know how closely involved Hadrian was in the design of the estate, nor how directly it reflected or shaped his personality; see MacDonald and Pinto 1995: 14–23 for a plausible attempt to plug Hadrian into this landscape; Ricotti 2001 attempts a detailed mapping of Hadrian onto the estate. Also useful: Hoffmann 1998; Ghio 2002.

[19] Ball 2004; Newby 2005: 96–105. Cf. Juv. 4 on Domitian's Alban 'court'.

[20] Plin. *Ep.* 6.31.14–15.

[21] Raeder 1983: 287–90.

[22] First the Anio Vetus, later the Aqua Claudia and Anio Nouus.

[23] On the role of water, see MacDonald and Pinto 1995: 170–82; Ricotti 1998.

[24] Compare again with the extensive remodelling of the Palatine plateau in Rome, initiated to some extent by Nero but monumentalized by Domitian (MacDonald 1982: 47–74). That the Villa Adriana (anciently, Villa Tiburtina) was Hadrian's residence while notionally at Rome strengthens the connection. He had a plethora of other suburban villas, e.g. at Antium, Baiae, and Puteoli (where he died).

to the site (from the north, probably gained by road from a turn-off on the Via Tiburtina). The first impression of the estate from the low-lying route across the Campagna from Rome (a little south, but primarily west) highlights the villa's use of topography to enhance the designed qualities of the landscape. The monumental East and West Terraces took full advantage of the two valleys to showcase the scale and boldness of the design; Pember's imaginative reconstruction of Pliny's Laurentina (Figure 8) hints at the effect.[25] The bulk of the west façade of the East–West Terrace – about ninety-five metres wide, and supported by massive substructures (service quarters) – dominated the main access from the north and from the western route from Rome. Rotating about forty-five degrees, the East-West Terrace's long northern Ambulatory Wall confronted those approaching from the plain below and made a massive visual statement to travellers coming from the Via Tiburtina, whether guests (perhaps approaching the central '*Poecile*' entrance), or courtiers or functionaries (heading on towards the political spaces that dominated the villa's eastern range).[26]

This axial rotation means that the villa turns away from the city it replaces, and subtly demonstrates that the visitor is entering a world where Rome's traditional heart is not the primary point of reference. Assuming that the main access route swept across the Anio and the north-eastern valley ('Tempe'), the villa's use of the terrain as scenography may also have collapsed a range of features into one dramatic isovist: a vista taking in the East Terraces' bulk – and amblers enjoying the view (perhaps from the East Belvedere) – as well as, just possibly, the matching West Belvedere ('Roccabruna'). This was despite the density of buildings in the north-west quadrant of the site and the distance involved: as the crow flies, from the North ('Greek') Theatre it is nearly one and a half kilometres to the West Belvedere.

We can compare the contrastingly dialogic gaze between Rome and the Villa d'Este at nearby Tivoli (see Figure 21) to get a sense of the difference that orientation makes. Working for Cardinal Ippolito II d'Este, Pirro Ligorio took marble and ideas from Hadrian's Villa to create a hugely influential and symbolic fantasy landscape. He used Tivoli's natural cliffs to fashion panoramic and densely decorated

---

[25] At around 300 metres, the range of East and West Terraces is astounding. The West ('Academy Gardens') range becomes more human in scope with the Southern ('Academy') Range.

[26] Identified by Pirro Ligorio – excavating during the 1550s and 1560s – as the *Poecile* (i.e. evoking the Painted Stoa in Athens, where the philosopher Zeno once taught) and *c.*230 metres long. See Ligorio 1723: *passim*.

Figure 21 Tivoli, view towards Rome from the Villa d'Este. Note that the dome of St Peter's is visible on the skyline.

outdoor terraces and promenades, to embed faux-natural grottoes and formal and informal pools, and to showcase a bewildering array of fountains.[27] The 'Rometta' famously recreated Rome as a lower-terrace topographic water feature – the real city shimmers on the horizon behind the hyperreal version within which guests and owner could play at mastery of space and politics.[28] Now sadly incomplete, the scope and complexity of Ligorio's original vision (displayed in Giovanni Francesco Venturini's 1691 engraving) surely echoed in miniature the reinvented political villa created by Hadrian.

Despite these conjectures and comparisons, on the ground the site continues to tease visitors and to offer few satisfactory way-finding strategies. It is simultaneously too full of features and too lacking in three-dimensional coherence. Even the hypothetical itineraries proposed by Chiappetta (2008) are only presented as two-dimensional skeleton plans, which do not capture the complexity of interpretative challenges facing us today. Tall cypresses give some hints of the lush greenery that the sophisticated hydraulics must have helped to soften

[27] Coffin 1960, 2004: 83–105; Dernie 1996. In brief, see Nys 2000.
[28] Madonna 1991; Dernie 1997.

the plateau, setting off the sparkling white and, closer to, colourful marble walls and pavements (cf. Figure 9). Aurally, too, the site bears little relationship to its probable ancient design – the multiplicity of natural and artificial water courses and fountains must have made a delightful impact after a dusty ride or trip in an uncomfortable carriage, while the villa's height, from the plain, would have promised the murmur of refreshing breezes, rustling the plantings designed to soothe eyes and ears alike.[29] Greenery may have softened some of the potentially domineering monumentality, uniting built and natural environments in one designed, harmonious landscape.

Much of the impact of the relational qualities between spaces and structures is lost and has not yet been fully understood, and modern authorized itineraries offer no sense of how the original axial routes, avenues, and paths mediated between landscape and visitor, and perhaps also scripted the kind of visit available to different classes of visitor. As we have seen, a key villa activity was the philosophically engaged stroll, but today no traces of this activity can be mapped. Zones that now seem visually or spatially connected may have been designed as structurally and experientially separate.[30] Examples of 'lost' views might include one from the West Terrace across the 'Canopus', or from the East–West Terrace into the 'Stadium' Garden. We get no sense of the sensory delights or intellectual interest offered by a stroll to one of the Belvederes and, while the relationship between the Peristyle Pool Building, 'Stadium' Garden, and East–West Terrace seems structurally cluttered today, it must have originally made for interesting sightline patterns and provided an important sense of diminution in scale between the roofs of the first and last structures. The relationship between the upper park (not as now a fairly barren expanse with little to detain the eye, but complete with rotunda and grotto and, we must imagine, lush planting, statuary, and other landscape structures) and the 'Canopus' in its mini-valley (Figure 20) would once have been dialogic and complementary rather than mutually incomprehensible.

---

[29] Recall Vitruvius' comment that appropriate greenery has a physically beneficial effect on the eyes (5.9.5). Compare the dense greenery of frescoed plantings discussed above (Chapter VI), but also the importance of natural features more generally in painted and literary scenography. Ligorio's nearby Villa d'Este offers a useful analogue in terms of colour, shade, prospects, complexity, and sound (though on a comparatively minute scale). The Virtual Villa of Livia (Webography: *The Virtual Museum of the Ancient Via Flaminia*) suggests a sense of how elevation impacted on a villa's relationship with its approaches.

[30] For a general overview (urban morphology), see MacDonald 1986: 32–110; on Hadrian's Villa, see MacDonald and Pinto 1995: 78–138 (and *passim*). Jashemski and Ricotti 1992 discuss archaeological case studies.

Additional aspects that fail to cross over into a modern visit include the important relationship between sun and shade (outdoors, but also in the covered porticoes), the depth of shadow and quality of light at different times of day, the breeziness or stillness of particular avenues and configurations of outdoor space, and the physical difference between dusty grit (the main surface underfoot today) and the range of potential original paved and natural surfaces and terrains. All of these alter our perception of the villa as a meaningful space, and make the modern visitor's experience of a tour worlds apart from that of a guest, a visiting official, or a member of the imperial family in Hadrian's day. Its confusing, ruinous, but also often iconic topography shifts us unsettlingly between 'known' and 'unknowable' perceptual nodes. On my last visit – a baking-hot, thundery, and airless day – I lingered interminably, frustrated at the incomprehensible structures and blank spaces, willing them to come into focus (known, recognized sites, yet implacable to understanding), and tiredly zipped through the more immediately charming and iconic 'Canopus', shady 'Serapeum' (Scenic Canal and Triclinium), and 'Maritime Theatre' features.[31]

Missing too, of course, are the marble and flesh-and-blood figures who populated this landscape.[32] We speculated – discussing the Horti Sallustiani – on how a programme of statuary could script or at least endorse a series of possible itineraries through an estate. Hadrian's Tiburtine villa must similarly have made use of its valleys to create tempting stories amid which to ramble, and even to act out fantasies. As so often, and in common with so many sites extensively admired in previous centuries, working out who and what the villa's marble and bronze inhabitants were, and how they related to each other, eludes us.[33] We can only observe that the density of outdoor sculpture, while

[31] In a complex and agenda-setting study, Porteous 1990 explores how memory, sensory experience (including smell), imagination, ethics, and sense of self combine to generate individual and emotionally charted 'experiences' of place.

[32] It is not just Hadrian, his family, guests, and functionaries whose silence haunts this landscape. The physical effort and management of this estate (like others) was based on slave labour – voices mostly overlooked when enjoying a few days in the country; on daily life at the villa, see MacDonald and Pinto 1995: 183–97.

[33] Famous examples of the villa's silent inhabitants are two black marble centaurs (from Aphrodisias) and an extensively restored red marble faun (famous from Nathaniel Hawthorne's 1860 novel *The Marble Faun*), both in Rome's Musei Capitolini; and Egyptian and Egyptianizing statues (displayed to emphasize a connection with the Villa's 'Canopus'), in the Vatican Museums. Others include Graeco-Roman favourites such as Dionysus, Mercury, Apollo, Athena, Diana, Venus, Mars, Atalanta, Hercules, Fortuna, Muses, Amazons, Sileni, nymphs, caryatids, athletes, and gladiators. Images of Hadrian, Antinous (posthumously), and the imperial family also shared the estate with their flesh-and-blood counterparts, along with an array of marble beasts. See MacDonald and Pinto 1995: 141–51.

hard to gauge, is likely to have been at least in line with the kind of sculptural dispositions noted by Cicero when hunting for art.[34]

By the second century CE, art 'factories' in Athens, Alexandria, and Aphrodisias were producing often outstanding copies but also original pieces to satisfy increasingly demanding and sophisticated consumers keen to acquire the cachet of being a collector. 'Antiquities' also seem still to have been coming onto the market, and Hadrian's well-documented admiration for all things Greek must have made for an intensification in trade and production – following imperial fashion.[35] Stylistically, there must have been variability in quality, but semiotically the number, disposition, and eclectic subject matter of the statuary must have heightened the sense that this estate represented Hadrian's vision of the empire in microcosm.[36]

Conclusions, and looking ahead

Starting with thematic explorations of landscape, this *Survey* dug into how and why the natural world meant something more than food and drink, or a charming scene, in ancient Rome, and also questioned whether it figured in the development of a quintessential Roman mindset. A range of theoretical and methodological approaches opened up some of the problems and delights that we face when trying to understand how nature mattered urgently – aesthetically, productively, financially, philosophically – at a time when Rome was becoming a major Mediterranean power. Investigating Latin literary landscapes and setting them in context helps to sketch out what Romans thought (or wanted their friends, enemies, and rivals to think they thought) about the world they inhabited; but we always read within the constraints of our remove from a society whose vocabulary, syntax, *mores*, and values are two millennia from ours. We then turned to a set of significant images and sites, moving from muted pastoral

---

[34] E.g. Cic. *Att.* 1.1.5, 1.4.3, 1.8.2, 1.9.2, 1.10.3, 1.16.15, 13.40, 15.9; *Fam.* 7.23; *Leg.* 2.2, 6, 7, 3.13. Cicero knows that statuary transforms what surrounds it. See also Raeder 1983: 287–9; Leen 1991; Neudecker 1998; Narducci 2003. As noted in Chapter 5, Pliny's villas (as described) are remarkable for the absence of marble and statuary.

[35] For Hadrian as trendsetter, see Zanker 1996: 198–266 (contextualizing discussion).

[36] Surviving and identified statuary (Raeder 1983: 205–42) is short on 'state' or 'official' imagery; if so, this suggests that the villa reflected a strikingly individual perspective on state and empire alike.

corridor frescoes, through the immersive painted garden-room style, to the real gardens and parks of Rome's environs.

Drawing on what ancient authors wrote about the environment adds meaning to these physical sights and spaces. Nevertheless, despite our access to literary texts, the role of the ancient landscape as a kind of autobiographical statement, filled with the murmur of conversation, laughter, music, and footsteps, and coloured by the emblematic role of labour, is elusive.[37] Roman landscapes are always subordinated to human interest and ingenuity (artistic or practical) and, in the end, this fleeting human quality and the interpretative gap that keeps us guessing about what real and depicted Roman landscapes meant to their original audiences are what makes their richness so hard to recapture. Like Forsyth (quoted above) we can think ourselves onto Columella's farm, and we can still stroll along Hadrian's terraces, but we struggle to make a direct connection with the daily reality of Roman landscape's autocratic, numinous, and ideational meaning, and we fill in the gaps with our own concerns. Whether walking physically across these ancient spaces or traversing them in the mind's eye, we enrich them as 'realandimagined' sites. The place of the observer is never straightforwardly resolvable as simply a position in space.[38] Space, too, we have seen, is experienced subjectively and through personal, cultural, social, and historical filters. Every space has its own uniquely nuanced vocabulary and syntax, and no two observers will accentuate it identically.

Nevertheless this *Survey*'s case studies do leave us with an identifiable and culturally significant Roman interest in how 'landscape' tells on the figures who designed, described, and inhabited it. This fascination with the scenic backdrop and its affective qualities coloured all aspects of elite Roman life – and was central to the murky world of countless agricultural slaves who worked to make the countryside and parklands fit the ideal. Individual responses and patterns of movement relating to specific sites and descriptions may be irrecoverable, and day-to-day experience of landscape for most citizens is lost, but as we have seen – even when farming is ostensibly the focus – depicted and textualized ethnoscapes were typically designed to produce or stimulate particular kinds of physical and intellectual activity, or sensory response. The

---

[37] Hadrian's Villa demonstrates the disappearance of the 'service' aspects of a villascape. See Chiappetta 2008: 158–9 (the subterranean service routes); compare, for example, Calke Abbey, Derbyshire, UK.

[38] Royo and Gruet 2008: 391.

contemporary Green agenda and anxiety about climate change give us a chance to re-engage with concerns that ancient Romans might have understood as integral to a meaningful interest in landscape: how to cohabit harmoniously with capricious *Natura*, how to benefit sustainably from the environment, and how to place humankind productively within a complexly interconnected universe.[39] We may not always fully understand the resonances, but we can see the kinds of issue that crop up frequently enough to develop an interpretative pattern.

Underpinning ancient interest in landscape was its role as a signal that nature was on one's side, and this typically meant more than simply good farming practice and putting food on the plate. At Rome in particular, defining the environment and mapping one's place within it, metaphorically or literally, was part of a more-or-less explicit and ongoing process of self-fashioning articulated by wealthy, ambitious, and educated citizens, a process which trickled down through the practice of daily life, colouring non-elite Romans' experience of their collective role in history and place in the cosmos. This book hopes to encourage further reflection on how understanding Roman identity went hand in hand with exploring, inhabiting, and cultivating the landscape in the widest possible sense. Landscape, we may eventually conclude, matters, in interesting and sometimes surprising ways, and constantly encourages viewers, readers, and passers-through to explore farther on and further in.

---

[39] The most influential modern discussion of how and why viewing the countryside as a site of Golden Age nostalgia is a politicized act is R. Williams 1973. Surveying the environmental agenda, see e.g. Bignell 2009; Danvers 2009.

BIBLIOGRAPHY

Ackerman, J. S. 1990. *The Villa. Form and Ideology of Country Houses*. London, Thames and Hudson.

Adams, G. W. 2006. *The Suburban Villas of Campania and their Social Function*. BAR International Series 1542. Oxford, Archaeopress.

—— 2008. *Rome and the Social Role of Élite Villas in its Suburbs*. BAR International Series 1760. Oxford, Archaeopress.

Adembri, B. 2000, *Hadrian's Villa. Guide*. Translated by E. De Sena. Milan, Electa.

Agache, S. 1987. 'L'actualité de la Villa Publica en 55–54 av. J.-C.', in Pietri 1987: 211–34.

—— 2008. 'La villa comme image de soi (Rome antique, des origines à la fin de la République', in Galand-Hallyn 2008: 15–44.

Alcock, S. E. 1993. *Graecia Capta. The Landscapes of Roman Greece*. Cambridge, Cambridge University Press.

—— 2002. *Archaeologies of the Greek Past. Landscape, Monuments, and Memories*. Cambridge, Cambridge University Press.

—— 2007. 'The Essential Countryside: The Greek World', in Alcock and Osborne 2007: 120–38.

——, Cherry, J. F., and Davis, J. L. 1994. 'Intensive Survey, Agricultural Practice and the Classical Landscape of Greece', in I. Morris (ed.), *Classical Greece. Ancient Histories and Modern Archaeologies*. Cambridge, Cambridge University Press: 137–70.

—— and Osborne, R. (eds.) 2007. *Classical Archaeology*. Malden, MA, Blackwell.

Alden Smith, R. 2005. *The Primacy of Vision in Virgil's Aeneid*. Austin, TX, University of Texas Press.

Allison, P. M. 1992. 'The Relationship Between Wall-decoration and Room-type in Pompeian Houses: A Case Study of the Casa della Caccia Antica', *JRA* 5: 235–49.

Alpers, P. 1979. *The Singer of the Eclogues. A Study of Virgilian Pastoral*. Berkeley, CA, University of California Press.

—— 1996. *What is Pastoral?* Chicago, IL, University of Chicago Press.

Anderson, B. 2006. *Imagined Communities. Reflections on the Origin and Spread of Nationalism*. Second revised edition, London, Verso.

Anderson, M. L. 1987. *Pompeiian Frescoes in the Metropolitan Museum of Art*. New York, Metropolitan Museum of Art.

Ando, C. 2002. 'Vergil's Italy: Ethnography and Politics in First-century Rome', in D. S. Levene and D. Nelis (eds.), *Clio and the Poets. Augustan Poetry and the Traditions of Ancient Historiography*. Leiden, Brill: 123–42.

Andreae, B. 1996. *Am Birnbaum . Gärten und Parks im antiken Rom in den Vesuvstädten und in Ostia*. Mainz, Philipp von Zabern.

Andrews, M. 1999. *Landscape and Western Art*. Oxford, Oxford University Press.

Anschuetz, K. F., Wilshusen, R. H., and Scheick, C. L. 2001. 'An Archaeology of Landscapes: Perspectives and Directions', *Journal of Archaeological Research* 9: 157–211.

Argenio, R. 1970. 'La villa sorrentina di Pollio Felice (C. Papinii Statii *Silvarum* liber II,2)', *Rivista di Studi Classici* 18: 186–95.

Armstrong, D., Fish, J., Johnston, P. A., and Skinner, M. B. (eds.) 2004. *Vergil, Philodemus, and the Augustans.* Austin, TX, University of Texas Press.

Arnold, D. 2008. '(Auto)biographies and Space', in D. Arnold and J. R. Sofaer (eds.), *Biographies and Space. Placing the Subject in Art and Architecture.* London, Routledge: 6–16.

Ashcroft, B., Griffiths, G., and Tiffin, H. 2002. *The Empire Writes Back. Theory and Practice in Post-colonial Literatures.* Second edition, London, Routledge.

Assmann, J. 1995. 'Collective Memory and Cultural Identity', translated by J. Czaplicka, *New German Critique* 65: 125–33.

――― 2006. *Religion and Cultural Memory.* Translated by R. Livingstone. Stanford, CA, Stanford University Press.

Attema, P. 1996. 'Inside and Outside the Landscape: Perceptions of the Pontine Region', *Archaeological Dialogues* 3: 176–95.

――― 2005. 'Early Urbanization between 800 and 600 BC in the Pontine Region (South Lazio), the Salento Isthmus (Apulia), and the Sibaritide (Northern Calabria)', in R. Osborne and B. Cunliffe (eds.), *Mediterranean Urbanization 800–600 BC.* Proceedings of the British Academy 126. Oxford, Oxford University Press: 113–42.

Augé, M. 1995. *Non-Places. Introduction to an Anthropology of Supermodernity.* Translated by J. Howe. London, Verso.

Azara, P. 2008. 'Landscape: Live Nature. Towards the Construction of the Image of the Landscape in the West', in G. Maciocco (ed.), *Urban Landscape Perspectives.* Berlin, Springer: 43–60.

Bachelard, G. 1994. *The Poetics of Space.* Translated by M. Jolas. Second English edition, Boston, MA, Beacon.

Bahn, P. 1996. *Archaeology. A Very Short Introduction.* Oxford, Oxford University Press.

Bal, M. 1985. *Narratology. Introduction to the Theory of Narrative.* Toronto, University of Toronto Press.

Ball, L. F. 1994. 'A Reappraisal of Nero's *Domus Aurea*', in L. La Follette, C. Pavolini, M.-A. Tomei, et al. *Rome Papers. The Baths of Trajan Decius, Iside e Serapide nel Palazzo, a late Domus on the Palatine and Nero's Golden House. JRA* Supplement 11. Portsmouth, RI, Journal of Roman Archaeology: 183–254.

――― 2004. *The Domus Aurea and the Roman Architectural Revolution.* Cambridge, Cambridge University Press.

Bannon, C. J. 2009. *Gardens and Neighbors. Private Water Rights in Roman Italy.* Ann Arbor, MI, University of Michigan Press.

Barker, G. W. and Lloyd, J. (eds.) 1991. *Roman Landscapes. Archaeological Survey in the Mediterranean Region.* London, British School at Rome.

Barnes, T. J. and Duncan, J. S. (eds.) 1992. *Writing Worlds.* London, Routledge.

Barnett, R. 2007. 'Sacred Groves: Sacrifice and the Order of Nature in Ancient Greek Landscapes', *Landscape Journal* 26: 252–69.

Baroin, C. 1998. 'La maison romaine comme image et lieu de mémoire', in C. Auvray-Assayas (ed.), *Images romaines*. Études de Littérature Ancienne 9. Paris, Presses de L'École Normale Supérieure: 177–91.

Barthes, R. 1967. *Elements of Semiology*. Translated by A. Lavers and C. Smith. London, Jonathan Cape.

——— 1986. 'The Reality Effect', in *The Rustle of Language*. Translated by R. Howard. New York, Hill and Wang: 141–8.

——— 1993. *Mythologies*. Translated by A. Lavers. London, Vintage.

Bartman, E. 1991. 'Sculptural Collecting and Display in the Private Realm', in Gazda 1991: 71–88.

Batstone, W. 1997. 'Virgilian Didaxis: Value and Meaning in the *Georgics*', in Martindale 1997a: 125–44.

Baumann, H. 1993. *The Greek Plant World in Myth, Art and Literature*. Translated and augmented by W. T. Stearn and E. R. Stearn. Portland, OR, Timber.

Beagon, M. 1992. *Roman Nature. The Thought of Pliny the Elder*. Oxford, Clarendon Press.

Beard, M. 1987. ' A Complex of Times: No More Sheep on Romulus' Birthday', *PCPhS* 33: 1–15.

——— 1998. 'Imaginary *Horti*: Or up the Garden Path', in Cima and La Rocca 1998: 23–32.

——— and Henderson, J. 2001. *Classical Art. From Greece to Rome*. Oxford, Oxford University Press.

——— , North, J., and Price, S. 1998. *Religions of Rome. Volume I: A History*. 2 vols, Cambridge, Cambridge University Press.

Beckley, B. (ed.) 2001. *Sticky Sublime*. New York, Allworth.

Bek, L. 1980. *Towards Paradise on Earth. Modern Space Conception in Architecture – A Creation of Renaissance Humanism*. Analecta Romana Instituti Danici 9. Odense, Odense University Press.

Bender, B. (ed.) 1993. *Landscape. Politics and Perspectives*. Oxford, Berg.

Benjamin, W. 1999. *Illuminations*. Edited by H. Arendt and translated by H. Zohn. London, Pimlico.

Bennett, J. 2002. *Thoreau's Nature. Ethics, Politics and the Wild*. Second edition, Lanham, MD, Rowman & Littlefield.

Bérard, C. and Bron, C. 1986. 'Bacchos au coeur de la cité: le thiase dionysiaque dans l'espace politique', in *L'association dionysiaque dans les sociétés anciennes*. Rome, L'École Française de Rome: 13–27.

Berger, J. 1972. *Ways of Seeing*. London, BBC, and Harmondsworth, Penguin.

Bergmann, B. 1991. 'Painted Perspectives of a Villa Visit: Landscape as Status and Metaphor', in Gazda 1991: 49–70.

——— 1992. 'Exploring the Grove: Pastoral Space on Roman Walls', in Hunt 1992b: 21–46.

——— 1994. 'The Roman House as Memory Theatre: The House of the Tragic Poet in Pompeii', *ABull* 76: 225–56.

——— 1995a. 'Greek Masterpieces and Roman Recreative Fictions', *HSPh* 97: 79–120.

——— 1995b. 'Visualizing Pliny's Villas', *JRA* 8: 406–20.

——— 1999. 'Rhythms of Recognition: Mythical Encounters in the Roman Landscape', in F. de Angelis and S. Muth (eds.), *Im Spiegel des Mythos. Bilderwelt und Lebenswelt*. Wiesbaden, L. Reichert: 81–107.

——— 2002. 'Art and Nature in the Villa at Oplontis', in T. McGinn, P. Carafa, N. de Grummond, B. Bergmann, and T. Najbjerg (eds.), *Pompeian Brothels, Pompeii's Ancient History, Mirrors and Mysteries, Art and Nature at Oplontis, and the Herculaneum 'Basilica'*. *JRA* Supplement 47. Portsmouth, RI, Journal of Roman Archaeology: 87–120.

——— 2007. 'Housing and Households: The Roman World', in Alcock and Osborne 2007: 224–43.

——— 2008. 'Staging the Supernatural: Interior Gardens of Pompeian Houses', in Mattusch 2008: 53–69.

Berns, G. 1976. 'Time and Nature in Lucretius' *De Rerum Natura*', *Hermes* 104: 477–92.

Beyen, H. G. 1948. 'Les domini de la Villa de la Farnésine', in *Studia varia Carolo Guiliemo Vollgraf a discipulis oblata*. Amsterdam, North Holland: 3–21.

Bhabha, H. K. 1990a. 'Introduction: Narrating the Nation', in Bhabha 1990b: 1–7.

——— (ed.) 1990b. *Nation and Narration*. London, Routledge.

——— 1994. *The Location of Culture*. London, Routledge.

Bignell, B. 2009. 'Beauty as a Way of Knowing: The Redemption of Knowing through the Experience of Beauty', in Stibbe 2009: 191–7.

Bilde, P. G. 2005. 'The Roman Villa by Lake Nemi: From Nature to Culture – Between Private and Public', in Santillo Frizell and Klynne 2005.

Birksted, J. (ed.) 2000. *Landscapes of Memory and Experience*. London, Spon.

Bjur, H. and Santillo Frizell, B. (eds.) 2009. *Via Tiburtina. Space, Movement and Artefacts in the Urban Landscape*. Rome, Swedish Institute in Rome.

Bloomer, W. M. 1997. *Latinity and Literary Society at Rome*. Philadelphia, PA, University of Pennsylvania Press.

Blum, H. 1969. *Die Antike Mnemotechnik*. Hildesheim, Georg Olms.

Boatwright, M. T. 1998. 'Luxuriant Gardens and Extravagant Women: The *Horti* of Rome between Republic and Empire', in Cima and La Rocca 1998: 71–82.

——— 2009. 'Hadrian in London', *AJA* 113: 121–8.

Bodel, J. 1994. *Graveyards and Groves. A Study of the Lex Lucerina*. Special issue *AJAH* 11.

——— 1997. 'Monumental villas and villa monuments', *JRA* 10: 5–35.

Bradley, G., Isayev, E., and Riva, C. (eds.) 2007. *Ancient Italy. Regions without Borders*. Exeter, University of Exeter Press.

Bragantini, I. 1998a. 'Ambulacro F–G', in Di Mino 1998: 114–23.

——— 1998b. 'Le Decorazioni', in Di Mino 1998: 15–22.

——— and de Vos, M. (eds.) 1982. *Museo Nazionale Romano, le pitture II,1. Le decorazione della Villa Romana della Farnesina*. Rome, De Luca.

Braund, D. and Gill, C. (eds.) 2003. *Myth, History and Culture in Republican Rome. Studies in Honour of T. P. Wiseman*. Exeter, University of Exeter Press.

Braund, S. H. 1989. 'City and Country in Roman Satire', in S. H. Braund (ed.), *Satire and Society in Ancient Rome*. Exeter, University of Exeter Press: 23–47.

Breed, B. W. 2006. *Pastoral Inscriptions. Reading and Writing Virgil's* Eclogues. London, Duckworth.

Bremmer, J. N. 2004. *Greek Religion*, Greece & Rome New Surveys in the Classics 24. Oxford, Oxford University Press.

Brennan, T. 1990. 'The National Longing for Form', in Bhabha 1990b: 44–70.

Briant, P. 2002. *From Cyrus to Alexander. A History of the Persian Empire.* Translated by P. T. Daniels. Winona Lake, IN, Eisenbraun.

Brilliant, R. 1975. Review of A. Alföldi, *Die Zwei Lorbeerbäume des Augustus* (Bonn, 1973), *AJA* 79: 392–3.

Brockmeier, J. 2002. 'Remembering and Forgetting: Narrative as Cultural Memory', *Culture & Psychology* 8: 15–43.

Broise, H. and Jolivet, V. 1987. 'Recherches sur les Jardins de Lucullus', in Pietri 1987: 747–61.

——— 1996. 'Horti Lucullani', in *LTUR*, iii.67–70.

——— 1999. 'Horti Lucullani', in *LTUR*, iv.265–7.

Bruhl, A. 1953. *Liber Pater. Origine et expansion du culte dionysiaque à Rome et dans le monde romain.* Bibliothèque des Écoles Françaises d'Athènes et de Rome 175. Paris, Bibliothèque des Écoles Française D'Athènes et de Rome.

Brunt, P. A. 1965a. '*Amicitia* in the Late Roman Republic', *PCPhS* 2: 1–20.

——— 1965b. 'Italian Aims at the Time of the Social War', *JRS* 55: 90–109.

Budd, M. 2002. *The Aesthetic Appreciation of Nature.* Oxford, Oxford University Press.

Bugh, G. R. (ed.) 2006. *The Cambridge Companion to the Hellenistic World.* Cambridge, Cambridge University Press.

Burgin, V. 1996. *In/different Spaces. Place and Memory in Visual Culture.* Berkeley, CA, University of California Press.

Burkert, W. 1985. *Greek Religion. Archaic and Classical.* Translated by J. Raffan. Oxford, Blackwell.

Campbell, B. 2000. *The Writings of the Roman Land Surveyors. Introduction, Text, Translation, and Commentary.* London, Society for the Promotion of Roman Studies.

Cancik, H. 1968. 'Eine epikureische Villa: Statius, *Silv.* II 2: Villa Surrentina', *AU* 11: 62–75.

——— 1985–6. 'Rome as a Sacred Landscape: Varro and the End of Republican Religion in Rome', *VRel* 4/5: 250–63.

Caneva, G and Bohuny, L. 2003. 'Botanic Analysis of Livia's Painted Flora (Prima Porta, Roma)', *Journal of Cultural Heritage* 4: 149–55.

Canter, H. V. 1939. 'Praise of Italy in Classical Authors II', *CJ* 34: 396–409.

Carandini, A. 1985. *Settefinestre. Una villa schiavistica nell'Etruria romana.* 3 vols, Modena, Panini.

——— 2007. *Roma. Il primo giorno.* Rome, Laterza.

Carey, S. 2002. 'A Tradition of Adventures in the Imperial Grotto', *G&R* 49: 44–61.

Carpano, C. M. 2000. 'Gli Horti Sallustiani', in V. Moretti (ed.), *Il recupero dell'Aula Adrianea degli Horti Sallustiani.* Rome, Arti Grafiche La Moderna: 19–24.

Carrara, M. 2005. 'La villa di Livia a Prima Porta da *praedium suburbanum* a *villa Caesarum*', in Santillo Frizell and Klynne 2005.

Carroll, L. 2007. *Through the Looking Glass, and What Alice Found There.* Facsimile reprint of the 1872 edition, Rockville, MD, Wildside.

Carroll, M. 1992. 'The Gardens of Greece from Homeric to Roman Times', *Journal of Garden History* 12: 84–101.

—— 2003. *Earthly Paradises. Ancient Gardens in History and Archaeology*. London, British Museum Press.

Casey, E. S. 1993. *Getting Back into Place. Toward a Renewed Understanding of the Place-World*. Bloomington, IN, Indiana University Press.

—— 2000. *Remembering. A Phenomenological Study*. Second edition, Bloomington, IN, Indiana University Press.

—— 2001. 'Between Geography and Philosophy: What Does It Mean to Be in the Place-World?', *Annals of the Association of American Geographers* 91: 683–93.

Castriota, D. 1995. *The Ara Pacis Augustae and the Imagery of Abundance in Later Greek and Early Roman Imperial Art*. Princeton, NJ, Princeton University Press.

Chambers, I. 1994. *Migrancy, Culture, Identity*. Abingdon, Routledge.

Chandler, D. 2007. *Semiotics. The Basics*. Second edition, London, Routledge.

Chard, C. 1999. *Pleasure and Guilt on the Grand Tour. Travel Writing and Imaginative Geography, 1600–1830*. Manchester, Manchester University Press.

Charlesworth, M. 2003. 'Movement, Intersubjectivity, and Mercantile Morality at Stourhead', in Conan 2003a: 264–85.

Chiappetta, F. 2008. *I percorsi antichi di Villa Adriana*. Rome, Quasar.

Chinn, C. M. 2007. 'Before Your Very Eyes: Pliny *Epistulae* 5.6 and the Ancient Theory of Ekphrasis', *CPh* 102: 265–80.

Christian, K. 2008. 'Landscapes of Ruin and the Imagination in the Antiquarian Gardens of Renaissance Rome', in M. Conan (ed.), *Gardens and Imagination. Cultural History and Agency*. Washington, DC, Dumbarton Oaks Research Library: 117–37.

Cima, M. 1986. 'Dagli scavi dell'Esquilino all'interpretazione dei monumenti', in Cima and La Rocca 1986: 37–52.

—— 1996. 'Horti Lamiani', in *LTUR*, iii.61–4.

—— and La Rocca, E. (eds.) 1986. *Le tranquille dimore degli dei. La residenza imperiale degli Horti Lamiani*. Venice, Cataloghi Marsilio.

—— —— (eds.) 1998. *Horti romani. Atti del Convegno Internazionale, Roma, 4–6 Maggio 1995*. Rome, L'Erma di Bretschneider.

—— and Talamo, E. 2008. *Gli horti di Roma antica*. Milan, Electa.

Claridge, A. 1997–8. 'The Villas of the Laurentine Shore', *RPAA* 70: 307–17.

Clarke, J. R. 1991. *The Houses of Roman Italy, 100 B.C.–A.D. 250. Ritual, Space, and Decoration*. Berkeley, CA, University of California Press.

—— 1996. 'Landscape Paintings in the Villa of Oplontis', *JRA* 9: 81–107.

—— 2005. 'Roman Domestic Interiors: Propaganda or Fashion?', in Galinsky 2005: 264–78.

Clarke, M. L. 1973. 'The Garden of Epicurus', *Phoenix* 27: 386–7.

Clay, D. 2009. 'The Athenian Garden', in J. Warren, (ed.), *The Cambridge Companion to Epicureanism*. Cambridge, Cambridge University Press: 9–28.

Clay, J. S. 1981. 'The Old Man in the Garden: *Georgics* 4.116–148', *Arethusa* 14: 57–65.

Clifford, J. 1997. *Routes. Travel and Translation in the Late Twentieth Century*. Cambridge, MA, Harvard University Press.

Coarelli, F. 1971–2. 'Il complesso pompeiano del Campo Marzio e la sua decorazione scultorea', *RPAA* 44: 99–122.

—— 1996. 'Horti Caesaris (ad Portam Collinam)', in *LTUR*, iii.55.

Coffin, D. R. 1960. *The Villa d'Este at Tivoli*. Princeton, NJ, Princeton University Press.

—— 2004. *Pirro Ligorio. The Renaissance Artist, Architect, and Antiquarian*. University Park, PA, Pennsylvania State University Press.

Cole, S. G. 2004. *Landscapes, Gender, and Ritual Space. The Ancient Greek Experience*. Berkeley, CA, University of California Press.

Coleman, K. M. 1986. 'The Emperor Domitian and Literature', in *ANRW*, ii.32.5: 3087–115.

—— 1988. *Statius*. Silvae *IV*. Oxford, Clarendon Press.

—— 1990. 'Fatal Charades: Roman Executions Staged as Mythological Enactments', *JRS* 80: 44–73.

Conan, M. 1986. 'Nature into Art: Gardens and Landscapes in the Everyday Life of Ancient Rome', *Journal of Garden History* 4: 348–56.

—— (ed.) 2003a. *Landscape Design and the Experience of Motion*. Dumbarton Oaks Colloquium on the History of Landscape Architecture 24. Washington, DC, Dumbarton Oaks Research Library.

—— 2003b. 'Landscape Metaphors and Metamorphosis of Time', in Conan 2003a: 288–317.

—— (ed.) 2007. *Middle East Garden Traditions. Unity and Diversity. Questions, Methods and Resources in a Multicultural Perspective*. Washington, DC, Dumbarton Oaks Research Library.

Cooper, D. E. 2006. *A Philosophy of Gardens*. Oxford, Oxford University Press.

Corbeill, A. 2002. 'Political Movement: Walking and Ideology in Republican Rome', in Fredrick 2002: 182–215.

Cornell, T. J. 1996. 'Hannibal's Legacy: The Effects of the Hannibalic War on Italy', in T. Cornell, B. Rankov, and P. Sabin (eds.), *The Second Punic War. A Reappraisal*. BICS Supplement 67. London, Institute of Classical Studies: 97–117.

—— and Lomas, K. (eds.) 1995. *Urban Society in Roman Italy*. London, UCL Press.

Cosgrove, D. E. 1998. *Social Formation and Symbolic Landscape*. Second edition, Madison, WI, University of Wisconsin Press.

—— 2007. *Geography and Vision. Seeing, Imagining and Representing the World*. London, I. B. Tauris.

Cowan, R. 2009. 'Virgil's Cucumber Again: Columella 10.378–92', *CQ* 59: 286–9.

Cox, B. and Forshaw, J. 2009. *Why Does E=MC²?* Cambridge, MA, Da Capo Press.

Cubitt, G. 2007. *History and Memory*. Manchester, Manchester University Press.

Cunliffe, B., Gosden, C., and Joyce, R. A. (eds.) 2009. *The Oxford Handbook of Archaeology*. Oxford, Oxford University Press.

Cuomo, S. 2000. 'Divide and Rule: Frontinus and Roman Land-surveying', *SHPS* 31: 189–202.

Daniels, S. 1989. 'Marxism, Culture, and the Duplicity of Landscape', in R. Peet and N. Thrift (eds.), *New Models in Geography. The Political-economy Perspective*. London, Unwin Hyman: 196–220.

—— and Cosgrove, D. 1988. 'Introduction: Iconography and Landscape', in D. Cosgrove and S. Daniels (eds.), 1988. *The Iconography of Landscape. Essays on the Symbolic Representation, Design and Use of Past Environments*. Cambridge, Cambridge University Press: 1–10.

Danvers, J. 2009. 'Being-in-the-World: The Ability to Think about the Self in Interconnection and Interdependence with the Surrounding World', in Stibbe 2009: 185–90.

D'Arms, J. H. 1970. *Romans on the Bay of Naples*. Cambridge, MA, Harvard University Press.

—— 1998. 'Between Public and Private: The *epulum publicum* and Caesar's *Horti Trans Tiberim*', in Cima and La Rocca 1998: 33–44.

Davies. J. C. 1971. 'Was Cicero Aware of Natural Beauty?', *G&R* 18: 152–65.

Davis, J. L. 2007. 'Doing Archaeology in the Classical Lands: The Greek World', in Alcock and Osborne 2007: 53–68, 85–8.

Davis, P. J. 1987. 'Structure and Meaning in the *Eclogues* of Calpurnius Siculus', *Ramus* 16: 32–54.

de Certeau, M. 1984. *The Practice of Everyday Life*. Translated by S. Rendall. Berkeley, CA, University of California Press.

De Franceschini, M. 1991. *Villa Adriana. Mosaici, pavimenti, edifici*. Rome, L'Erma di Bretschneider.

—— 2006. '*Continuatio* e *renovatio* nella Villa Adriana in Tivoli', in S. Sande and L. Hodne (eds.), *Continuatio et Renovatio*, special issue, *AAAH* 20 (n.s. 6): 79–103.

de Grummond, N. T. and Ridgway, B. S. (eds.) 2000. *From Pergamon to Sperlonga. Sculpture and Context*. Berkeley, CA, University of California Press.

De Lacy, P. 1964. 'Distant Views: The Imagery of Lucretius 2', *CJ* 60: 49–55.

Deleuze, G. 2004. *Difference and Repetition*. Translated by P. Patton. London, Continuum.

de Ligt, L., and Northwood, S. (eds.) 2008. *People, Land, and Politics. Demographic Developments and the Transformation of Roman Italy 300 BC–AD 14*. Leiden, Brill.

della Portella, I. (ed.) 2004. *The Appian Way. From its Foundation to the Middle Ages*. Translated by S. Sartarelli. Los Angeles, CA, J. Paul Getty Trust.

Demetz, P. 1958. 'The Elm and the Vine: Notes toward the History of a Marriage Topos', *PMLA* 73: 521–32.

Denard, H. 2002. 'Virtuality and Performativity: Recreating Rome's Theatre of Pompey', *PAJ: A Journal of Performance and Art* 24: 25–43.

Dench, E. 1995. *From Barbarians to New Men. Greek, Roman, and Modern Perceptions of Peoples of the Central Apennines*. Oxford, Oxford University Press.

—— 1996. 'Images of Italian Austerity from Cato to Tacitus', in M. Cébeillac-Gervasoni (ed.), *Les élites municipales de l'Italie péninsulaire des Gracques à Néron*. Naples, Ecole Française de Rome: 247–54.

—— 1998. 'Austerity, Excess, Success, and Failure in Hellenistic and Early Imperial Italy', in M. Wyke (ed.), *Parchments of Gender. Deciphering the Bodies of Italy*. Oxford, Oxford University Press: 121–46.

—— 2005. *Romulus' Asylum. Roman Identities from the Age of Alexander to the Age of Hadrian*. Oxford, Oxford University Press.

de Neeve, P. W. 1992. 'A Roman Landowner and his Estates: Pliny the Younger', *SIFC* 10: 335–44.

Dennett, D. C. 1991. *Consciousness Explained*. Boston, MA, Little Brown.

Dernie, D. 1996. *The Villa d'Este at Tivoli*. London, Academy.

—— 1997. 'The Use and Meaning of Materials in the Garden of the Villa d'Este at Tivoli', *Architectural Research Quarterly* 2.3: 64–73.

de Vos, M. 1982. 'Corridoio rettilineo F, corridoio anulare G', in Bragantini and de Vos 1982: 337–75.

———— 1983. 'Funzione e decorazione dell'Auditorium di Mecenate', in G. Pisani Sartorio and L. Quilici (eds.), *Roma capitale 1870–1911. L'archeologia in Roma capitale tra sterro e scavo.* Venice, Marsilio: 231–47.

———— 1991. 'Nuove pitture egittizzanti di epoca Augustea', in C. Morigini Govi, S. Curto, and S. Pernigotti Bologne (eds.), *L'Egitto fuori dell'Egitto. Dalla riscoperta all'Egittologia.* Bologna, Cooperativa Libreria Universitaria: 121–43.

Dilke, O. A. W. 1971. *The Roman Land Surveyors. An Introduction to the Agrimensores.* Newton Abbot, David and Charles.

Di Mino, M. R. S. (ed.) 1998. *La villa della Farnesina in palazzo Massimo alle Terme.* Milan, Electa.

di Pasquale, G. and Paolucci, F. 2007. *Il giardino antico da Babilonia a Roma. Scienza, arte e natura.* Livorno, Sillabe.

Dobbins, J. J. and Foss, P. W. (eds.) 2007. *The World of Pompeii.* London, Routledge.

Dolciotti, A. M. 1998a. 'Giardino L', in Di Mino 1998: 92–3.

———— 1998b. 'La Scoperta', in Di Mino 1998: 7–9.

Doody, A. 2007. 'Virgil the Farmer? Critiques of the *Georgics* in Columella and Pliny', *CPh* 102: 180–97.

Dorter, K. 1971. 'Imagery and Philosophy in Plato's *Phaedrus*', *JHPh* 9: 279–88.

DuBois, P. 2006. 'The History of the Impossible: Ancient Utopia', *CPh* 101: 1–14.

Duncan, J. and Ley, D. (eds.) 1993. *Place/Culture/Representation.* London, Routledge.

du Prey, P. de la Ruffinière. 1994. *The Villas of Pliny. From Antiquity to Posterity.* Chicago, IL, University of Chicago Press.

Duret, L. and Néraudau, J.-P. 2001. *Urbanisme et métamorphoses de la Rome antique.* Second edition, Paris, Les Belles Lettres.

Dyson, S. L. 2003. *The Roman Countryside.* London, Duckworth.

Eco, U. 1984. *Semiotics and the Philosophy of Language.* Bloomington, IN, Indiana University Press.

———— 1986. *Travels in Hyperreality.* Translated by W. Weaver. San Diego, CA, Harcourt Brace Jovanovich.

Edwards, C. 1993. *The Politics of Immorality in Ancient Rome.* Cambridge, Cambridge University Press.

———— 1996. *Writing Rome. Textual Approaches to the City.* Cambridge, Cambridge University Press.

———— 2003. 'Incorporating the Alien: The Art of Conquest', in Edwards and Woolf 2003: 44–70.

———— and Woolf, G. (eds.) 2003. *Rome the Cosmopolis.* Cambridge, Cambridge University Press.

Edwards, M. 1987. '*Locus horridus* and *locus amoenus*', in Whitby, Hardie, and Whitby, 1987: 267–76.

Ehrlich, T. L. 1989. 'The Waterworks of Hadrian's Villa', *Journal of Garden History* 9: 161–76.

———— 2002. *Landscape and Identity in Early Modern Rome. Villa Culture at Frascati in the Borghese Era.* Cambridge, Cambridge University Press.

Elkins, J. and DeLue, R. (eds.) 2008. *Landscape Theory.* New York, Routledge.

Elsner, J. 1994. 'Constructing Decadence: The Representation of Nero as Imperial Builder', in J. Elsner and J. Masters (eds.), *Reflections of Nero. Culture, History and Representation*. London, Duckworth: 112–27.

———— 1995. *Art and the Roman Viewer. The Transformation of Art from the Pagan World to Christianity*. Cambridge, Cambridge University Press.

———— 2007. 'Viewing Ariadne: From Ekphrasis to Wall-painting in the Roman World', *CPh* 102: 20–44.

Empson, W. 1935. *Some Versions of Pastoral*. London, Chatto and Windus.

Erasmo, M. 2008. *Reading Death in Ancient Rome*. Columbus, OH, Ohio State University Press.

Evans, R. 2003. 'Searching for Paradise: Landscape, Utopia and Rome', *Arethusa* 36: 285–307.

———— 2008. *Utopia Antiqua. Readings of the Golden Age and Decline at Rome*. London, Routledge.

Evans, V. 2004. *The Structure of Time. Language, Meaning and Temporal Cognition*. Amsterdam, John Benjamins.

———— and Green, M. C. 2006. *Cognitive Linguistics. An Introduction*. Edinburgh, Edinburgh University Press.

Fairclough, H. R. 1930. *Love of Nature among the Greeks and Romans*. London, George G. Harrap & Co.

Fantham, E. 1992. 'The Role of Evander in Ovid's *Fasti*', *Arethusa* 25: 155–71.

———— 2004. *The Roman World of Cicero's* De oratore. Oxford, Oxford University Press.

Fantuzzi M. and Papanghelis, T. (eds.) 2006. *Brill's Companion to Greek and Latin Pastoral*. Leiden, Brill.

Farney, G. D. 2007. *Ethnic Identity and Aristocratic Competition in Republican Rome*. Cambridge, Cambridge University Press.

Farrar, L. 2000. *Ancient Roman Gardens*. Revised edition, Stroud, Sutton.

Farrell, J. 1991. *Vergil's* Georgics *and the Traditions of Ancient Epic. The Art of Allusion in Literary History*. Oxford, Oxford University Press.

———— 1997. 'The Phenomenology of Memory in Roman Culture', *CJ* 92: 373–83.

———— 2001. *Latin Language and Latin Culture from Ancient to Modern Times*. Cambridge, Cambridge University Press.

Fauconnier, G. 1994. *Mental Spaces. Aspects of Meaning Construction in Natural Language*. Second edition, Cambridge, Cambridge University Press.

Favro, D. 1994. 'The Street Triumphant: The Urban Impact of Roman Triumphal Parades', in Z. Çelik, D. Favro, and R. Ingersoll (eds.), *Streets. Critical Perspectives on Public Space*. Berkeley, CA, University of California Press: 151–64.

———— 1996. *The Urban Image of Augustan Rome*. Cambridge, Cambridge University Press.

Feeney, D. 1998. *Literature and Religion at Rome. Cultures, Contexts, and Beliefs*. Cambridge, Cambridge University Press.

———— 2007. *Caesar's Calendar. Ancient Time and the Beginnings of History*. Berkeley, CA, University of California Press.

Feldherr, A. 1997. '*Caeci auaritia*: Avarice, History and Vision in Livy V', in C. Deroux (ed.), *Studies in Latin Literature and Roman History 8*. Collection Latomus 239. Brussels, Latomus: 268–77.

Fentress, E. 2007. 'Around the Temple: The New Galleries of the Capitoline Museum', *AJA* 111: 365–9.

Fentress, J. and Wickham, C. 1992. *Social Memory*. Oxford, Blackwell.

Ferrari, G. R. F. 1987. *Listening to the Cicadas. A Study of Plato's* Phaedrus. Cambridge, Cambridge University Press.

Flower, H. I. 1996. *Ancestor Masks and Aristocratic Power in Roman Culture*. Oxford, Oxford University Press.

———— (ed.) 2004. *The Cambridge Companion to the Roman Republic*. Cambridge, Cambridge University Press.

———— 2006. *The Art of Forgetting. Disgrace and Oblivion in Roman Political Culture*. Chapel Hill, NC, University of North Carolina Press.

Fludernik, M., Freeman, D. C., and Freeman, M. H. 1999. 'Metaphor and Beyond: An Introduction', *Poetics Today* 20: 383–96.

Fontana-Giusti, G. K. 2007. 'Urban Strolling as the Measure of Quality', *arq: Architectural Research Quarterly* 11: 255–64.

Forsyth, J. 1835. *Remarks on Antiquities, Arts, and Letters, during an Excursion in Italy, in the Years 1802 and 1803*. Fourth edition, London, John Murray.

Forsythe, G. 2005. *A Critical History of Early Rome. From Prehistory to the First Punic War*. Berkeley, CA, University of California Press.

Forte, M. (ed.) 2007. *La villa di Livia. Un percorso di ricerca di archeologia virtuale*. Rome, L'Erma di Bretschneider.

Förtsch, R. 1993. *Archäologischer Kommentar zu den Villenbriefen des jüngeren Plinius*. Mainz, Zabern.

Foucault, M. 1986. 'Of Other Spaces', translated by J. Miskowiec, *Diacritics: A Review of Contemporary Criticism* 16: 22–7.

———— 1988. *The Care of the Self. The History of Sexuality, Vol. 3*. Translated by R. Hurley. London, Allen Lane.

Foucher, L. 1981. 'Le cult de Bacchus sous l'empire romain', in *ANRW*, ii.17.2: 684–702.

Foxhall, L., Jones, M., and Forbes, H. 2007. 'Human Ecology and the Classical Landscape: Greek and Roman Worlds', in Alcock and Osborne 2007: 91–117.

Fowler, D. 2000. 'The Ruin of Time: Monuments and Survival at Rome', in *Roman Constructions*. Oxford, Oxford University Press: 193–217.

Frazer, A. 1992. 'The Roman Villa and the Pastoral Ideal', in Hunt 1992b: 49–61.

———— (ed.) 1998. *The Roman Villa. Villa Urbana*. Philadelphia, PA, University of Pennsylvania Museum.

Fredrick, D. (ed.) 2002. *The Roman Gaze. Vision, Power, and the Body*. Baltimore, MD, John Hopkins University Press.

French, R. 1994. *Ancient Natural History. Histories of Nature*. London, Routledge.

Freud, S. 1963. *Civilization and its Discontents*. Translated by J. Riviere, edited by J. Strachey. London, Hogarth Press.

Frischer, B., Crawford, J., and de Simone, M. 2006. *The 'Horace's Villa' Project. 1997–2003*. BAR International Series 1588. Oxford, Archaeopress.

Fritter, C. 2002. *Poetry, Space, Landscape. Toward a New Theory*. Cambridge, Cambridge University Press.

Fuentes-Utrilla, P., López-Rodríguez, R. A., and Gil, L. 2004. 'The Historical Relationship of Elms and Vines', *Investigación Agraria, Sistemas y Recursos Forestales* 13: 7–15.

Gabba, E. 1994. 'Rome and Italy: The Social War', in J. A. Crook, A. Lintott, and E. Rawson (eds.), *The Last Age of the Roman Republic, 146–43 B.C. The Cambridge Ancient History* 9. Cambridge, Cambridge University Press: 104–28.

Gabriel, M. M. 1955. *Livia's Garden Room at Prima Porta*. New York, New York University Press.

Gagliardo, M. C. and Packer, J. E. 2006. 'A New Look at Pompey's Theater: History, Documentation, and Recent Excavation', *AJA* 110: 93–122.

Galand-Hallyn, P. (ed.) 2008. *La villa et l univers familial de l Antiquité à la Renaissance*. Paris, Presses de l'Université Paris-Sorbonne.

Gale, M. 1994. *Myth and Poetry in Lucretius*. Cambridge, Cambridge University Press.

Galinsky, K. (ed.) 2005. *The Cambridge Companion to The Age of Augustus*. Cambridge, Cambridge University Press.

Gallini, C. 1970. *Protesta e integrazione nella Roma antica*. Bari, Laterza.

Gärdenfors, P. 2000. *Conceptual Spaces. The Geometry of Thought*. Cambridge, MA, MIT Press.

Gargola, D. J. 1995. *Lands, Laws, and Gods. Magistrates and Ceremony in the Regulation of Public Lands in Republican Rome*. Chapel Hill, NC, University of North Carolina Press.

——— 2004. 'The Ritual of Centuriation', in C. F. Konrad (ed.), *Augusto augurio. Rerum humanarum et divinarum commentationes in honorem Jerzy Linderski*. Stuttgart, Franz Steiner: 123–49.

Garnsey, P. 2000. 'The Land', in A. K. Bowman, P. Garnsey, and D. Rathbone (eds.), *The High Empire, A.D. 70–192. The Cambridge Ancient History* 11. Cambridge, Cambridge University Press: 679–709.

Garrison, D. 1992. 'The *locus inamoenus*: Another Part of the Forest', *Arion* 2: 98–114.

Gazda, E. K. (ed.) 1991. *Roman Art in the Private Sphere*. Ann Arbor, MI, University of Michigan Press.

——— (ed.) 2002. *The Ancient Art of Emulation. Studies in Artistic Originality and Tradition from the Present to Classical Antiquity*. MAAR Supplement 1. Ann Arbor, MI, University of Michigan Press.

Geymonat, M. 2000. 'Immagini letterarie e reali del paesaggio di montagna in Virgilio', *Philologus* 144: 81–9.

Ghio, M. 2002. 'Sotto l'occhio di Adriano', in Reggiani 2002: 211–16.

Giesecke, A. L. 1999. 'Lucretius and Virgil's Pastoral Dream', *Utopian Studies* 10: 1–15.

——— 2001. 'Beyond the Garden of Epicurus: The Utopics of the Ideal Roman Villa', *Utopian Studies* 12: 13–32.

——— 2007. *The Epic City. Urbanism, Utopia, and the Garden in Ancient Greece and Rome*. Cambridge, MA, Harvard University Press.

Gifford, T. 1999. *Pastoral*. Abingdon, Routledge.

Gill, C. 1995. *Greek Thought*. Greece & Rome New Surveys in the Classics 25. Oxford, Oxford University Press.

Gillespie, S. and Hardie, P. (eds.) 2007. *The Cambridge Companion to Lucretius*. Cambridge, Cambridge University Press.

Gillis, D. J. 1967. 'Pastoral Poetry in Lucretius', *Latomus* 26: 339–62.

Gizzi, S. 2002. 'Il verde a Villa Adriana come questione generale di restauro', in Reggiani 2002: 217–35.

Glare, P. G. W. (ed.) 1982. *Oxford Latin Dictionary*. Oxford, Clarendon Press.

Gleason, K. L. 1990. 'The Garden Portico of Pompey the Great: An Ancient Public Park Preserved in the Layers of Rome', *Expedition* 32.2: 4–13.

———— 1994. '*Porticus Pompeiana*: A New Perspective on the First Public Park of Ancient Rome', *Journal of Garden History* 14: 13–27.

Golledge, R. G. (ed.) 1999. *Wayfinding Behavior. Cognitive Mapping and Other Spatial Processes*. Baltimore, MD, Johns Hopkins University Press.

Gombrich, E. H. 1960. *Art and Illusion*. London, Phaidon.

Görler, W. 1988. 'From Athens to Tusculum: Gleaning the Background of Cicero's *De oratore*', *Rhetorica* 6: 215–35.

Gowers, E. 2000. 'Vegetable Love: Virgil, Columella and Garden Poetry', *Ramus* 29: 127–48.

Gowing, A. 2005. *Empire and Memory. The Representation of the Roman Republic in Imperial Culture*. Cambridge, Cambridge University Press.

Grahame, M. 2000. *Reading Space. Social Interaction and Identity in the Houses of Pompeii. A Syntactical Approach to the Interpretation and Analysis of Built Space*. BAR International Series 886. Oxford, Archaeopress.

Grau, O. 2003. *Virtual Art. From Illusion to Immersion*. Translated by G. Custance. Cambridge, MA, MIT Press.

Green, C. M. C. 1997. 'Free as a Bird: Varro *de Re Rustica* 3', *AJPh* 118: 427–48.

Greenblatt, S. (1980) *Renaissance Self-fashioning. From More to Shakespeare*. Chicago, IL, University of Chicago Press.

Griesbach, J. 2005. 'Villa e mausoleo: trasformazioni nel concetto della memoria nel suburbio romano', in Santillo Frizell and Klynne 2005.

Grimal, P. 1938. 'Les métamorphoses d' Ovide et la peinture paysagiste à l'époque d'Auguste', *REL* 16: 145–61.

———— 1945. 'La Colline de Janus', *RA* 24: 56–87.

———— 1984. *Les jardins romains. Essai sur le naturalisme romain*. Third edition, Paris, Fayard.

Gros, P. 1987. 'La fonction symbolique des edifices théâtraux dans le paysage urbain de la Rome augustéene', in Pietri 1987: 319–43.

———— 1999. 'Porticus Pompei', in *LTUR*, iv.148–9.

Gruen, E. S. 1990. 'The Bacchanalian Affair', in *Studies in Greek Culture and Roman Policy*. Cincinnati Classical Studies n.s. 7. Leiden, Brill: 34–78.

———— 1992. *Culture and National Identity in Republican Rome*. Ithaca, NY, Cornell University Press.

Gruet, B. 2006. *La rue à Rome, miroir de la ville. Entre l émotion et la norme*. Paris, Presses de l'Université Paris-Sorbonne.

Gualtieri, M. 2008. 'Lucanian Landscapes in the Age of "Romanization" (Third to First Centuries BC): Two Case Studies', in de Ligt and Northwood 2008: 387–413.

Guarino, C. and Bruno, S. 2002. 'Il restauro del verde in Villa Adriana', in Reggiani 2002: 204–10.

Gutzwiller, K. 1991. *Theocritus' Pastoral Analogies. The Formation of a Genre*. Madison, WI, University of Wisconsin Press.

———— 2007. *A Guide to Hellenistic Literature*. Malden, MA, Blackwell.

Guzzo, P. G., Howe, T. N., Bonifacio, G., and Sodo, A. M. (eds.) 2004. *In Stabiano. Exploring the Ancient Seaside Villas of the Roman Elite*. Castellammare di Stabia, Nicola Longobardi.

Halbwachs, M. 1992. *On Collective Memory*. Edited and translated by L. A. Coser. Chicago, IL, University of Chicago Press.

Hales, S. 2003. *Roman Houses and Social Identity*. Cambridge, Cambridge University Press.

Halperin, D. M. 1983. *Before Pastoral. Theocritus and the Ancient Tradition of Bucolic Poetry*. New Haven, CT, Yale University Press.

Hardie, P. 1992. 'Augustan Poets and the Mutability of Rome', in A. Powell (ed.), *Roman Poetry and Propaganda in the Age of Augustus*. Bristol, Bristol Classical Press: 59–82.

———— 1998. *Virgil*. Greece & Rome New Surveys in the Classics 28. Oxford, Oxford University Press.

———— 2006. 'Statius' Ovidian Poetics and the Tree of Atedius Melior (*Silvae* 2.3)', in Nauta, van Dam, and Smolenaars 2006: 207–21.

Harnad, S. 1987. 'Category Induction and Representation', in S. Harnad (ed.), *Categorical Perception. The Groundwork of Cognition*. Cambridge, Cambridge University Press: 535–65.

Harris, D. 1999. 'The Postmodernization of Landscape: A Critical Historiography', *JSAH* 58: 434–43.

Harrison, S. J. 2004. 'Virgil's *Corycius senex* and Nicander's *Georgica*: Georgics 4.116–48', in M. Gale (ed.), *Latin Epic and Didactic Poetry. Genre, Tradition and Individuality*. Swansea, Classical Press of Wales: 109–23.

———— 2005. 'Vergil and the *Mausoleum Augusti*: Georgics 3.12–18', *AClass* 48: 185–8.

Hartswick, K. 2004. *The Gardens of Sallust. A Changing Landscape*. Austin, TX, University of Texas Press.

Harvey, K. (ed.) 2009. *History and Material Culture*. London, Routledge.

Haselberger, L., Romano, D. G., and Dumser, E. A. (eds.) 2002. *Mapping Augustan Rome*. *JRA* Supplement 50. Portsmouth, RI, Journal of Roman Archaeology.

Haskell, F. and Penny, N. 1981. *Taste and the Antique. The Lure of Classical Sculpture, 1500–1900*. New Haven, CT, Yale University Press.

Hass, P. 1998. *Der locus amoenus in der Antiken Literatur. Zu Theorie und Geschichte eines Literarischen Motivs*. Bamberg, Wissenschaftlicher.

Häuber, C. 1996. 'Horti Maecenatis', in *LTUR*, iii.70–3.

———— 1998. 'The Esquiline Horti: New Research', in Frazer 1998: 55–64.

Helmreich, A. 2002. *The English Garden and National Identity. The Competing Styles of Garden Design, 1870–1914*. Cambridge, Cambridge University Press.

Henderson, J. 1998. 'Virgil, *Eclogue* 9: Valleydiction', *PVS* 23: 149–76.

———— 2002a. 'Columella's Living Hedge: The Roman Gardening Book', *JRS* 92: 110–33.

———— 2002b. *Pliny's Statue. The Letters, Self-portraiture and Classical Art*. Exeter, University of Exeter Press.

———— 2003. 'Portrait of the Artist as a Figure of Style: P.L.I.N.Y.'s Letters', *Arethusa* 36: 115–25.

———— 2004a. *HORTVS. The Roman Book of Gardening*. London, Routledge.

———— 2004b. *Morals and Villas in Seneca's Letters. Places to Dwell*. Cambridge, Cambridge University Press.

Hepple, L. W. 2001. '"The Museum in the Garden": Displaying Classical Antiquities in Elizabethan and Jacobean England', *Garden History* 29: 109–20.

Herman, V. 1999. 'Deictic Projection and Conceptual Blending in Epistolarity', *Poetics Today* 20: 523–41.

Heslin, P. 2007. 'Augustus, Domitian and the So-called Horologium Augusti', *JRS* 97: 1–20.

Hill, D. K. 1944. 'The Temple above Pompey's Theatre', *CJ* 39: 360–6.

———— 1981. 'Some Sculpture from Roman Domestic Gardens', in MacDougall and Jashemski 1981: 83–94.

Hillier, B. 2003a. 'The Architectures of Seeing and Going: Or, are Cities shaped by Bodies or Minds? And is there a Syntax of Spatial Cognition?', *Proceedings of the 4th International Space Syntax Symposium*, London, <http://www.spacesyntax.net/SSS4.htm>, accessed 30 November 2009.

———— 2003b. 'The Knowledge that Shapes the City: The Human City Beneath the Social City', *Proceedings of the 4th International Space Syntax Symposium*, London, <http://www.spacesyntax.net/SSS4.htm>, accessed 30 November 2009.

———— and Hanson, J. 1984. *The Social Logic of Space*. Cambridge, Cambridge University Press.

———— and Penn, A. 2004. 'Rejoinder to Carlo Ratti', *Environment and Planning B: Planning and Design* 31: 501–11.

Hindin, G. 2008. 'The Beautiful Recollected: Memory and Beauty in Plato's *Phaedrus*', in A.-T. Tymieniecka (ed.), *Beauty's Appeal. Measure and Excess.* Analecta Husserliana: The Yearbook of Phenomenological Research 97. Dordrecht, Springer: 13–19.

Hinds, S. 2002. 'Landscape with Figures: Aesthetics of Place in the *Metamorphoses* and its Tradition', in P. Hardie (ed.), *The Cambridge Companion to Ovid*. Cambridge, Cambridge University Press: 122–49.

Hirsch, E. and O'Hanlon, M. (eds.) 1995. *The Anthropology of Landscape. Perspectives on Place and Space*. Oxford, Clarendon Press.

Hodos, T. 2010. 'Local and Global Perspectives in the Study of Social and Cultural Identities', in S. Hales and T. Hodos (eds.), *Material Culture and Social Identities in the Ancient World*. Cambridge, Cambridge University Press: 3–31.

Hoffmann, A. 1998. 'Villa Hadriana: Raum, Licht und Konstruktion', in Frazer 1998: 65–76.

Hölscher, T. 2004. *The Language of Images in Roman Art*. Translated by A. Snodgrass and A. Künzl Snodgrass. Cambridge, Cambridge University Press.

Horden, P. and Purcell, N. 2000. *The Corrupting Sea. A Study of Mediterranean History*. Oxford, Blackwell.

Howe, T. N. 2004. 'Powerhouses: The Seaside Villas of Campania in the Power Culture of Rome', in Guzzo et al. 2004: 15–32.

Hubbard, T. K. 1996. 'Calpurnius Siculus and the Unbearable Weight of Tradition', *Helios* 23: 67–89.

———— 1998. *The Pipes of Pan. Intertextuality and Literary Filiation in the Pastoral Tradition From Theocritus to Milton.* Ann Arbor, MI, University of Michigan Press.

Hughes, J. D. 1994. *Pan's Travail. Environmental Problems of the Ancient Greeks and Romans.* Baltimore, MD, Johns Hopkins University Press.

Hunt, J. D. 1991. 'The Garden as Cultural Object', in S. Wrede and W. H. Adams (eds.), *Denatured Visions. Landscape and Culture in the Twentieth Century.* New York, Museum of Modern Art: 19–32.

———— (ed.) 1992a. *Garden History. Issues, Approaches, Methods.* Dumbarton Oaks Colloquium on the History of Landscape Architecture 13. Washington, DC, Dumbarton Oaks Research Library.

———— (ed.) 1992b. *The Pastoral Landscape.* Studies in the History of Art 36. Washington, DC, National Gallery of Art.

———— 1996. *Garden and Grove. The Italian Renaissance Garden in the English Imagination 1600–1750.* Philadelphia, PA, University of Pennsylvania Press.

———— 1999. 'Introduction: The Immediate Garden and the Larger Landscape', in J. D. Hunt (ed.), *The Immediate Garden and the Larger Landscape.* Special issue of *Studies in the History of Gardens and Designed Landscapes* 1: 3–6.

———— 2000. *Greater Perfections. The Practice of Garden Theory.* Philadelphia, PA, University of Pennsylvania Press.

———— 2003. '"Lordship of the Feet": Toward a Poetics of Movement in the Garden', in Conan 2003a: 187–214.

Hurst, H. 2007. 'Doing Archaeology in the Classical Lands: The Roman World', in Alcock and Osborne 2007: 69–88.

Huskinson, J. 2000a. 'Elite Culture and the Identity of Empire', in Huskinson 2000b: 95–123.

———— (ed.) 2000b. *Experiencing Rome. Culture, Identity and Power in the Roman Empire.* London, Routledge.

Hutton, W. 2005. *Describing Greece. Landscape and Literature in the* Periegesis *of Pausanias.* Cambridge, Cambridge University Press.

Huyssen, A. 2003. *Present Pasts. Urban Palimpsests and the Politics of Memory.* Stanford, CA, Stanford University Press.

Ingerson, A. E. 1994. 'Tracking and Testing the Nature–Culture Dichotomy', in C. Crumley (ed.), *Historical Ecology. Cultural Knowledge and Changing Landscapes.* Santa Fe, NM, School of American Research: 30–41.

Ingold, T. 2000. *The Perception of the Environment. Essays on Livelihood, Dwelling and Skill.* London, Routledge.

Innes, D. C. 2002. 'Longinus and Caecilius: Models of the Sublime', *Mnemosyne* 55: 259–84.

Isayev, E. 2007. 'Why Italy?', in Bradley, Isayev, and Riva 2007: 1–20.

Jaccottet, A.-F. 2003. *Choisir Dionysos. Les associations dionysiaques ou la face cachée du dionysisme. Vol. I: Text; Vol. II: Documents.* Zürich, Akanthus.

Jaeger, M. 1997. *Livy's Written Rome.* Ann Arbor, MI, University of Michigan Press.

Jashemski, W. F. 1979/93. *The Gardens of Pompeii: Herculaneum and the Villas Destroyed by Vesuvius,* 2 vols, New Rochelle, NY, A. D. Caratzas.

———— 1981. 'The Campanian Peristyle Garden', in MacDougall and Jashemski 1981: 29–48.

—— 2002. 'Plants: Evidence from Wall Paintings, Mosaics, Sculpture, Plant Remains, Graffiti, Inscriptions, and Ancient Authors', in Jashemski and Meyer 2002: 80–216.

—— 2007. 'Gardens', in Dobbins and Foss 2007: 487–98.

—— and Meyer, F. G. (eds.) 2002. *The Natural History of Pompeii*. Cambridge, Cambridge University Press.

—— and Ricotti, E. Salza Prina. 1992. 'Preliminary Excavations in the Gardens of Hadrian's Villa: The Canopus Area and the Piazza d'Oro', *AJA* 96: 579–95.

Jay, M. 1993. *Downcast Eyes. The Denigration of Vision in Twentieth-century French Thought*. Berkeley, CA, University of California Press.

Jehne, M., and Pfeilschifter, R. (eds.) 2006. *Herrschaft ohne Integration? Rom und Italien in Republikanischer Zeit*. Studien zur Alten Geschichte 4. Frankfurt, Alte Geschichte.

Jellicoe, G., Waymark, J., and Jellicoe, S. 1995. *The Landscape of Man. Shaping the Environment from Prehistory to the Present Day*. Third edition, London, Thames and Hudson.

Jenkyns, R. 1998. *Virgil's Experience. Nature and History; Times, Names, and Places*. Oxford, Oxford University Press.

Johnson, W.R. 1990. 'Messalla's Birthday: The Politics of Pastoral', *Arethusa* 23: 95–113.

—— 2004. 'A Secret Garden: *Georgics* 4.116–148', in Armstrong et al. 2004: 75–83.

Jones, F. (forthcoming). *Virgil's Garden: Bucolic Space in the* Eclogues. London, Duckworth.

Jones, S. 1997. *The Archaeology of Ethnicity. Constructing Identities in the Past and Present*. London, Routledge.

Kehoe, D. P. 2007. 'The Early Roman Empire: Production', in W. Scheidel, I. Morris, and R. P. Saller (eds.), *The Cambridge Economic History of the Greco-Roman World*. Cambridge, Cambridge University Press: 543–69.

Kellum, B. A. 1990. 'The City Adorned: Programmatic Display at the Aedes Concordiae Augustae', in K. Raaflaub and M. Toher (eds.), *Between Republic and Empire. Interpretations of Augustus and his Principate*. Berkeley, CA, University of California Press: 276–308.

—— 1994. 'The Construction of a Landscape in Augustan Rome: The Garden Room at the Villa *ad Gallinas*', *ABull* 76: 211–24.

King, N. 2000. *Memory, Narrative, Identity. Remembering the Self*. Edinburgh, Edinburgh University Press.

Kingsbury, N. and Richardson, T. (eds.) 2005. *Vista. The Culture and Politics of Gardens*. London, Frances Lincoln.

Klynne, A. 2005. 'The Laurel Grove of the Caesars: Looking in and Looking out', in Santillo Frizell and Klynne 2005.

—— and Liljenstolpe, P. 2000a. 'Investigating the Gardens of the Villa of Livia', *JRA* 13: 220–33.

—— —— 2000b. 'Where to Put Augustus? A Note on the Placement of the Prima Porta Statue', *AJP* 121: 121–8.

Koortbojian, M. 1996. '*In commemorationem mortuorum*: Text and Image along the "Streets of Tombs"', in J. Elsner (ed.), *Art and Text in Roman Culture*. Cambridge, Cambridge University Press: 210–33.

Kraus, C. S. 1994. 'No Second Troy: Topoi and Refoundation in Livy, Book V', *TAPhA* 124: 267–89.

Krieger, M. 1992. *Ekphrasis. The Illusion of the Natural Sign*. Baltimore, MD, Johns Hopkins University Press.

Kronenberg, L. J. 2000. 'The Poet's Fiction: Virgil's Praise of the Farmer, Philosopher, and Poet at the End of *Georgics* 2', *HSPh* 100: 341–60.

––––––– 2009. *Allegories of Farming from Greece to Rome*. Cambridge: Cambridge University Press.

Kuttner, A. L. 1995. 'Republican Rome Looks at Pergamon', in *Greece in Rome. Influence, Integration, Resistance*, special issue of *HSPh* 97: 157–78.

––––––– 1998. 'Prospects of Patronage: Realism and *romanitas* in the Architectural Vistas of the 2nd Style', in Frazer 1998: 93–107.

––––––– 1999a. 'Culture and History at Pompey's Museum', *TAPhA* 129: 343–73.

––––––– 1999b. 'Hellenistic Images of Spectacle, from Alexander to Augustus', in B. Bergmann and C. Kondoleon (eds.), *The Art of Ancient Spectacle*. Washington, DC, National Gallery of Art: 97–123.

––––––– 1999c. 'Looking Outside Inside: Ancient Roman Garden Rooms', in J. D. Hunt (ed.), *The Immediate Garden and the Larger Landscape*. Special issue of *Studies in the History of Gardens and Designed Landscapes* 1: 7–35.

––––––– 2003. 'Delight and Danger in the Roman Water Garden: Sperlonga and Tivoli', in Conan 2003a: 103–56.

Lakoff, G. and Johnson, M. 2003. *Metaphors We Live By*. Revised edition, Chicago, IL, University of Chicago Press.

Larmour, D. H. J. and Spencer, D. 2007a. '*Roma, recepta*: A Topography of the Imagination', in Larmour and Spencer 2007b: 1–60.

––––––– (eds.) 2007b. *The Sites of Rome: Time, Space, Memory*. Oxford, Oxford University Press.

La Rocca, E. 1986. 'Il lusso come espressione di potere', in Cima and La Rocca 1986: 3–35.

––––––– 2008. *Lo spazio negato. La pittura di paesaggio nella cultura artistica greca e romana*. Milan, Electa.

Laurence, R. 1997. 'Writing the Roman Metropolis', in Parkins 1997: 1–20.

––––––– 1999. *The Roads of Roman Italy. Mobility and Cultural Change*. London, Routledge.

––––––– and Newsome, D. J. (eds.) in press 2011. *Rome, Ostia and Pompeii. Movement and Space*. Oxford, Oxford University Press.

Lavagne, H. 1988. *Operosa Antra. Recherches sur la grotte à Rome de Sylla à Hadrien*, Bibliothèque des Écoles Françaises d'Athènes et de Rome 272. Rome, École Française de Rome.

Leach, E. W. 1973. 'Corydon Revisited: An Interpretation of the Political *Eclogues* of Calpurnius Siculus', *Ramus* 2: 53–97.

––––––– 1974. *Virgil's Eclogues. Landscapes of Experience*. Ithaca, NY, Cornell University Press.

––––––– 1975. 'Neronian Pastoral and the World of Power', *Ramus* 4: 204–30.

––––––– 1980. 'Sacral-idyllic Landscape Painting and the Poems of Tibullus' First Book', *Latomus* 39: 47–79.

——— 1985. 'Landscape and the Prosperous Life. The Discrimination of Genre in Augustan Literature and Painting', in R. Winkes (ed.), *The Age of Augustus*. Providence, RI, Center for Old World Archaeology and Art, Brown University: 189–95.

——— 1988. *The Rhetoric of Space. Literary and Artistic Representations of Landscape in Republican and Augustan Rome*. Princeton, NJ, Princeton University Press.

——— 1990. 'The Politics of Self-presentation: Pliny's *Letters* and Roman Portrait Sculpture', *ClAnt* 9: 14–39.

——— 1993. 'Horace's Sabine Topography in Lyric and Hexameter Verse', *AJPh* 114: 271–302.

——— 1998. 'Personal and Communal Memory in the Reading of Horace's *Odes*, Books 1–3', *Arethusa* 31: 43–74.

——— 2003. '*Otium* as *luxuria*: Economy of Status in the Younger Pliny's *Letters*', *Arethusa* 36: 147–65.

——— 2004. *The Social Life of Painting in Ancient Rome and on the Bay of Naples*. Cambridge, Cambridge University Press.

Lee, E. N. 1978. 'The Sense of an Object: Epicurus on Seeing and Hearing', in P. K. Machamer and R. G. Turnbull (eds.), *Studies in Perception. Interrelations in the History of Philosophy and Science*. Columbus, OH, Ohio State University Press: 27–59.

Leen, A. 1991. 'Cicero and the Rhetoric of Art', *AJPh* 112: 229–45.

Lefebvre, H. 1991. *The Production of Space*. Translated by D. Nicholson-Smith. Oxford, Blackwell.

Lehmann, P. W. 1953. *Roman Wall Paintings from Boscoreale in the Metropolitan Museum of Art*. Cambridge, MA, Archaeological Institute of America.

Ligorio, P. 1723. *Descrittione della superba e magnificentissima Villa Hadriana*. Parallel Latin/Italian texts, in J. G. Graevius (ed.), *Thesaurus antiquitatum et historiarum Italiae, Etruriae, Umbriae, Sabinorum et Lati*, viii.4. Leiden, Petrus van der Aa.

Liljenstolpe, P. and Klynne, A. 1997–8. 'The Imperial Gardens of the Villa of Livia at Prima Porta: A Preliminary Report on the 1997 Campaign', *ORom* 22–3: 127–47.

Linderski, J. 1985. 'The Dramatic Date of Varro, *de Re Rustica*, Book III and the Elections in 54', *Historia* 34: 248–54.

——— 1989. 'Garden Parlors: Nobles and Birds', in R. I. Curtis (ed.), *Studia Pompeiana et Classica in Honor of Wilhelmina F. Jashemski*. Volume 2, New Rochelle, NY, A. D. Caratzas: 105–27.

——— 2001. '"*Imago hortorum*": Pliny the Elder and the Gardens of the Urban Poor', *CPh* 96: 305–8.

Ling, R. 1977. 'Studius and the Beginnings of Roman Landscape Painting', *JRS* 67: 1–16.

Littlewood, A. R. 1987. 'Ancient Literary Evidence for the Pleasure Gardens of Roman Country Villas', in MacDougall 1987: 9–30.

Lloyd, R. B. 1982. 'Three Monumental Gardens on the Marble Plan', *AJA* 86: 91–101.

Lock, G. 2009. 'Human Activity in a Spatial Context', in Cunliffe, Gosden, and Joyce 2009: 169–88.

Lomas, K. 1993. *Rome and the Western Greeks, 350 BC–AD 200. Conquest and Acculturation in Southern Italy*. London, Routledge.

—— 1996. *Roman Italy, 338 BC–AD 200. A Sourcebook*. London, UCL Press.

—— 2000. 'Cities, States, and Ethnic Identity in Southeast Italy', in K. Lomas and E. Herring (eds.), *The Emergence of State Identities in Italy*. London, Accordia Research Institute, University of London: 79–90.

—— 2004. 'Italy During the Roman Republic, 338–31 B.C.', in Flower 2004: 199–224.

Loughrey, B. 1984. *The Pastoral Mode. A Casebook*. London, Macmillan.

Lowenthal, D. 1961. 'Geography, Experience, and Imagination: Towards a Geographical Epistemology', *Annals of the Association of American Geographers* 51: 241–60.

Lowrie, M. 2003. 'Rome: City and Empire', *CW* 97: 57–68.

Lugli, G. 1938. 'La pianta dell'antica casa della Farnesina', *MEFRA* 55: 5–27.

Lynch, K. 1960. *The Image of the City*. Cambridge, MA, MIT Press.

Lyne, R. O. A. M. 1974. '*Scilicet et tempus veniet*: Virgil, *Georgics* 1.463–514', in T. Woodman and D. West (eds.), *Quality and Pleasure in Latin Poetry*. Cambridge, Cambridge University Press: 47–66.

McCracken, G. 1935. 'Cicero's Tusculan Villa', *CJ* 30: 261–77.

MacDonald, W. L. 1982. *The Architecture of the Roman Empire, Volume I. An Introductory Study*. Revised edition, New Haven, CT, Yale University Press.

—— 1986. *The Architecture of the Roman Empire, Volume II. An Urban Appraisal*. New Haven, CT, Yale University Press.

—— and Pinto, J. A. 1995. *Hadrian's Villa and its Legacy*. New Haven, CT, Yale University Press.

MacDougall, E. B. (ed.) 1987. *Ancient Roman Villa Gardens*. Dumbarton Oaks Colloquium on the History of Landscape Architecture 10. Washington, DC, Dumbarton Oaks Research Library.

—— and Jashemski, W. (eds.) 1981. *Ancient Roman Gardens*. Dumbarton Oaks Colloquium on the History of Landscape Architecture 7. Washington, DC, Dumbarton Oaks Research Library.

McEvilley, T. 2001. 'Turned Upside Down and Torn Apart', in Beckley 2001: 57–83.

McEwen, I. K. 1995. 'Housing Fame: In the Tuscan Villa of Pliny the Younger', *Res* 27: 11–24.

—— 2003. *Vitruvius. Writing the Body of Architecture*. Cambridge, MA, MIT Press.

Mackie, N. 1989. 'Urbanity in a Roman Landscape: The *Eclogues* of Calpurnius Siculus', *Landscape Research* 14: 9–14.

Madonna, M. L. 1991. 'La "Rometta" di Pirro Ligorio in Villa d'Este a Tivoli: un incunabolo tridimensionale', in M. Fagiolo (ed.), *Roma antica. L immagine delle grandi città Italiane* 1. Rome, Caponi: unpaginated.

Maggiulli, G. 1995. *Incipiant siluae cum primum surgere. Mondo vegetale e nomenclatura della flora di Virgilio*. Rome, Gruppo Editoriale Internazionale.

Maltby, R. 1991. *A Lexicon of Ancient Latin Etymologies*. ARCA 25. Leeds, Francis Cairns.

Martindale, C. (ed.) 1997a. *The Cambridge Companion to Virgil*. Cambridge, Cambridge University Press.

—— 1997b. 'Green Politics: The *Eclogues*', in Martindale 1997a: 107–24.

Marvin, M. 2002. 'The Ludovisi Barbarians: The Grand Manner', in Gazda 2002: 205–33.

Marx, L. 2000. *The Machine in the Garden. Technology and the Pastoral Ideal in America.* Second edition, New York, Oxford University Press.

Marzano, A. 2008. 'Science, Art, Nature: Ancient Gardens in All their Variety', *AJA* 112.2 online Museum Review, <http://www.ajaonline.org/pdfs/museum_reviews/ AJA1122_Marzano.pdf>, accessed 17 June 2010.

Mattusch, C. (ed.) 2008. *Pompeii and the Roman Villa. Art and Culture around the Bay of Naples.* London, Thames and Hudson.

Mayer, J. W. 2005. *Imus ad villam. Studien zur Villeggiatur im stadtrömischen Suburbium in der späten Republik und frühen Kaiserzeit.* Geographica Historica 20. Stuttgart, Franz Steiner.

Mayer, R. G. 2006. 'Latin Pastoral after Virgil', in Fantuzzi and Papanghelis 2006: 451–66.

Mazzoleni, D. and Pappalardo, U. 2004. *Domus. Wall Painting in the Roman House.* Translated by A. L. Jenkens. Los Angeles, CA, J. Paul Getty Museum.

Meban, D. 2008. 'Temple Building, *Primus* Language, and the Proem to Virgil's Third *Georgic*', *CPh* 103: 150–74.

Meiggs, R. 1982. *Trees and Timber in the Ancient Mediterranean World.* Oxford, Clarendon Press.

Meinig, D. W. 1979a. 'The Beholding Eye: Ten Versions of the Same Scene', in Meinig 1979b: 33–48.

——— (ed.) 1979b. *The Interpretation of Ordinary Landscapes. Geographical Essays.* New York, Oxford University Press.

Merleau-Ponty, M. 1964. 'Eye and Mind', translated by C. Dallery, in J. M. Edie (ed.), *The Primacy of Perception.* Evanston, IL, Northwestern University Press: 159–90.

——— 2002. *Phenomenology of Perception.* Translated by C. Smith. Abingdon, Routledge.

Mielsch, H. 1987. *Die römische Villa. Architektur und Lebensform.* Munich, C. H. Beck.

Mikalson, J. D. 2005. *Ancient Greek Religion.* Oxford, Blackwell.

——— 2006. 'Greek Religion: Continuity and Change in the Hellenistic Period', in Bugh 2006: 208–22.

Miles, M. M. 2008. *Art as Plunder. The Ancient Origins of Debate about Cultural Property.* New York, Cambridge University Press.

Miller, A. 1995. 'Magisterial Visions: Recent Anglo-American Scholarship on the Represented Landscape', *American Quarterly* 47: 140–51.

Miller, M. 1993. *The Garden as an Art.* Albany, NY, State University of New York Press.

Mitchell, W. J. T. 1986. *Iconology. Image, Text, Ideology.* Chicago, IL, University of Chicago Press.

——— 1994a. 'Imperial Landscape', in Mitchell 1994b: 5–34.

——— (ed.) 1994b. *Landscape and Power.* Chicago, IL, University of Chicago Press.

Moatti, C. 2006. 'Translation, Migration and Communication in the Roman Empire: Three Aspects of Movement in History', *ClAnt* 25: 109–40.

Moltesen, M. 1998. 'The Sculptures from the *Horti Sallustiani* in the Ny Carlsberg Glyptotek', in Cima and La Rocca 1998: 175–88.

Montiglio, S. 2000. 'Wandering Philosophers in Classical Greece', *JHS* 120: 86–105.

Moore, C. W., Mitchell, W. J., and Turnbull Jr, W. 1993. *The Poetics of Gardens.* Cambridge, MA, MIT Press.

Moore, F. G. 1906. 'Cicero's Amaltheum', *CPh* 1: 121–6.

Moormann, E. M. 2007. 'Villas Surrounding Pompeii and Herculaneum', in Dobbins and Foss 2007: 435–54.

Morley, N. 1997. 'Cities in Context: Urban Systems in Roman Italy', in Parkins 1997: 42–58.

——— 2003. 'Migration and the Metropolis', in Edwards and Woolf 2003: 147–57.

Mouritsen, H. 1998. *Italian Unification. A Study in Ancient and Modern Historiography. BICS* Supplement 70. London, Institute of Classical Studies.

Myers, K. S. 2000. '*Miranda fides:* Poet and Patrons in Paradoxographical Landscapes in Statius' *Silvae*', *MD* 44: 103–38.

——— 2005. '*Docta otia*: Garden Ownership and Configurations of Leisure in Statius and Pliny the Younger', *Arethusa* 38: 103–29.

Narducci, E. 2003. 'La memoria della grecità nell'immaginario delle ville ciceroniane', in M. Citroni (ed.), *Memoria e identità. La cultura romana costruisce la sua immagine.* Florence, Università degli Studi di Firenze, Dipartamento di Scienze dell'Antichità 'Giorgio Pasquali': 119–48.

Nauta, R. R. 2002. *Poetry for Patrons. Literary Communication in the Age of Domitian.* Leiden, Brill.

——— , van Dam, H.-J., and Smolenaars, J. J. L. (eds.) 2006. *Flavian Poetry.* Leiden, Brill.

Neisser, U. 1989. 'Domains of Memory', in P. R. Solomon, G. R. Goethals, C. M. Kelly, and B. R. Stephens (eds.), *Memory. Interdisciplinary Approaches.* New York, Springer: 67–83.

Neudecker, R. 1998. 'The Roman Villa as a Locus of Art Collections', in Frazer 1998: 77–91.

Nevett, L. 1997. 'Perceptions of Domestic Space in Roman Italy', in B. Rawson and P. Weaver (eds.), *The Roman Family in Italy. Status, Sentiment, Space.* Oxford, Oxford University Press: 281–98.

Newby Z. 2002. 'Sculptural Display in the So-called Palaestra of Hadrian's Villa', *MDAI(R)* 109: 59–82.

——— 2005. *Greek Athletics in the Roman World. Victory and Virtue.* Oxford, Oxford University Press.

Newlands, C. 1987. 'Urban Pastoral: The Seventh *Eclogue* of Calpurnius Siculus', *ClAnt* 6: 330–46.

——— 2002. *Statius' Silvae and the Poetics of Empire.* Cambridge, Cambridge University Press.

——— 2004. 'Statius and Ovid: Transforming the Landscape', *TAPhA* 134: 133–55.

Newmyer, S. T. 1984. 'The Triumph of Art over Nature: Martial and Statius on Flavian Aesthetics', *Helios* 11: 1–7.

Nicolet, C. 1991. *Space, Geography and Politics in the Early Roman Empire.* Translated by H. Leclerc. Ann Arbor, MI, University of Michigan Press.

Niebisch, A. 2008. 'Symbolic Space: Memory, Narrative, Writing', in G. Backhaus and J. Murungi (eds.), *Symbolic Landscapes.* Dordrecht, Springer: 323–37.

Nightingale, A. W. 2001. 'On Wandering and Wondering: *Theôria* in Greek Philosophy and Culture', *Arion* 9: 23–58.

Nisbet, R. G. M. 1978. '*Felicitas* at Surrentum (Statius, *Silvae* II.2)', *JRS* 68: 1–11.

Nora, P. 2001. 'General Introduction', in P. Nora (ed.), *Rethinking France. Les Lieux de Mémoire. Vol. 1. The State*. Translated by M. Trouille. Chicago, IL, University of Chicago Press: vii–xxii.

Nys, P. 2000. 'The Villa d'Este Storyboard', in Birksted 2000: 223–44.

Oakley, S. 1993. 'The Roman Conquest of Italy', in Rich and Shipley 1993: 9–37.

Olick, J. K. 2003. 'Introduction', in *States of Memory. Continuities, Conflicts, and Transformations in National Retrospection*. Durham, NC, Duke University Press: 1–16.

Olwig, K. R. 1996. 'Recovering the Substantive Nature of Landscape', *Annals of the Association of American Geographers* 86: 630–53.

Opper, T. 2008. *Hadrian. Empire and Conflict*. London, British Museum Press.

Orlin, E. M. 2008. 'Octavian and Egyptian Cults: Redrawing the Boundaries of Romanness', *AJPh* 129: 231–53.

Osborne, R. 1987. *Classical Landscape with Figures. The Ancient Greek City and its Countryside*. London, Sheridan House.

—— 1992. 'Classical Greek Gardens: Between Farm and Paradise', in Hunt 1992a: 373–91.

O'Sullivan, T. M. 2006. 'The Mind in Motion: Walking and Metaphorical Travel in the Roman Villa', *CPh* 101: 133–52.

—— 2007. 'Walking with Odysseus: The Portico Frame of the Odyssey Landscapes', *AJPh* 128: 497–532.

Otis, B. 1963. *Virgil. A Study in Civilized Poetry*. Oxford, Clarendon Press.

Pagán, V. E. 2005. *Conspiracy Narratives in Roman History*. Austin, TX, University of Texas Press.

—— 2006. *Rome and the Literature of Gardens*. London, Duckworth.

Pailler, J.-M. 1988. *Bacchanalia. La répression de 186 av. J.-C. à Rome et en Italie. Vestiges, Images, Tradition*. Bibliothèque des Écoles Françaises d'Athènes et de Rome 270. Rome, Ecole Française de Rome.

Palmer, R. E. A. 1990. *Studies of the Northern Campus Martius in Ancient Rome*. TAPhS 80.2. Philadelphia, PA.

Papaioannou, S. 2003. 'Founder, Civilizer and Leader: Vergil's Evander and his Role in the Origins of Rome', *Mnemosyne* 56: 680–702.

Papi, E. 1996. 'Horti Caesaris', in *LTUR*, iii.55–6.

Parkins, H. (ed.) 1997. *Roman Urbanism. Beyond the Consumer City*. London, Routledge.

Parry, A. 1957. 'Landscape in Greek Poetry', *YClS* 15: 3–29.

Parry, H. 1964. 'Ovid's *Metamorphoses*: Violence in a Pastoral Landscape', *TAPhA* 95: 268–82.

Paschalis, M. (ed.) 2007. *Pastoral Palimpsests. Essays in the Reception of Theocritus and Virgil*. Rethymnon Classical Studies 3. Herakleion, Crete University Press.

Patterson, A. 1987. *Pastoral and Ideology. From Virgil to Valéry*. Berkeley, CA, University of California Press.

Patterson, J. R. 2000. 'On the Margins of the City of Rome', in V. M. Hope and E. Marshall (eds.), *Death and Disease in the Ancient City*. London, Routledge: 85–103.

—— 2006. *Landscapes and Cities. Rural Settlement and Civic Transformation in Early Imperial Italy*. Oxford, Oxford University Press.

Pavlovskis, Z. 1973. *Man in an Artificial Landscape. The Marvels of Civilization in Imperial Rome.* Leiden, Brill.

Pease, A. S. 1952. 'A Sketch of the Development of Ancient Botany', *Phoenix* 6: 44–51.

Pelgrom, J. 2008. 'Settlement Organization and Land Distribution in Latin Colonies Before the Second Punic War', in de Ligt and Northwood 2008: 333–72.

Pellicer, A. 1966. *Natura. Étude sémantique et historique du mot latin.* Paris, Presses Universitaires de France.

Pember, C. F. 1947. 'The Country House of a Roman Man of Letters', *Illustrated London News* 5653, 23 August; 220–1.

Perkell, C. G. 1981. 'On the Corycian Gardener of Vergil's Fourth *Georgic*', *TAPhA* 111: 167–77.

———— 1989. *The Poet's Truth. A Study of the Poet in Virgil's* Georgics. Berkeley, CA, University of California Press.

Perkins, P. 2000. 'Power, Culture and Identity in the Roman Economy', in Huskinson 2000b: 183–212.

Peters, W. J. T. 1963. *Landscape in Romano-Campanian Mural Painting.* Assen, Van Gorcum.

Peterson, A. L. 2001. *Being Human. Ethics, Environment, and Our Place in the World.* Berkeley, CA, University of California Press.

Petsalis-Diomidis, A. 2007. 'Landscape, Transformation, and Divine Epiphany', in S. Swain, S. Harrison, and J. Elsner (eds.), *Severan Culture.* Cambridge, Cambridge University Press: 250–89.

Pietri, C. (ed.) 1987. *L'urbs. Espace urbain et histoire. Actes du colloque international organisé par le Centre National de la Recherche Scientifique et l'École Française de Rome (Rome, 8–12 Mai 1985).* Collection de l'École Française de Rome 98. Rome, École Française de Rome.

Pinon, P. and Culot, M. (eds.) 1982. *La Laurentine et l'invention de la villa romaine.* Paris, Éditions du Moniteur.

Pinto, J. 1993. 'Giovanni Battista Piranesi's Plan of Hadrian's Villa', *Princeton University Library Chronicle* 55: 63–84.

Piranomonte, M. (ed.) 2007. *Un paradiso ritrovato. Scavi al Villino Fassi.* Rome, De Luca.

Poggiolo, R. 1975. *The Oaten Flute. Essays on Pastoral Poetry and the Pastoral Ideal.* Cambridge, MA, Harvard University Press.

Pollard, A. M. 2009. 'Measuring the Passage of Time: Achievements and Challenges in Archaeological Dating', in Cunliffe, Gosden, and Joyce 2009: 145–68.

Pollard, E. A. 2009. 'Pliny's *Natural History* and the Flavian *Templum Pacis*: Botanical Imperialism in First-century CE Rome', *Journal of World History* 20: 309–38.

Pollitt, J. J. 1978. 'The Impact of Greek Art on Rome', *TAPhA* 108: 155–74.

Porphyrios, D. 1983. 'Pliny's Villa at Laurentum', *Architectural Design* 53: 2–7.

Porteous, J. D. 1990. *Landscapes of the Mind. Worlds of Sense and Metaphor.* Toronto, University of Toronto Press.

Porter, J. I. 2007. 'Lucretius and the Sublime', in Gillespie and Hardie 2007: 167–84.

Pöschl, V. 1964. *Die Hirtendichtung Virgils.* Heidelberg, C. Winter.

Potter, J. 1996. *Representing Reality. Discourse, Rhetoric and Social Construction.* London, Sage.

Potter, T. W. 1987. *Roman Italy*. Berkeley, CA, University of California Press.

Purcell, N. 1987a. 'Tomb and Suburb', in H. von Hesberg and P. Zanker (eds.), *Römische Gräberstraßen. Selbstdarstellung – Status – Standard*. Munich, C. H. Beck: 25–41.

⸻ 1987b. 'Town in Country and Country in Town', in MacDougall 1987: 187–203.

⸻ 1990. 'The Creation of Provincial Landscape: The Roman Impact on Cisalpine Gaul', in T. Blagg and M. Millett (eds.), *The Early Roman Empire in the West*. Oxford, Oxbow: 6–29.

⸻ 1995. 'The Roman Villa and the Landscape of Production', in Cornell and Lomas 1995: 151–80.

⸻ 1996a. 'The Roman Garden as a Domestic Building', in I. Barton (ed.), *Roman Domestic Buildings*. Exeter, University of Exeter Press: 121–51.

⸻ 1996b. 'Rome and the Management of Water: Environment, Culture and Power', in G. Shipley and J. Salmon (eds.), *Human Landscapes in Classical Antiquity. Environment and Culture*. London, Routledge: 180–212.

⸻ 1998. 'Alla scoperta di una costa residenziale romana: il *litus Laurentinum* e l'archeologia dell'otium', in M. G. Lauro (ed.), *Castelporziano III. Campagne di scavo e restauro 1987–1991*. Rome, Viella: 11–32.

⸻ 2007. 'Urban Spaces and Central Places: The Roman World', in Alcock and Osborne 2007: 182–202.

Putnam, M. C. J. 1970. *Virgil's Pastoral Art. Studies in the Eclogues*. Princeton, NJ, Princeton University Press.

Raeder, J. 1983. *Die statuarische Ausstattung der Villa Adriana bei Tivoli*. Frankfurt, Peter Lang.

Ranaldi, A. 2001. *Pirro Ligorio e l'interpretazione delle ville antiche*. Rome, Quasar.

Rathbone, D. W. 2003. 'The Control and Exploitation of *ager publicus* in Italy under the Roman Republic', in J.-J. Aubert (ed.), *Tâches publiques et entreprise privée dans le monde romain*. Genève, Université de Neuchâtel: 135–78.

⸻ 2008. 'Poor Peasants and Silent Sherds', in de Ligt and Northwood 2008: 305–32.

Rea, J. A. 2007. *Legendary Rome. Myth, Monuments, and Memory on the Palatine and Capitoline*. London, Duckworth.

Reay, B. 2005. 'Agriculture, Writing and Cato's Aristocratic Self-fashioning', *ClAnt* 24: 331–61.

Reed, J. D. 2007. *Virgil's Gaze. Nation and Poetry in the Aeneid*. Princeton, NJ, Princeton University Press.

Reeder, J. C. 1997a. 'The Statue of Augustus from Prima Porta and the Underground Complex', in C. Deroux (ed.), *Studies in Latin Literature and Roman History VIII*. Collection Latomus 239. Brussels, Latomus: 287–308.

⸻ 1997b. 'The Statue of Augustus from Prima Porta, the Underground Complex, and the Omen of the *Gallina Alba*', *AJPh* 118: 89–118.

⸻ 2001. *The Villa of Livia ad Gallinas Albas. A Study in the Augustan Villa and Garden*. Archaeological Transatlantica 20. Providence, RI, Brown University.

Reggiani, A. M. (ed.) 2002. *Villa Adriana, paesaggio antico e ambiente moderno. Atti del Convegno a Roma 23–24 Giugno 2000*. Milan, Mondadori Electa.

Rehak, P. 2006. *Imperium and Cosmos. Augustus and the Northern Campus Martius*. Madison, WI, University of Wisconsin Press.

Renan, E. 1990. 'What is a Nation?', translated by M. Thom, in Bhabha 1990b: 8–22.

Renfrew, C. 2005. 'Cognitive Archaeology', in C. Renfrew and P. Bahn (eds.), *Archaeology. The Key Concepts*. Abingdon, Routledge: 41–5.

——— and Bahn, P. 2008. *Archaeology. Theories, Methods and Practice*. Fifth edition, London, Thames and Hudson.

Rich, J. 1993. 'Fear, Greed and Glory: The Causes of Roman War-making in the Middle Republic', in Rich and Shipley 1993: 38–68.

——— and Shipley, G. (eds.) 1993. *War and Society in the Roman World*. London, Routledge.

——— and Wallace-Hadrill, A. (eds.) 1991. *City and Country in the Ancient World*. London, Routledge.

Ricoeur, P. 1977. *The Rule of Metaphor. Multi-disciplinary Studies in the Creation of Meaning in Language*. Translated by R. Czerny, K. McLaughlin, and J. Costello. Toronto, University of Toronto Press.

——— 1984/5/8. *Time and Narrative (Temps et Récit)*. 3 vols, translated by K. McLaughlin and D. Pellauer. Chicago, IL, University of Chicago Press.

——— 2004. *Memory, History, Forgetting*. Translated by K. Blamey and D. Pellauer. Chicago, IL, University of Chicago Press.

Ricotti, E. Salza Prina. 1984. 'La cosa della Villa Magna: il Laurentinum di Plinio il Giovane', in *Atti della Accademia Nazionale dei Lincei, classe de scienze morali, storiche e filologiche rendiconti 38* (series 8). Rome, Accademia Nazionale dei Lincei: 339–58.

——— 1987. 'The Importance of Water in Roman Garden Triclinia', in MacDougall 1987: 135–84.

——— 1998. 'Adriano: architettura del verde e dell'acqua', in Cima and La Rocca 1998: 363–400.

——— 2001. *Villa Adriana. Il sogno di un imperatore*. Rome, L'Erma di Bretschneider.

Ridgway, B. S. 1981. 'Greek Antecedents of Garden Sculpture', in MacDougall and Jashemski 1981: 7–28.

——— 2000. 'The Sperlonga Sculptures: The Current State of Research', in de Grummond and Ridgway 2000: 78–91.

Riggsby, A. M. 1997. '"Public" and "Private" in Roman Culture: The Case of the *Cubiculum*', *JRA* 10: 36–56.

——— 1998. 'Self and Community in the Younger Pliny', *Arethusa* 31: 75–97.

Riikonen, H. 1976. 'The Attitude of Roman Poets and Orators to the Countryside as a Place for Creative Work', *Arctos* 10: 75–85.

Roncayolo, M. 2006. 'The Scholar's Landscape', translated by R. C. Holbrook, in P. Nora (ed.), *Rethinking France. Les Lieux de Mémoire. Vol. 2. Space*, translated by D. P. Jordan. Chicago, IL, University of Chicago Press: 343–82.

Roselaar, S. T. 2008. 'Regional Variations in the Use of the *ager publicus*', in de Ligt and Northwood 2008: 573–602.

Rosen, R. M. and Sluiter, I. (eds.) 2006. *City, Countryside and the Spatial Organization of Value in Classical Antiquity*. *Mnemosyne* Supplement 279. Leiden, Brill.

Rosenmeyer, T. G. 1969. *The Green Cabinet. Theocritus and the European Pastoral Lyric*. Berkeley, CA, University of California Press.

———— 2000. 'Seneca and Nature', *Arethusa* 33: 99–119.

Rosenstein, N. S. 2004. *Rome at War. Farms, Families, and Death in the Middle Republic.* Chapel Hill, NC, University of North Carolina Press.

Rousseau, D. 2008. 'La présentation au public des villae romaines: des ruines aux reconstitutions *in situ*', in C. Pieri (ed.), *Idées et débats. De la restitution en archéologie/Archaeological Restitution.* Paris, Éditions du Patrimoine (and <http://editions.monuments-nationaux.fr/en/online-books/bdd/livree/9>): 222–35.

Royo, M. and Gruet, B. 2008. 'Décrire Rome: fragment et totalité, la ville ancienne au risque du paysage', in P. Fleury and O. Desbordes (eds.), *Roma illustrata.* Caen, Presses Universitaires de Caen: 377–92.

Rüpke, J. 2004. '*Acta aut agenda*: Relations of Script and Performance', in A. Barchiesi, J. Rüpke, and S. Stephens (eds.), *Rituals in Ink. A Conference on Religion and Literary Production in Ancient Rome, Held at Stanford University in February 2002.* Munich, Franz Steiner: 23–43.

Saenger, P. 1990. 'The Separation of Words and the Order of Words: The Genesis of Medieval Reading', *Scrittura e Civiltà* 14: 49–74.

Said, E. 1993. *Culture and Imperialism.* London, Chatto and Windus.

Saint-Martin, F. 1990. *Semiotics of Visual Language.* Bloomington, IN, Indiana University Press.

Sallares, R. 2002. *Malaria and Rome. A History of Malaria in Ancient Italy.* Oxford, Oxford University Press.

Santillo Frizell, B. and Klynne, A. (eds.) 2005. *Roman Villas around the Urbs. Interaction with Landscape and Environment. Proceedings of a Conference Held at the Swedish Institute in Rome, September 17–18, 2004.* Rome, <http://www.isvroma.it/public/SV/index.php?option=com_content&task=view&id=40&Itemid=55>, accessed 22 November 2009 (unpaginated).

Sauron, G. 1987. ' Le complexe pompéien du Champ de Mars: nouveauté urbanistique à finalité idéologique', in Pietri 1987: 457–73.

———— 1994. *Quis deum? L'expression plastique des idéologies politiques et religieuses à Rome à la fin de la République et au début du Principat.* Bibliothèque des Écoles Françaises d'Athènes et de Rome 285. Rome, École Française de Rome.

———— 2007. 'Un *amaltheum* dans la villa d'Oplontis/Torre Annunziata?', *RSP* 18: 41–6.

Schama, S. 1995. *Landscape and Memory.* London, HarperCollins.

Scheid, J. 1993. '*Lucus, nemus*: qu'est-ce qu'un bois sacré?', in O. de Cazanove and J. Scheid (eds.), *Les bois sacrés.* Naples, Centre Jean Bérard: 13–20.

Scheidel, W. 2004. 'Human Mobility in Roman Italy, 1: The Free Population', *JRS* 94: 1–26.

Schiesaro, A. 2007. 'Lucretius and Roman Politics and History', in Gillespie and Hardie 2007: 41–58.

Schrijvers, P. H. 2006. 'Silius Italicus and the Roman Sublime', in Nauta, van Dam, and Smolenaars 2006: 97–111.

Schroeder, F. M. 2004. 'Philodemus: *Avocatio* and the Pathos of Distance in Lucretius and Vergil', in Armstrong et al. 2004: 139–56.

Sciarrino, E. 2004. 'Putting Cato the Censor's *Origines* in its Place', *ClAnt* 23: 323–57.

Scully, S. 1988. 'Cities in Italy's Golden Age', *Numen* 35: 69–78.

Segal, C. P. 1963. 'Nature and the World of Man in Greek Literature', *Arion* 2: 19–53.

—— 1965. '*Tamen cantabitis Arcades*: Exile and Arcadia in *Eclogues One* and *Nine*', *Arion* 4: 238–66.

—— 1969. *Landscape in Ovid's* Metamorphoses. *A Study in the Transformations of a Literary Symbol*. Wiesbaden, Franz Steiner.

—— 1981. *Poetry and Myth in Ancient Pastoral. Essays on Theocritus and Virgil*. Princeton, NJ, Princeton University Press.

Settis, S. 2002. *Le pareti ingannevoli. La villa di Livia e la pittura di giardino*. Milan, Electa.

Sharples, R. W. 2006. 'Philosophy for Life', in Bugh 2006: 223–40.

Sharrock, A. 2002. 'Looking at Looking: Can You Resist a Reading?', in Fredrick 2002: 265–95.

Short, W. M. 2008. 'Thinking Places, Placing Thoughts: Spatial Metaphors of Mental Activity in Roman Culture', *I Quaderni del Ramo d'Oro* 1: 106–29, <http://www.qro.unisi.it/frontend/>, accessed 17 June 2010.

Silberberg-Pierce, S. 1980. 'Politics and Private Imagery: The Sacral-idyllic Landscapes in Augustan Art', *Art History* 3: 241–51.

Skoie, M. 2006. 'City and Countryside in Virgil's *Eclogues*', in Rosen and Sluiter 2006: 297–325.

—— and Velázquez, S. B. (eds.) 2006. *Pastoral and the Humanities. Arcadia Re-inscribed*. Exeter, University of Exeter Press.

Small, J. P. 1997. *Wax Tablets of the Mind. Cognitive Studies of Memory and Literacy in Classical Antiquity*. London, Routledge.

Smith, A. D. 1999. *Myths and Memories of the Nation*. Oxford, Oxford University Press.

Smith, A. T. 2003. *The Political Landscape. Constellations of Authority in Early Complex Polities*. Berkeley, CA, University of California Press.

Smith, C. 2007. 'Latium and the Latins: The Hinterland of Rome', in Bradley, Isayev, and Riva 2007: 161–78.

Smith, J. T. 1997. *Roman Villas. A Study in Social Structure*. London, Routledge.

Smolenaars, J. J. L. 2006. 'Ideology and Poetics along the Via Domitiana: Statius *Silvae* 4.3', in Nauta, van Dam, and Smolenaars 2006: 223–44.

Snyder, G. 1990. *The Practice of the Wild. Essays*. San Francisco, CA, North Point.

Soja, E. 1996. *Thirdspace. Journeys to Los Angeles and Other Real-and-Imagined Places*. Cambridge, MA, Blackwell.

Spencer, D. 2005. 'Lucan's Follies: Memory and Ruin in a Civil War Landscape', *G&R* 52: 46–69.

—— 2006. 'Horace's Garden Thoughts: Rural Retreats and the Urban Imagination', in Rosen and Sluiter 2006: 239–74.

—— 2007. 'Rome at a Gallop: Livy on Not Gazing, Jumping, or Toppling into the Void', in Larmour and Spencer 2007b: 61–101.

—— 2008. 'Singing in the Garden: Statius' *plein air* Lyric (after Horace)', in J. Blevins (ed.), *Dialogism and Lyric Self-fashioning. Bakhtin and the Voices of a Genre*. Selinsgrove, PA, University of Susquehanna Press: 66–83.

Spirn, A. W. 1998. *The Language of Landscape*. New Haven, CT, Yale University Press.

Spivak, G. C. 1987. *In Other Worlds. Essays in Cultural Politics*. New York, Methuen.

Spurr, M. S. 1986. *Arable Cultivation in Roman Italy c. 200 B.C.–c. A.D. 100*. Journal of Roman Studies Monographs 3. London, Society for the Promotion of Roman Studies.

Stafford, B. M. 2001. 'The Epiphanic Sublime', in Beckley 2001: 177–82.

Stamper, J. W. 2005. *The Architecture of Roman Temples. The Republic to the Middle Empire*. Cambridge, Cambridge University Press.

Stefani, G. and Borgoncino, M. 2006. 'Il giardino dipinto della Casa del Bracciale d'Oro a Pompei', in T. Budetta (ed.), *Il giardino. Realtà e imaginario nell arte antica*. Castellammare di Stabia, N. Longobardi: 71–84.

Steil, L. (ed.) 1987. *Tradition and Architecture. Palaces, Public Buildings and Houses*. Special edition of *Architectural Design* 57.5–6.

Steinby, E. M. (ed.) 1993–2000. *Lexicon topographicum urbis Romae*. 6 vols, Rome, Laterza.

Stein-Hölkeskamp, E. and Hölkeskamp, K.-J. (eds.) 2006. *Erinnerungsorte der Antike. Die römische Welt*. Munich, C. H. Beck.

Stewart, A. F. 1977. 'To Entertain an Emperor: Sperlonga, Laokoon and Tiberius at the Dinner Table', *JRS* 67: 76–90.

Stibbe, A. (ed.) 2009. *The Handbook of Sustainable Literacy. Skills for a Changing World*. Totnes, Green Books, <http://arts.brighton.ac.uk/stibbe-handbook-of-sustainability>, accessed 17 June 2010.

Strocka, V. M. 2007. 'Domestic Decoration: Painting and the "Four Styles"', in Dobbins and Foss 2007: 302–22.

Stronach, D. 1989. 'The Royal Garden at Pasargadae: Evolution and Legacy', in de Meyer, L. and Haerinck, E. (eds.), *Archaeologia Iranica et Orientalis. Miscellanea in honorem Louis Vanden Berghe I*. Gent, Peeters: 475–502.

Sundermann, M. 1984. 'Pliny's Villa Laurentum 1982', in D. Porphyrios (ed.), *Leon Krier. Houses, Places, Cities*. Special edition of *Architectural Design* 54.7–8: 120–5.

——— 1987a. 'Villa Laurentium de Plinius', in Steil 1987: 9–13.

——— 1987b. 'Villa Tuscum de Plinius', in Steil 1987: 14–15.

Syme, R. 1964. *Sallust*. Berkeley, CA, University of California Press.

Tacoli, C. 1998. 'Rural–Urban Interactions: A Guide to the Literature', *Environment and Urbanization* 10: 147–66.

Taisne, A. 1978. 'Peintures de villas chez Stace', *Caesarodunum* 13: 40–53.

Takács, S. A. 2000. 'Politics and Religion in the Bacchanalian Affair of 186 B.C.E.', *HSPh* 100: 301–10.

Talamo, E. 1998. 'Gli *horti* di Sallustio a Porta Collina', in Cima and La Rocca 1998: 113–69.

Tanzer, H. 1924. *Villas of Pliny the Younger*. New York, Columbia University Press.

Tatum, W. J. 2006. 'The Final Crisis (69–44)', in N. Rosenstein and R. Morstein-Marx (eds.), *A Companion to the Roman Republic*. London, Wiley-Blackwell, 190–211.

Taylor, M. C. 2002. *The Moment of Complexity. Emerging Network Culture*. Chicago, IL, University of Chicago Press.

Taymor, J. 2000. *Titus. The Illustrated Screenplay, Adapted from the Play by William Shakespeare*. New York, Newmarket Press.

Temelini, M. A. 2006. 'Pompey's Politics and the Presentation of his Theatre-Temple Complex, 61–52 BCE', *Studia Humaniora Tartuensia* 7.A.4: 1–14, <http://www.ut.ee/klassik/sht/2006/temelini1.pdf>, accessed 23 June 2010.

Temporini, H. and Haase, W. (eds.) 1972–. *Aufstieg und Niedergang der römischen Welt*. Berlin, Walter de Gruyter.

Terrenato, N. 2001. 'The Auditorium Site in Rome and the Origins of the Villa', *JRA* 14: 5–32.

–––––– 2007. 'The Essential Countryside: The Roman World', in Alcock and Osborne 2007: 139–61.

Theodorakopoulos, E. 2010. *Ancient Rome at the Cinema. Story and Spectacle in Hollywood and Rome*. Exeter, Bristol Phoenix Press.

Thomas, M. L. and Clarke, J. R. 2007. 'The Oplontis Project 2005–6: Observations on the Construction History of Villa A at Torre Annunziata', *JRA* 20: 222–32.

Thomas, R. F. 1982. *Lands and Peoples in Roman Poetry. The Ethnographic Tradition*. Cambridge Philological Society Supplement 7. Cambridge, Cambridge University Press.

–––––– 1988. *Virgil*. Georgics, 2 vols, Cambridge, Cambridge University Press.

–––––– 1995. '*Vestigia ruris*: Urbane Rusticity in Virgil's *Georgics*', in *Greece in Rome. Influence, Integration, Resistance*. Special edition of *HSPh* 97: 197–214.

–––––– 2004–5. 'Torn Between Jupiter and Saturn: Ideology, Rhetoric and Culture Wars in the *Aeneid*', *CJ* 100: 121–47.

Thoreau, H. D. 1906. 'Walking', in F. H. Allen and B. Torrey (eds.), *The Writings of Henry D. Thoreau*. Boston, MA, Houghton Mifflin: 205–48.

–––––– 2004. *The Writings of Henry D. Thoreau. A Week on the Concord and Merrimack Rivers*. Introduction by J. McPhee. Princeton, NJ, Princeton University Press.

Thrift, N. 2004. 'Intensities of Feeling: The Spatial Politics of Affect', *Geografiska Annaler Series B* 86: 57–78.

Tilley, C. 1994. *A Phenomenology of Landscape. Places, Paths and Monuments*. Oxford, Berg.

Tilly, B. 1947. *Vergil's Latium*. Oxford, Basil Blackwell.

Toll, K. 1997. 'Making Roman-ness and the *Aeneid*', *ClAnt* 16: 34–56.

Treggiari, S. 2003. 'Ancestral Virtues and Vices: Cicero on Nature, Nurture and Presentation', in Braund and Gill 2003: 139–64.

Turner, T. 2005. *Garden History. Philosophy and Design 2000 BC to 2000 AD*. Abingdon, Spon.

Tybout, R. A. 2001. 'Roman Wall-painting and Social Significance', *JRA* 14: 33–56.

–––––– 2007. 'Rooms with a View: Residences Built on Terraces along the Edge of Pompeii (Regions VI, VII and VIII)', in Dobbins and Foss 2007: 407–20.

van Buren, A. W. and Kennedy, R. M. 1919. 'Varro's Aviary at Casinum', *JRS* 9: 59–66.

van Eck, C. 2000. '"The Splendid Effects of Architecture, and its Power to Affect the Mind": The Workings of Picturesque Association', in Birksted 2000: 245–58.

Van Valen, L. 1973. 'A New Evolutionary Law', *Evolutionary Theory* 1: 1–30.

Varela, F., Thompson, E., and Rosch, E. 1991. *The Embodied Mind. Cognitive Science and Human Experience*. Cambridge, MA, MIT Press.

Vasaly, A. 1993. *Representations. Images of the World in Ciceronian Oratory*. Berkeley, CA, University of California Press..

Vautier, D. 2007. *Tous les chemins mènent à Rome. Voyages d artistes du XVIe au XIXe siècle*. Brussels, Fonds Mercator.

Venturi, M. F. 1989. 'Homer's Garden', *Journal of Garden History* 9: 86–94.

Vermeule, C. 1968. 'Graeco-Roman Statues: Purpose and Setting – II: Literary and Archaeological Evidence for the Display and Grouping of Graeco-Roman Sculpture', *Burlington Magazine* 110, no. 788: 607–13.

Versluys, M. J. 2002. *Aegyptiaca Romana. Nilotic Scenes and the Roman Views of Egypt.* Leiden, Brill.

Verzár-Bass, M. 1998. 'A proposito dei mausolei negli *horti* e nelle *villae*', in Cima and La Rocca 1998: 401–24.

Vessey, D. W. T. 1981. 'Atedius Melior's Tree: Statius *Silvae* 2.3', *CPh* 76: 46–52.

Villedieu, F. (ed.) 2001. *Il giardino dei Cesari. Dai pallazi antichi alla Vigna Barberini, sul Monte Palatino. Scavi dell'École française de Rome, 1985–1999.* Rome, Quasar.

von Blanckenhagen, P. H. and Alexander, C. 1990. *The Augustan Villa at Boscotrecase.* Mainz, Philipp von Zabern.

von Stackelberg, K. T. 2009. *The Roman Garden. Space, Sense, and Society.* Abingdon, Routledge.

von Ungern-Sternberg, J. 2004. 'The Crisis of the Republic', trans. by H. I. Flower, in Flower 2004: 89–109.

Wachtel, N. (1990) 'Remember and Never Forget', in M.-N. Bourguet, L. Valensi, and N. Wachtel (eds.), *Between Memory and History.* Chur, Harwood Academic Publishers: 101–29.

Wallace-Hadrill, A. 1982. 'The Golden Age and Sin in Augustan Ideology', *P&P* 95: 19–36.

——— 1983. '*Ut pictura poesis*? Review of J. M. Croisille, *Poésie et art figuré de Néron aux Flaviens.* Collection Latomus 179. Brussels, Latomus, 1982. 2 vols', *JRS* 73: 180–3.

——— (ed.) 1989. *Patronage in Ancient Society.* London, Routledge.

——— 1994. *Houses and Society in Pompeii and Herculaneum.* Princeton, NJ, Princeton University Press.

——— 1998a. '*Horti* and Hellenization', in Cima and La Rocca 1998: 1–12.

——— 1998b. 'The Villa as Cultural Symbol', in Frazer 1998: 43–53.

——— 2005. '*Mutatas formas*: The Augustan Transformation of Roman Knowledge', in Galinsky 2005: 55–84.

——— 2007. 'The Development of the Campanian House', in Dobbins and Foss 2007: 279–91.

——— 2008. *Rome's Cultural Revolution.* Cambridge, Cambridge University Press.

Walter, U. 2004. *Memoria und res publica. Zur Geschichtskultur im republikanischen Rom.* Frankfurt, Antike.

Warnock, S., and Brown, N. 1998. 'Putting Landscape First', *Landscape Design* 268: 44–6.

Watkin, D. 1992. 'Architecture', in R. Jenkyns (ed.), *The Legacy of Rome. A New Appraisal.* Oxford, Oxford University Press: 329–65.

Weis, H. A. 2000. 'Odysseus at Sperlonga: Hellenistic Hero or Roman Heroic Foil?', in de Grummond and Ridgway 2000: 111–65.

Welch, T. S. 2001. '*Est locus uni cuique suus*: City and Status in Horace's *Satires* 1.8 and 1.9', *ClAnt* 20: 165–92.

——— 2008. 'Horace's Journey through Arcadia', *TAPhA* 138: 47–74.

Werth, P. 1999. *Text Worlds. Representing Conceptual Space in Discourse.* Harlow, Longman.

Whitby, M., Hardie, P., and Whitby, M. (eds.) 1987. *Homo Viator. Classical Essays for John Bramble.* Bristol, Bristol Classical Press.

White, K. D. 1967. 'Latifundia', *BICS* 14: 62–79.

—— 1973. 'Roman Agricultural Writers I: Varro and his Predecessors', in *ANRW*, i.4: 439–97.

White, M. J. 2003. 'Stoic Natural Philosophy (Physics and Cosmology)', in B. Inwood (ed.), *The Cambridge Companion to the Stoics.* Cambridge, Cambridge University Press: 124–52.

Williams, J. 2003. *Gilles Deleuze's 'Difference and Repetition'. A Critical Introduction and Guide.* Edinburgh, Edinburgh University Press.

Williams, M. F. 1991. *Landscape in the* Argonautica *of Apollonius Rhodius.* Frankfurt, Peter Lang.

Williams, R. 1973. *The Country and the City.* London, Chatto and Windus.

Wiseman, T. P. 1994. '*Conspicui postes tectaque digna deo*: The Public Image of Aristocratic and Imperial Houses in the Late Republic and Early Empire', in *Historiography and Imagination. Eight Essays on Roman Culture.* Exeter, University of Exeter Press: 98–115 (= Pietri 1987: 395–413).

—— 1998. 'A Stroll on the Rampart', in Cima and La Rocca 1998: 13–22.

Witcher, R. E. 2005. 'The Extended Metropolis: *Urbs*, *Suburbium* and Population', *JRA* 18: 120–38.

—— 2008. 'Regional Field Survey and the Demogaphy of Roman Italy', in de Ligt and Northwood 2008: 273–303.

—— 2009. 'The Countryside', in A. Erskine (ed.), *A Companion to Ancient History.* Oxford, Blackwell: 462–73.

Witek, F. 2006. *Vergils Landschaften. Versuch einer Typologie literarischer Landschaft.* Spudasmata 111. Hildesheim, Olms.

Wolschke-Bulmahn, J. (ed.) 1997. *Nature and Ideology. Nature and Garden Design in the Twentieth Century.* Dumbarton Oaks Colloquium on the History of Landscape Architecture 18. Washington, DC, Dumbarton Oaks.

Wyler, S. 2006. 'Roman Replications of Greek Art at the Villa Della Farnesina', *Art History* 29: 213–32.

—— 2008. 'Le dionysisme dans les villas romaines: initiation familiale ou contre-modèle social?', in Galand-Hallyn 2008: 61–77.

Wylie, J. 2007. *Landscape.* Abingdon, Routledge.

Yates, F. A. 1966. *The Art of Memory.* London, Routledge and Kegan Paul.

Yegül, F. 1992. *Baths and Bathing in Classical Antiquity.* Cambridge, MA, MIT Press.

Yntema, D. 2008. 'Polybius and the Field Survey Evidence from Apulia', in de Ligt and Northwood 2008: 373–85.

Young, T. and Riley, R. (eds.) 2002. *Theme Park Landscapes. Antecedents and Variations.* Dumbarton Oaks Colloquium on the History of Landscape Architecture 20. Washington, DC, Dumbarton Oaks.

Yu, N. 1996. 'Thoreau's Critique of the American Pastoral in a Week'. *Nineteenth-century Literature* 51: 304–26.

Zanker, P. 1988. *The Power of Images in the Age of Augustus.* Translated by A. Shapiro. Ann Arbor, MI, University of Michigan Press.

—— 1996. *The Mask of Socrates. The Image of the Intellectual in Antiquity.* Translated by A. Shapiro. Berkeley, CA, University of California Press.

Zarmakoupi, M. 2008. 'Designing the Landscapes of the Villa of Livia at Prima Porta', in D. Kurtz, C. Meyer, D. Saunders, A. Tsingarida, and N. Harris (eds.), *Essays in Classical Archaeology for Eleni Hatzivassiliou 1977–2007*. BAR International Series 1796. Oxford, Archaeopress: 269–76.

——— in press. '*Porticus* and *Cryptoporticus* in Luxury Villa Architecture', in K. Cole, E. Poehler, and M. Flohr (eds.), *Pompeii. Cultural Standards, Practical Needs*. Oxford, Oxbow.

Zeiner, N. K. 2005. *Nothing Ordinary Here. Statius as Creator of Distinction in the Silvae*. New York, Routledge.

Zerubavel, E. 2003. *Time Maps. Collective Memory and the Social Shape of the Past*. Chicago, IL, University of Chicago Press.

Zetzel, J. E. G. 1997. 'Rome and its Traditions', in Martindale 1997a: 188–203.

——— 2003. 'Plato with Pillows: Cicero on the Uses of Greek Culture', in Braund and Gill 2003: 119–38.

WEBOGRAPHY

(All sites last accessed on 17 June 2010.)

Archaeolog, <http://traumwerk.stanford.edu/archaeolog/>.

Archaeology News, <http://www.archaeologynews.org/>.

Awesome Billboards and Outdoor Advertising. Billboardom, <http://billboardom.blogspot.com/>.

Catena Digital Archive of Historic Gardens and Landscapes <http://www.lunacommons.org/luna/servlet/BardBar~1~1>

Curran, L. C. 'Domus Aurea', at *Maecenas. Images of Greece and Rome*, <http://wings.buffalo.edu/AandL/Maecenas/rome/domus_aurea/thumbnails_contents.html>.

De Franceschini, M. *Villa Adriana*, <http://www.villa-adriana.net/>.

De Haas, T. C. A. *The Pontine Region Project*, <http://www.rug.nl/let/onderzoek/onderzoekinstituten/gia/CurrentResearch/pontineregionproject?lang=en>.

'Early Roman Calendar', at *Calendars Through the Ages*, <http://www.webexhibits.org/calendars/calendar-roman.html>.

Extraordinary and Attractive Billboards, <http://10steps.sg/inspirations/artworks/50-extraordinary-and-attractive-billboards/>.

Frischer, B. *Virtual World Heritage Laboratory. The Hadrian's Villa Project*, <http://vwhl.clas.virginia.edu/villa.html>.

Garden Visit, <http://www.gardenvisit.com/>.

Hadrian. Empire and Conflict, <http://www.britishmuseum.org/hadrian>.

Hadrian's Villa and the California Garden, <http://www.gardenconservancy.org/images/DavidStreatfield.pdf>.

Horti Sallustiani, <http://www.horti-sallustiani.it/index.jsp>.

Iconoclasm, <http://www.iconoclasm.dk/?p=266>.

LacusCurtius, 'Greek and Roman Authors', at <http://penelope.uchicago.edu/Thayer/E/Roman/Texts/>.

The Latin Library, <http://www.thelatinlibrary.com/>.

Lawrence, C. (a) 'Home Page', at *The Roman Mysteries*, <http://romanmysteries.com/pages/50-Home_Page>.

Lawrence, C. (b) 'Serendipity in Surrentum', at *Roman Mysteries Blog*, <http://flavias.blogspot.com/2009/04/serendipity-in-surrentum.html>.

Lawrence, C. (c) 'Villa di Pollio Felici', at *Roman Mysteries Blog*, <http://flavias.blogspot.com/2005/06/villa-di-pollio-felice.html>.

Lawrence, C. (d) 'A Visit to Laurentum', at *The Roman Mysteries*, <http://romanmysteries.com/pages/94-Laurentum_Visit>.

Ministero per i Beni e le Attività Culturali. *Palatino/Vigna Barberini. Riemerge una Imponente Struttura di Epoca Neroniana*, <http://www.beniculturali.it/mibac/export/MiBAC/sito-MiBAC/Contenuti/Ministero/UfficioStampa/ComunicatiStampa/visualizza_asset.html_854392074.html>.

Museo dell'Ara Pacis, <http://en.arapacis.it/museo/l_ara_pacis_nel_campo_marzio>.

Neilson, H. *The Long Island City Sundial*, <http://licsundial.net/>.

Nova Roma. *Roman Calendar*, <http://www.novaroma.org/nr/Roman_calendar>.

Oberly, N. 'Reality, hyperreality (1)', at *Theories of Media. Keywords Glossary*, <http://csmt.uchicago.edu/glossary2004/realityhyperreality.htm>.

The Oplontis Project, <http://www.oplontisproject.org/index.html>.

Perseus Digital Library, <http://www.perseus.tufts.edu/>.

Ricotti, E. S. P. 'Villa Adriana', at *Eugenia Salza Prina Ricotti. Sito Web Ufficiale*, <http://www.espr-archeologia.it/categoria_en/1/Villa-Adriana>.

Rogue Classicism, <http://rogueclassicism.com/>.

Romano, D. G. et al. *Digital Augustan Rome.* <http://digitalaugustanrome.org/>.

Solarium/Horologium Augusti at the University of Oregon, Eugene, <http://darkwing.uoregon.edu/~klio/solarium/solarium_project.htm>.

Stanford Digital Forma Urbis Romae Project, <http://formaurbis.stanford.edu/>.

'Street of Tombs', at *Bryn Mawr's Visual Resources. High Resolution Image – Italy, Pompeii*, <http://www.brynmawr.edu/library/visualresources/lanterns/lrgimage/italy/pompeii/LX000529.html>.

Villa Sciarra, <http://www.sovraintendenzaroma.it/i_luoghi/ville_e_parchi_storici/ville_dei_nobili/villa_sciarra>.

The Virtual Museum of the Ancient Via Flaminia, <http://www.vhlab.itabc.cnr.it/flaminia/>.

INDEX